"It is often very hard to see the obvious—that is, something as basic as the eloquence required for the proclamation of the gospel. But Beitler helps us recognize that the simple truth has an unmistakable eloquence, which is why it matters that we take lessons from the classical rhetorical tradition. Readers of this book will discover that the rhetorical task and questions of the truth of what we believe cannot be separated."

Stanley Hauerwas, author of *The Character of Virtue: Letters to a Godson*

"In *Seasoned Speech*, James Beitler gives us a deep and subtle meditation on the many rhetorics of Christian witness—the enormously varied ways that the language of extraordinary and ordinary saints bear forth the gospel. To read this book is to be impressed by the author's scholarship but still more by the love with which he explores the relationship between our words and the Word."

Alan Jacobs, distinguished professor of humanities, honors program, Baylor University

"James E. Beitler's extraordinary and thoughtful book re-establishes the centrality of rhetorical theory for the practice of Christian witness. He examines the ethos of notable Christian rhetors, from C. S. Lewis to Marilynne Robinson, and organizes his discussion according to seasons in the liturgical calendar, demonstrating the connection between Christian witness and worship. These deeply theological reflections remind readers that rhetoric is not merely flowery language but is grounded in wisdom and truth. This is an important book for Christian scholars of rhetoric and lay Christians alike."

Christine J. Gardner, associate professor and chair of the department of communication arts, Gordon College

"This is an enlightening and fascinating exploration of five witnesses to the Christian faith and gospel. Even more, these diverse truth bearers—C. S. Lewis, Dorothy Sayers, Dietrich Bonhoeffer, Desmond Tutu, and Marilynne Robinson—function as lenses through which James Beitler III shows how the Word, liturgy, and life weave together rhetorically in faithful witness in differing contexts. Beitler's treatment is itself a keen example of seasoned speech, an embodied and intensely personal witness tinged with liturgical overtones. The effect of Beitler's evocative analysis is twofold: to encourage the reader to a self-examination of one's own Christian self, and to invite the reader to participate in the kind of embodied witness that Christian existence entails."

André Resner, professor of homiletics and liturgics, Hood Theological Seminary

"In today's toxic communication climate, the apostle Paul's admonition that our speech should 'always be gracious' (Col 4:6) seems impossibly naive. One factor that fuels our skepticism is that we have no models of what gracious persuasion looks like in practical ways. How can we be both gracious and convicted in our communication? We are indebted to James Beitler for offering us vivid examples of Christian communicators—Lewis, Sayers, Bonhoeffer, Tutu, Robinson—who spoke timely truth marked by creativity, passion, and respect. Even if you are familiar with Beitler's subjects, his insights cast them in a new and invigorating light."

Tim Muehlhoff, professor of communication, Biola University, author of *Winsome Persuasion: Christian Influence in a Post-Christian World*

"Christians not only have the responsibility to understand the gospel but also to share it with others. This task is inspired by the Spirit through human agency—lives lived, deeds done, and words spoken. All are important and complementary but each is a special charism. This book is about the charism of the spoken word and what we can learn from the masters of the craft in persuading others to follow Christ. Because the communicators discussed are all among my favorites, I am biased in commending it to potential readers. But I hope my few words will persuade you to take up and read and become better witnesses to the Word. This is a well-crafted and timely book."

John de Gruchy, emeritus professor, University of Cape Town

"Beautifully written, this book explores the diverse rhetorical strategies of five influential Christians, arguing that their different communication styles celebrate and sustain the power of Pentecost. In the process of interpreting what makes their tongues burn with illuminating power, Beitler provides a lucid introduction to the history of rhetoric, calling Christians to participate in shared liturgical practices so that communal worship might ignite new ways to speak truth into culture."

Crystal Downing, codirector of the Marion E. Wade Center, author of *Changing Signs of Truth* and *Salvation from Cinema*

SEASONED

SPEECH

RHETORIC IN THE LIFE OF THE CHURCH

JAMES E. BEITLER III

IVP Academic

An imprint of InterVarsity Press
Downers Grove, Illinois

InterVarsity Press
P.O. Box 1400, Downers Grove, IL 60515-1426
ivpress. com
email@ivpress.com

InterVarsity Press® is the book-publishing division of InterVarsity Christian Fellowship/USA®, a movement of students and faculty active on campus at hundreds of universities, colleges, and schools of nursing in the United States of America, and a member movement of the International Fellowship of Evangelical Students. For information about local and regional activities, visit intervarsity. org.

Scripture quotations, unless otherwise noted, are from The Holy Bible, English Standard Version, copyright © 2001 by Crossway Bibles, a division of Good News Publishers. Used by permission. All rights reserved.

Letter excerpts from Dorothy L. Sayers appearing on pages 70-72 and 80-84 used by permission of the estate of Dorothy L. Sayers, represented by David Higham Associates, Ltd.

Cover design: Cindy Kiple
Interior design: Daniel van Loon
Images: photo of C. S. Lewis: © National Portrait Gallery, London
  photo of Dorothy Sayers: © Alpha Historica / Alamy Stock Photo
  photo of Dietrich Bonhoeffer: © Scherl/Süddeutsche Zeitung Photo / Alamy Stock Photo
  photo of Marilynne Robinson: © photo of Marilynne Robinson / Jamie Clifford/AROHO 2011
  photo of Archbishop Desmond TuTu: © Nicholas Roberts / AFP / Getty Images

ISBN 978-0-8308-5244-4 (print)
ISBN 978-0-8308-7120-9 (digital)

Printed in the United States of America ∞

InterVarsity Press is committed to ecological stewardship and to the conservation of natural resources in all our operations. This book was printed using sustainably sourced paper.

Library of Congress Cataloging-in-Publication Data
A catalog record for this book is available from the Library of Congress.

P	25	24	23	22	21	20	19	18	17	16	15	14	13	12	11	10	9	8	7	6	5	4	3	2	1
Y	38	37	36	35	34	33	32	31	30	29	28	27	26	25	24	23	22	21	20	19					

For James and Arne

CONTENTS

ACKNOWLEDGMENTS

It seems fitting to me that I write these words in the period of ordinary time between Pentecost and Advent. Ordinary time—the "numbered, counted out" weeks that make up the majority of the liturgical year—is not simply Christianity's off-season.[1] Simon Chan describes it as "the time of the church, the time in which the church is to live out its calling in the world."[2] And Amy Plantinga Pauw writes, "An account of church in ordinary time encourages Christians to acknowledge and reflect on the fullness of their relationship to the triune God, which includes their relationship to God as Creator. . . . It encourages Christians to think about the texture of their daily life in community."[3] Reflecting on my relationship to God and on my common life with others, I am filled with gratitude. For me at least, the speech of ordinary time must be seasoned with thanksgiving.

This book simply wouldn't exist but for the support, kindness, and generosity of others. Thank you, first, to Tim Larsen and Alan Jacobs, who offered me guidance, feedback, and encouragement at various stages of the project; Jeffry Davis and Ken Chase, who served as readers on a paper that led to the book's central argument; Lisa Hemphill, who helped me with the editing process and drafted an

---

[1] Amy Plantinga Pauw, *Church in Ordinary Time: A Wisdom Ecclesiology* (Grand Rapids: Eerdmans, 2017), 1.

[2] Simon Chan, *Liturgical Theology: The Church as Worshiping Community* (Downers Grove, IL: InterVarsity Press, 2006), 164.

[3] Pauw, *Church in Ordinary Time*, 3.

initial version of the indexes; and Rick Gibson, Nicole and Chris Mazzarella, and Matt Milliner, who provided support and good cheer throughout the writing process. I'm also grateful to my three church communities—Trinity Church of Livonia, Trinity Presbyterian Church in Providence, and All Souls Anglican Church in Wheaton— out of whose lives this project emerged. I owe special thanks to my pastors: Rev. Michael Van Horn, Rev. David Sherwood, and Father Martin Johnson. Thank you for all you have taught me about worship and witness.

At Wheaton College, my work has been generously supported by a grant from the G. W. Aldeen Memorial Fund, a Junior Faculty Development Grant from the Alumni Association, several faculty travel grants, and a sabbatical grant. I received helpful feedback on the second chapter of the book when I presented it at Wheaton's Humanities Colloquium for faculty (organized by Tim Larsen and Tiffany Eberle Kriner) and later in Christine Colón's Wade Center authors course. My own research at the Wade Center benefited greatly from the knowledge and assistance of Laura Schmidt, Elaine Hooker, and Marjorie Lamp Mead. Thanks also go to my wonderful faculty colleagues in the English department (some of whom I've already mentioned and will happily mention again): Christina Bieber-Lake, Drew Bratcher, Christine Colón, Sharon Coolidge, Jeffry Davis, Susan Dunn-Hensley, the late Brett Foster, Jeffrey Galbraith, Alison Gibson, Rick Gibson, Tiffany Eberle Kriner, the late Roger Lundin, Nicole Mazzarella, Miho Nonaka, Leland Ryken, Wayne Martindale, Kim Sasser, and Ben Weber. Other members of the Wheaton community who have supported and encouraged me along the way include Chris Armstrong, Jill Baumgaertner, Tim Blackmon, Margaret Diddams, Marie Friesema, Stan Jones, Tracy McKenzie, Sarah Miglio, Philip Ryken, Dan Treier, and Nancy Underwood. My work at the college has also benefited from the help of several teaching assistants: Traver Carlson, Rachel Mudra, Rachel Post, and Angela Webster. Thank you all.

It has been a joy to work with InterVarsity Press on this book. Thank you to everyone who has contributed to its publication. I'm particularly grateful to David Congdon for taking an initial interest in the project and to David McNutt for providing me with insightful editorial comments and shepherding my book through the publication process. Thank you as well to my two anonymous readers for their helpful remarks about the project. I also want to express appreciation to IVP for allowing a version of chapter one to appear in the journal *Religion and the Arts*.

Lastly, thank you to my family. My interest in this project stemmed, in part, from seeds planted by my grandparents: James and Evelyn Beitler, and Raymond and LuEtta Frey. Throughout their lives, all four of my grandparents witnessed to the truth of the gospel; however, they did so in remarkably different ways. As I spent time with them, I came to realize that Christian witness testifies to the truth of Jesus Christ in many tongues and voices (a theme of chapter six). Meeting Karl and Jackie Kempe and hearing stories about Doris and Arnold Eklund—my wife's four grandparents—only reinforced this idea in my mind. And while such a notion is by no means a novel one, one of my personal reasons for writing this book was simply to reflect more on the wonderful diversity that characterizes the church's witness.

I'm also especially grateful to Jim and Melissa Beitler and to David and Karen Kempe for your constant love and support—and for modeling the Christian life for me, Brita, and our boys. (What is true of my grandparents is also true of my sons' grandparents, and I'm exceedingly grateful for that.) I'm also grateful for the love and support of Genevieve and David, Joe and Colleen, Tim and Megan, and Ashley and Zach.

Most important, thank you to my wife, Brita, and my two boys, James and Arne. You're the spice of my life, and I love you dearly. May your lives always be seasoned with love.

INTRODUCTION
The Rhetoric of Christian Witness

Let your speech always be gracious, seasoned with salt, so that
you may know how you ought to answer each person.

Colossians 4:6

Before converting to Christianity, Augustine of Hippo had been teaching rhetoric—the study and practice of the art of persuasion—to students in Milan. But upon his conversion, he decided to resign from his prestigious teaching position there. Augustine would leave "the market of speechifying," he explains in *The Confessions,* "so that young boys who were devoting their thoughts . . . to lying follies and legal battles, should no longer buy from [his] mouth the weapons for their frenzy."[1] Augustine had tasted "the real and all-surpassing sweetness" of the Lord, and he no longer wanted to teach students who sought to use rhetoric to make sinfulness seem desirable.[2] Considered apart from his other writings, Augustine's account of his conversion and ensuing career change in *The Confessions* might seem like a strange way to begin a book that aims, as the present work does, to illustrate and inspire faithful rhetorical activity in the life of the church. But the story does not end there.

---

[1]Augustine, *The Confessions*, trans. Maria Boulding, O.S.B. (New York: Vintage, 1998), 171.
[2]Augustine, *Confessions*, 170-71.

Though he gave up his post at Milan, his newfound faith did not curtail his engagement with rhetoric as much as it repurposed it.[3] Augustine's subsequent writings reveal that he remained a master rhetorician (one who studies the art of persuasion) and a skilled rhetor (one who practices that art); however, his faith allowed him to carry out these activities with their proper end in view.[4] From his conversion onward, Augustine sought to use rhetoric to "give conviction to . . . truth" and, ultimately, to help guide people into the joy and rest of the triune God.[5]

Augustine's most thorough reflections on the relationship between Christianity and rhetoric occur in his groundbreaking book *On Christian Teaching*. Writing to readers who may worry that rhetoric is neither originally nor explicitly Christian, he argues that as long as rhetorical knowledge is in keeping with what Christians believe, we may put it into practice.[6] Otherwise, those people who use rhetoric to "expound falsehoods" will have an advantage over people of faith.[7] He asks, "Since rhetoric is used to give conviction to both truth and falsehood, who could dare to maintain that truth, which depends on us for its defence, should stand unarmed in the fight against falsehood?"[8] The implied answer is, of course, nobody. While Augustine does go on to insist that skillful rhetoric (and, more specifically, eloquence) is unnecessary to bring about another's salvation, he also contends that it can make Christian wisdom more palatable.[9] "We

---

[3]Nello Cipriani, "Rhetoric," in *Augustine Through the Ages: An Encyclopedia*, ed. Allan D. Fitzgerald et al. (Grand Rapids: Eerdmans, 1999), 724. Quentin J. Schultze makes a similar point in his foreword in Tim Muehlhoff and Richard Langer's book *Winsome Persuasion: Christian Influence in a Post-Christian World* (Downers Grove, IL: InterVarsity Press, 2017), xi-xii.

[4]Dave Tell convincingly argues that Augustine's decision to leave his teaching position "marks a fundamental affirmation of rhetoric" ("Augustine and the 'Chair of Lies': Rhetoric in The Confessions," *Rhetorica: A Journal of the History of Rhetoric* 38, no. 4 [2010]: 384).

[5]Augustine, *On Christian Teaching* (Oxford: Oxford University Press, 1997), 101.

[6]Augustine, *On Christian Teaching*, 64-65, 101-2.

[7]Augustine, *On Christian Teaching*, 101.

[8]Augustine, *On Christian Teaching*, 101.

[9]Augustine, *On Christian Teaching*, 105.

often have to take bitter medicines," he writes, "and we must always avoid sweet things that are dangerous: but what better than sweet things that give health, or medicines that are sweet? The more we are attracted by sweetness, the easier it is for medicine to do its healing work."[10] Truth presented persuasively is sweet medicine.

For Christian students seeking to learn how to offer this sweet medicine to others—that is, "to speak eloquently as well as wisely"— Augustine points out that the church is full of examples to follow. In fact, there are so many models that "even for students with the leisure to read it is more likely that their time will run out than that these authors will be exhausted."[11] Faithful rhetoric flourishes in the church.

More than fifteen hundred years later, Augustine's reflections on rhetoric are as relevant as they have ever been, and contemporary Christians stand to benefit greatly from renewed attention to the subject. This opportunity exists because, despite the church's frequent attempts at persuasion both inside and outside its walls, Christians do not typically discuss acts of witness in terms of the rhetorical tradition, and such acts are rarely accompanied by rhetorical reflection. Though rhetoric is taught in Christian classical education programs, writing and communication courses at Christian colleges, and some seminary classes, it is seldom mentioned in church settings. In sermons and Sunday school classes, one is much more likely to hear the topic of witness discussed in terms of apologetics. While these discussions may touch on rhetoric, the approaches championed by apologists often represent only a small slice of what the rhetorical tradition has to offer the church.[12] What is more, Christian publishers have

---

[10]Augustine, *On Christian Teaching*, 105.

[11]Augustine, *On Christian Teaching*, 105.

[12]In a paper presented at the 2016 Rhetoric Society of America conference, Catherine Riley made a parallel argument about preaching, claiming that there is a need for more rhetorical instruction in the field of homiletics. She noted that handbooks on preaching rarely mention rhetoric

often left the subject of rhetoric to university presses, and on the rare occasion that rhetoric does make an appearance in a book from a Christian press, the subject is usually explored indirectly—again, usually under the guise of apologetics.[13]

To describe this state of affairs using the language of twentieth-century rhetorician Kenneth Burke, members of Christian congregations tend to engage in *rhetorica utens* (rhetorical practice) without sufficiently engaging in *rhetorica docens* (rhetorical theory).[14] In light of the wealth of resources that the rhetorical tradition offers speakers and writers who hope to communicate with their audiences more effectively, such uncritical practice almost certainly results in missed opportunities for witness.[15] It also hampers the church's ability to critique and reform its own acts of proclamation, increasing the likelihood that Christians will actually alienate the very people they are trying to reach. All too often, in the process of attempting to persuade others of the good news of Jesus Christ, Christians take on rhetorical

---

by name. She also referenced a survey she conducted of syllabi from homiletics courses; only six of forty-one syllabi mentioned rhetoric.

[13]Os Guinness's fine book *Fool's Talk: Recovering the Art of Christian Persuasion* (Downers Grove, IL: InterVarsity Press, 2015) is representative in this regard. Guinness rightly acknowledges *both* the "immense debt that apologetics owes to . . . rhetoric" *and* the need for Christians to be circumspect about embracing the whole of the rhetorical tradition (39-41). It is, however, beyond the scope of Guinness's project to thoroughly explore rhetoric's possibilities and limitations for Christian witness.

[14]Kenneth Burke, *Language as Symbolic Action: Essays on Life, Literature, and Method* (Berkeley: University of California Press, 1966), 36; James Jasinski, *Sourcebook on Rhetoric: Key Concepts in Contemporary Rhetorical Studies* (Thousand Oaks, CA: Sage, 2001), xiv.

[15]As a result of Christians' failure to adequately engage in rhetorical reflection, we have limited the number of resources at our disposal for effective witness, contributing to an overemphasis on apologetics and an increasingly narrow conception of the genre of testimony. In *Looking Before and After: Testimony and the Christian Life* (Grand Rapids: Eerdmans, 2008), Alan Jacobs makes the point that Christian testimonies tend to follow a specific formula ("I once was lost, but now am found"), and—without dismissing that formula—he invites readers to reflect on the fact that there are "many genres of the Christian life, each of which emphasizes or enacts one aspect of Jesus' life and teaching" (29). In light of this fact, Jacobs suggests that Christians would do well to mine Scripture and the Christian tradition for other exemplars. I would contend that what is true of Christian testimony is true of the rhetoric of Christian witness more generally. By exploring the writings of influential Christians, the current project highlights, to borrow language from Jacobs, a "repertoire" of rhetorical resources that readers might learn from and remake in their own contexts.

postures that are inimical to the proclamation of the gospel.[16] When we do so, we need more than theology to return us to right practice. We also need theologically informed rhetorical reflection, which offers resources both to evaluate our communicative practices and to revise those practices in ways that are consistent with the one who chose the form of the cross as his primary bearing in relation to the world.[17]

---

[16]After articulating problematic ways that some American evangelicals have attempted to participate in "public and political life," Mark Allan Steiner rightly remarks that "a significant dimension of these problems is *rhetorical*—created, shaped, reinforced, and naturalized by how evangelicals use and are used by symbols as they conceptualize what their faith is, how it is to be practiced authentically and how it might enter into public dialogue and political activism" (Mark Allan Steiner, "Reconceptualizing Christian Public Engagement: 'Faithful Witness' and the American Evangelical Tradition," *Journal of Communication and Religion* 32, no. 2 [2009]: 291). I also agree with Steiner's subsequent claim: "To the degree that this is so, a transformation in evangelical rhetorical practices could significantly and positively change these more fundamental understandings about what being a Christian means and what authentic Christian living looks like." One of my aims in writing this book has been to point to specific examples of Christian rhetorical activity that might help to ignite such a transformation. To be clear, Steiner's aims in his article are more expansive than mine (295); nevertheless, some of my figures' rhetorical practices exemplify aspects of Steiner's model. For example, C. S. Lewis's writing often demonstrates "epistemological modesty," Marilynne Robinson's novels "embrace . . . complexity and mystery," and all of the figures demonstrate "a respect for the importance of *ethos*" (295).

[17]One excellent resource for responding to the current cultural and political moment is Richard J. Mouw's *Uncommon Decency: Christian Civility in an Uncivil World*, 2nd ed. (Downers Grove, IL: InterVarsity Press, 2010). Mouw advocates for a posture of "convicted civility," which encourages Christians in their beliefs and faith commitments while "nurturing a spirit that is authentically kind and gentle" (16). Even as I endorse Mouw's project and approach, I think it is worth noting that he uses the word *rhetoric* in a pejorative way, reinforcing the term's negative connotations. Mouw mentions the term when discussing "angry rhetoric" (48, 49), "accusatory rhetoric" (49), "heavy rhetoric" (49), and "all-or-nothing rhetoric," which serves as "a substitute for an honest wrestling with the issues" (53). Another helpful resource is Alan Noble's *Disruptive Witness: Speaking Truth in a Distracted Age* (Downers Grove, IL: InterVarsity Press, 2018). Noble explains that the "secularism and distraction" encouraged in contemporary American culture "[makes] it difficult for us to communicate the full weight and exclusiveness of the gospel" (61). He responds by offering "concrete, achievable, and meaningful actions to help the church preserve its witness" in our contemporary context (88). Noble does not, however, focus specifically on rhetorical action. A final valuable resource, which *does* draw on the rhetorical tradition, is Tim Muehlhoff and Richard Langer's *Winsome Persuasion: Christian Influence in a Post-Christian World* (Downers Grove, IL: InterVarsity Press, 2017). Muehlhoff and Langer employ rhetorical theory in their book as they work toward the goal of "helping Christians engage in helpful and constructive public conversations—even when talking to people with whom we radically disagree" (7, see also 8-9). More specifically, Muehlhoff and Langer discuss the rhetorical appeals (68), facets of *ēthos* (68-75, 78-79), and identification (118)—concepts that also appear in my project.

This book responds to the church's need for greater rhetorical reflection by inviting readers to consider the rhetorical artistry of five exemplars of Christian witness: C. S. Lewis, Dorothy L. Sayers, Dietrich Bonhoeffer, Desmond Tutu, and Marilynne Robinson. By exploring the rhetoric of these Christians, the book aims to help change perceptions about rhetoric in the church and to demonstrate the importance of rhetorical reflection in a variety of ecclesial and cultural contexts. Though the book's five central figures are not recognized first and foremost as rhetors or rhetoricians, their work brings into relief a long and immensely fruitful conversation between the rhetorical tradition and the Christian tradition, which begins in Paul's epistles and continues to the present.

On Christianity and Rhetoric

One of the primary reasons for the absence of *rhetorica docens* in Christian congregations may be that, outside of academic contexts, the term *rhetoric* is almost always used pejoratively.[18] The term's negative connotations have a long history. Plato, who is often presented as one of rhetoric's earliest detractors, circulated the view that rhetoric was inferior to dialectic (i.e., philosophy), suggesting that the former was concerned only with appearances, while the latter dealt with matters of truth.[19] In Plato's *Gorgias*, for example, Socrates famously dismisses rhetoric as a "knack," which involved acts of "flattery" and was comparable to "pastry baking" and "cosmetics."[20] While Socrates speaks more favorably of rhetoric in the *Phaedrus* (and even sketches some prerequisites for persuasive

---

[18]Some of what follows (such as my comments about Plato and Peter Ramus) is an abbreviated version of an oft-told account about rhetoric's place in the history of Western thought and in contemporary discourse. For another, helpful overview, see the introduction to rhetorician James Jasinski's superb *Sourcebook on Rhetoric* (xiii-xxxv).

[19]Jean Nienkamp, introduction to *Plato on Rhetoric and Language: Four Key Dialogues* (Mahwah, NJ: Hermagoras, 1999), 1.

[20]Plato, *Gorgias* 463b, in Nienkamp, ed., *Plato on Rhetoric and Language*.

practice), Plato has seldom been described as a champion of the art of persuasion.[21]

Christian Scripture has been read as dismissive of rhetoric as well, and the apostle Paul's first letter to the church at Corinth is often invoked in such discussions. In 1 Corinthians 2:1-5, Paul contends that he shared the gospel with the Corinthians without using "lofty speech" or "plausible words of wisdom." He did so, he tells them, in order that their faith would be built on God's might and not his own. God's strength would be the surer foundation. In a remark about these verses that betrays the lingering traces of the association between rhetoric and cosmetics, theologian Kevin Vanhoozer writes, "Paul seems to go out of his way to dissociate himself from orators who employ the rouge of rhetoric in order to make the gospel more attractive."[22] Vanhoozer's comment does not indicate that he believes that Paul rejects rhetoric outright, nor does it suggest that he believes that Christians should reject rhetoric; nevertheless, comments such as this subtly reinforce negative views about rhetoric, providing fodder for those who would claim that 1 Corinthians 2:1-5 should be read as a prohibition against all uses of rhetoric. For some, Jesus's remarks in Matthew 10:17-20 confirm the truth of such a prohibition. After warning his followers that they will be beaten and forced "to bear witness" in the sight of worldly powers and the peoples of the world, Jesus offers the following words of comfort: "When they deliver you over, do not be anxious how you are to speak or what you are to say, for what you are to say will be given to you in that hour. For it is not you who speak, but the Spirit of your Father speaking through you." When this promise is read alongside Paul's first letter to the Corinthians, it is easy to see why some Christians may

---

[21]Nienkamp, introduction to _Plato on Rhetoric and Language_, 14-15; Plato, _Phaedrus_ 277b-c, in Nienkamp, ed., _Plato on Rhetoric and Language_.

[22]Kevin Vanhoozer, _The Drama of Doctrine: A Canonical Linguistic Approach to Christian Theology_ (Louisville: Westminster John Knox, 2005), 414.

be hesitant to advocate for the study and practice of persuasion in their congregations.

Writing in the sixteenth century, the French humanist Peter Ramus reinforced Plato's views by distinguishing rhetoric from philosophy and restricting the subject matter of the former. Ancient rhetoricians such as Cicero had taught their students that rhetoric consisted of five canons: *invention*, the practice of finding ideas, arguments, and means of persuasion; *arrangement*, the practice of ordering them; *style*, the practice of expressing them artfully; *memory*, the practice of storing them in the mind and recollecting them as particular situations warranted; and *delivery*, their public performance or presentation. Ramus reduced the established canons of rhetoric from five to two, transferring invention, arrangement, and memory to the realm of philosophy. "Dialectic," Ramus argues in *Brutinae Quaestiones*, "has three parts—invention of stratagems and arguments, arrangement of these through the syllogism and method, and then memory. . . . Yet what then will be left for rhetoric? Not only style in tropes and figures . . . but also delivery. This alone is the proper virtue of rhetoric."[23] Ramus's categories diminished rhetoric greatly. What once had been concerned with habits of mind and the intellect was reduced to matters of eloquence and stylistic embellishment. Ramus's representations of rhetoric, much like Plato's, framed rhetoric and truth as opposites, thereby contributing to public skepticism toward discourse described as rhetorical.[24]

---

[23]Peter Ramus, *Brutinae Quaestiones*, in *Peter Ramus's Attack on Cicero: Text and Translation of Ramus's* Brutinae Quaestiones, ed. James J. Murphy, trans. Carole Newlands (Davis, CA: Hermagoras, 1992), 17.

[24]Such skepticism toward rhetoric has been so powerful and persistent that when contemporary scholars of rhetoric write for non-specialists they almost always begin with a defense of their discipline. One fairly representative example appears at the beginning of Sharon Crowley and Debra Hawhee's popular textbook *Ancient Rhetorics for Contemporary Students*, 5th ed. (Boston: Pearson, 2012), 1.

Lest it seem that philosophers and theologians are solely responsible for the absence of *rhetorica docens* in Christian congregations, it should be noted that some members of the clergy as well as rhetoricians themselves may also be responsible for this state of affairs.[25] Pastors and priests influenced by the aforementioned views about rhetoric may be hesitant to talk openly about the subject in their churches for fear that their congregations will come to see them as calculating or, worse, disingenuous and manipulative. And rhetoricians uninformed about Christianity may represent Christians in a way that turns off believers to the discipline: it is not uncommon to read scholarship in rhetorical studies that misrepresents Christians or presents them in an unflattering light.[26] In light of negative representations of rhetoric by Christians and negative representations of Christians by rhetoricians, it is not surprising that one seldom hears talk about rhetoric within churches today.[27]

---

[25]Even St. Augustine does not always receive a pass on this point. For though he charts a way forward for the use of rhetoric among Christians, he does so, Thomas Amorose contends, in ways that limit rhetoric's scope. Amorose makes a compelling case that Augustine is partly responsible for the "constricting of rhetorical agency in early Christianity" ("Resistance to Rhetoric in Christian Tradition," in *Renovating Rhetoric in Christian Tradition*, ed. Elizabeth Vander Lei et al. [Pittsburgh: University of Pittsburgh Press, 2014], 140). He explains, "Augustine must confine the role of rhetor so that God's transforming love and the transforming, emotional force it exerts on human nature avoid corruption" (142). For my own part, I tend to think that Augustine did more to enliven rhetorical reflection among Christians than he did to limit it, and—while I view the scope of Christian rhetoric more broadly than Augustine does—I also appreciate his attempts to delimit the subject matter based on his convictions.

[26]Jeffry C. Davis and Adam Corbin note an example of such misrepresentation in their article "Problematizing the Center: Affirming Christian Identities and the Complexities of Faith," highlighting that Michael Mohon and J. Michael Rifenburg mistakenly conflate "Christian" and "fundamentalist Christian" when writing about their students' identities (*The Dangling Modifier* 21, no. 2 [2015]: 4). Sharon Crowley's *Toward a Civil Discourse: Rhetoric and Fundamentalism* (Pittsburgh: University of Pittsburgh Press, 2006) makes a similar mistake, calling for "a reinvigoration of the rhetorical arts" to address the deep divisions in our society yet failing to practice the kind of sensitivity to audience that she seems to be advocating for. As Mark Allan Steiner correctly observes, Crowley's "analysis prematurely discounts any edifying role for religious voices [in her proposal to promote civil discourse through rhetorical reflection] by conflating them into a 'theology-driven fundamentalism'" ("Reconceptualizing Christian Public Engagement," 292).

[27]In the concluding chapter of *Renovating Rhetoric in Christian Tradition*, Thomas Amorose offers a threefold explanation of Christianity's "resistance to rhetorical practices" that may also help explain why rhetoric is rarely discussed in churches (136). Amorose sketches "the anthropology,

And yet, despite negative views about rhetoric, it is also the case that many Christian thinkers *have* engaged or embraced the rhetorical tradition.[28] For example, Erasmus of Rotterdam, a Renaissance humanist as well as a Christian priest and theologian, wrote the rhetorical textbook *On Copia of Words and Ideas,* which promotes copiousness as a means of improving one's style and has implications for other rhetorical concepts such as revision and invention. Hugh Blair, George Campbell, and Richard Whately—who, among their various professional roles, were all ministers—championed the use of rhetoric in schools and seminaries during the late eighteenth and early nineteenth centuries.[29] And to cite just two contemporary scholars, David Cunningham and André Resner Jr. have recently advanced this conversation by publishing books that respectively explore theology as rhetorical and the intersections among theology, homiletics, and rhetoric.

This list is radically abridged—so much so, in fact, that one might make the claim that it is impossible to truly understand the Western rhetorical tradition apart from Christianity.[30] And as the brief survey

---

the hermeneutics, and the epistemology behind Christian tradition's relationship to rhetoric," highlighting specific Christian conceptions of human personhood, interpretation, and worldview that "hamper and limit the possibilities of rhetoric" (137-39). In their *Rhetorical Invention and Religious Inquiry* (New Haven: Yale University Press, 2000), Walter Jost and Wendy Olmsted offer a different explanation, writing that "rhetoricians with religious interests seem to be a rare breed, if not an endangered species, since the postmodern version of language holds that rhetoric *precludes* religious truth, which is typically cast as the final word in transcendental signifieds" (3).

[28]For examples, see Jost and Olmsted, *Rhetorical Invention and Religious Inquiry*; George A. Kennedy, *Classical Rhetoric and Its Christian and Secular Tradition from Ancient to Modern Times* (Chapel Hill: University of North Carolina Press, 1980); Jaroslav Pelikan, *Divine Rhetoric: The Sermon on the Mount as Message and as Model in Augustine, Chrysostom and Luther* (Crestwood, NY: St. Vladimir's Seminary Press, 2000), 3; Elizabeth Vander Lei et al., eds., *Renovating Rhetoric in Christian Tradition* (Pittsburgh: University of Pittsburgh Press, 2014).

[29]James L. Golden and Edward P. J. Corbett, *The Rhetoric of Blair, Campbell, and Whately*, rev. ed. (Carbondale: Southern Illinois University Press, 1990).

[30]My aim is not to be comprehensive here. For a more thorough account, see Kennedy's *Classical Rhetoric*. Kennedy discusses the rhetoric of the early church fathers, as well as many Christian writers from the Middle Ages, the Renaissance, and the seventeenth and eighteenth centuries (vii-viii). Two edited volumes that explore the intersections between Christianity

above suggests, Christian scholars and members of the clergy have been particularly active in engaging the tradition. For a whole host of reasons, it is vital that this engagement among scholars and clergy continue and expand; however, I want to suggest here that it is equally important that rhetorical reflection be recovered in, by, and for members of Christian congregations. I believe the people of God stand to benefit greatly from sustained and theologically responsible engagement with the Western rhetorical tradition.[31]

One reason for this is that Christians simply cannot avoid practicing rhetoric when witnessing. Rhetoric and truth are not opposites; rather, presentations of the truth are always rhetorical.[32] Given rhetoric's inevitability, it behooves Christians to reflect on rhetorical practice and learn how to do it well. Second, since all Christians are called to witness, the domain of rhetoric should not be occupied by seminarians, pastors, and scholars alone. All Christians should have access to the resources that the rhetorical tradition offers. Third, encouraging *rhetorica docens* among the laity has the potential to reinvigorate *rhetorica utens* in the church and enhance the church's witness. Members of the laity are too often encouraged to witness using simple formulas, and such approaches frequently fail to meet the demands

---

and rhetoric are Vander Lei et al., eds., *Renovating Rhetoric in Christian Tradition*, and Jost and Olmsted, eds., *Rhetorical Invention and Religious Inquiry*. Jaroslav Pelikan notes that, even as Christians drew upon classical rhetoric in their ecclesiastical and ecumenical discursive practices, aspects of classical rhetoric were also shaped by them (*Divine Rhetoric*, 21, 31). Pelikan notes, for example, that the "three Aristotelian 'genera of rhetorics, *symbouleutikon* ['deliberative'], *dikanikon* ['judicial'], *epideiktikon* ['demonstrative'],' would be profoundly modified when that principle of 'good words in the treating of the Word' was superimposed upon them" (31).

[31]One noteworthy example of the kind of engagement that I am advocating for here is the spring 2013 issue of *Comment Magazine*, which is devoted to the topic of persuasion. In his introduction to the issue, editor in chief James K. A. Smith defines persuasion as "a mode of convicted charity" ("The Lost Art of Persuasion," *Comment Magazine*, Spring 2013, 3). Though I do not return to this particular definition of persuasion throughout my project, I think the definition is an excellent one, and I believe that my rhetorical readings in the following chapters could be understood as an attempt to unpack how each of the book's figures practices such "convicted charity."

[32]Kenneth R. Chase, "Christian Rhetorical Theory: A New (Re)Turn," *Journal of Communication and Religion* 36, no. 1 (2013): 35-37.

of context or the specific needs of individuals. The writings of Aristotle, Cicero, Quintilian, Augustine, Erasmus, Blair, Campbell, Whately, Burke, Perelman and Olbrechts-Tyteca, Charland, Cunningham, Resner, and many others offer us resources to do better. By weaving excerpts of the writings of these figures into our Sunday school classes, Christian education classes, book discussions, and sermons, we can expand our repertoire of approaches to Christian witness, address audiences inside and outside of the church more effectively, and perhaps even learn how to participate in worship more fully. Recovering *rhetorica docens* in, by, and for the church may help us reinvigorate *rhetorica utens*.[33]

Recovering rhetorical reflection and reinvigorating our rhetorical practice must begin with Scripture's views about rhetoric.[34] As I have already noted, both Jesus and Paul made remarks that speak to the matter, and interpretations about their comments vary widely. However, in an article exploring 1 Corinthians 2:1-5, Matthew 10:17-20, and other relevant passages of Scripture, communication theorist Kenneth R. Chase observes that there is widespread agreement among Christian scholars that God works through our study and practice of rhetoric.[35] After reviewing the relevant literature on 1 Corinthians 2:1-5, Chase writes, "Paul's dissociation of human eloquence and divine power . . . does not establish a clean break between the suasive resources of rhetorical art and the spiritual power of divine wisdom"; instead, Paul's comments differentiate distinctly Christian rhetoric from non-Christian rhetoric.[36] Chase then goes on to argue against

---

[33]Muehlhoff and Langer's *Winsome Persuasion* offers one model of the sort of work that I have in mind here (8-9).

[34]Martin J. Medhurst made a similar claim when calling for "an explicitly Christian theory or approach to the study of rhetoric" in 2004 ("Religious Belief and Scholarship: A Complex Relationship," *Journal of Communication & Religion* 27, no. 1 [2004]: 40-47).

[35]Kenneth R. Chase, "Ethical Rhetoric and Divine Power: Reflections on Matthew 10:17-20 (and Parallels)," *Bulletin for Biblical Research* 22, no. 4 (2012): 201.

[36]Chase, "Ethical Rhetoric," 203.

the notion that rhetorical planning and the Spirit's power are some-how mutually exclusive, making the case that Jesus's instruction to his followers in Matthew 10:17-20 applies only in the circumstances men-tioned by Jesus in the passage—namely, those situations in which a disciple is pressured to witness by those in power.[37] Chase's readings suggest that Scripture allows for the study and practice of the art of persuasion, provided that one is sensitive to the demands of context and maintains a proper perspective about human rhetorical power in relation to both God's power and earthly powers. Such findings strike me as congruent with the rest of the biblical witness, which affirms and even celebrates the use of language across multiple genres for myriad purposes, including persuasion.

This does not mean, as Augustine suggested, that our witness will necessarily be compromised if we fail to engage in the study and prac-tice of rhetoric. God often acts powerfully in spite of our own actions. What is more, it is ultimately God who underwrites the church's rhe-torical practices and makes them persuasive (or not). It is necessary to admit, therefore, that there may be some limits to what we can say about the persuasiveness of the church's witness. As Jesus says to Nicodemus in the Gospel of John, "The wind blows where it wishes, and you hear its sound, but you do not know where it comes from or where it goes. So it is with everyone who is born of the Spirit" (Jn 3:8). But to admit that God works through our rhetorical practices—and, therefore, that we cannot know everything about how these practices function to persuade—is not to say that the persuasiveness of our witness is completely inscrutable to us. In light of that fact, I seek to

---

[37]Chase, "Ethical Rhetoric," 203-6. According to Chase, an important reason for Jesus's special instructions to his disciples in such situations is the following one: "When disciples are dragged before the authorities, they are coerced into a nexus of time and power that can only be effec-tively managed by divine empowerment. . . . The dynamic factors and forces calling forth an apologia exceed whatever rhetorical preparation the disciples could bring to bear in anticipation of that moment, overwhelming the truth of the witness and co-opting its message into the ideology of secular power" ("Ethical," 213).

call the church to engage in a more robust dialogue with the rhetorical tradition in hopes that such dialogue will help us better understand, and enhance the effectiveness of, our witness.

One of the tradition's—and this book's—key rhetorical concepts is *ēthos*.[38] According to Aristotle, *ēthos* is one of three rhetorical appeals by which a rhetor persuades an audience.[39] *Ēthos*, the appeal to one's character or credibility, accounts for the fact that a rhetor's ability to persuade an audience is tied to who the rhetor is or who he or she appears to be. Arguments from *ēthos* can take many different forms, and we can get a sense of this variety by considering the apostle Paul's rhetoric, which presents us with an argument from *ēthos* that flips the notion on its head. As André Resner Jr. has noted, the apostle Paul constructs a "reverse-*ēthos* argument" in his first letter to the church at Corinth.[40] Recognizing that one's weaknesses are actually strengths

---

[38]In order to be precise about the concept I am referring to in the book, I write *ēthos* with a macron over the first letter. In his book *Preacher and Cross: Person and Message in Theology and Rhetoric*, André Resner, Jr. gives a cogent rationale for the use of the macron, noting, "One difficulty that is immediately confronted in a study of *ēthos* from the rhetorical frame of reference is the confusion that exists over the spelling, pronunciation, and meaning of this word. The macron over the *ē* of *ēthos* is the diacritical marking used to transliterate the Greek letter *ēta*. It is pronounced with a long 'a' sound as in 'eight.' This macron differentiates *ēthos* from 'ethos,' a commonly used English word which has to do with 'customs,' 'beliefs,' or 'standards.' The confusion in the critical literature is due to the common practice of mistranslating *ēthos* into English without diacritical marking, and, most often, without even italics which would indicate that it is a foreign word and not the word 'ethos' which has become a functional word in the English language" (Grand Rapids: Eerdmans [1999], 2). Most of the scholars I cite in this book are referring to *ēthos* in their work; I retain these scholars' formatting decision when quoting them directly.

I focus on *ēthos* because it is one of the conceptual centerpieces of the Western rhetorical tradition and also because of my familiarity with the concept (James E. Beitler, "Making More of the Middle Ground: Desmond Tutu and the *Ethos* of the South African Truth and Reconciliation Commission," *Relevant Rhetoric: A New Journal of Rhetorical Studies* 3, no. 1 [Spring 2012]; *Remaking Transitional Justice in the United States: The Rhetorical Authorization of the Greensboro Truth and Reconciliation Commission* [New York: Springer, 2013], 18). Mark Allan Steiner's work offers additional justification for my emphasis. Steiner includes "respect for the importance of *ethos*" as the final feature of his "model for evangelical public and cultural engagement" ("Reconceptualizing Christian Public Engagement," 310, 313). I explore a few different definitions of *ēthos* throughout this book. For a fuller account of the concept, see Resner's book, which explores *ēthos* in classical rhetoric, the homiletic tradition, Paul's writings, and contemporary homiletic theory.

[39]Aristotle, *On Rhetoric* 1356a3-4.

[40]Resner, *Preacher and Cross*, 130.

when understood in light of the logic of the cross of Christ, Paul embraces the accusations of his detractors. He uses the critiques meant to undermine his rhetorical authority in order to justify that authority. Resner's observations remind us that, because Christians cling to the wisdom of the cross, our exploration of the rhetoric of Christian witness may reveal communicative postures and strategies that are at odds with what previous rhetoricians have taught us about persuasion.[41] This is not to say, however, that all of the rhetorical moves described in the proceeding pages will look identical to Paul's "reverse-*ēthos* argument." This book presents readers with a variety of ways that Christians have established *ēthos* when witnessing, both individually and collectively.[42] That said, in these pages I have tried to focus on rhetorics that all find their power in the gospel of Jesus Christ.

Rhetorics of Worship

Over the course of the book, I draw on the work of theologians such as Simon Chan, Stanley Hauerwas, Jennifer M. McBride, and John Webster to make the case that some of the most persuasive forms of Christian witness are constructed by the worshiping body of Christ.[43]

---

[41]Resner writes, "For Paul, true *ēthos* is derivative not of a social and cultural expectation but of an expectation (a divine call, commission, and empowerment) that arises from the nature of the gospel and the community of faith that is formed and sustained by the God-given and empowered *logos* (the cross-event-proclaimed)" (*Preacher and Cross*, 130).

[42]As we will see in later chapters, *ēthos* had both individual and communal dimensions for Aristotle and other ancient rhetoricians.

[43]Jennifer McBride's *The Church for the World: A Theology of Public Witness* (Oxford: Oxford University Press, 2012) jumpstarted my thinking on this topic. In the book, McBride makes the case that an important and neglected posture for the church to adopt when witnessing is "confession of sin unto repentant action" (11). McBride's point is a vital one for many American Christians to hear; however, she primarily explores one posture of witness, and—given the variety of situations that Christians find themselves in—there is a need to explore other postures that have been taken up by Christians as they have responded to the Great Commission. Reading McBride's book, I found myself thinking about the many ways that *worship practices* invite Christians to take on the posture of "confession of sin unto repentant action," and I realized that I could extend McBride's argument by considering other postures of witness that our worship practices invite us to adopt.

This argument extends recent work about the relationship between liturgy and Christian formation.[44]

In *Desiring the Kingdom: Worship, Worldview, and Cultural Formation,* philosopher James K. A. Smith suggests that the liturgies we participate in, whether they are Christian or not, order our loves and influence who we are, how we think and feel, and what we do in the world.[45] Smith goes on to demonstrate, in this book and subsequent ones, just how crucial Christian worship practices are, both for our spiritual formation and also for our educational, missional, and political endeavors. Jennifer M. McBride makes a related point in *Radical Discipleship: A Liturgical Politics of the Gospel*—a book that grew out of McBride's involvement with a justice-seeking Christian community in Atlanta, Georgia.[46] McBride's work in the community coincided with the seasons of the Christian year, which, she claims, brought the value of observing "a deeply liturgical life" home to her.[47] To emphasize this point, McBride organizes the chapters of her book according to the seasons of the Christian year.[48] Her account of her journey from Advent through Pentecost with the Atlanta-based community instructively highlights that, for those seeking to follow the gospel of Jesus Christ, one's own formation is indeed a matter of great import. But McBride's account also highlights that individual formation alone is insufficient: one's "personal transformation" also ought to be connected to "social and personal transformation."[49] Thus, her

---

[44]See, for example, James K. A. Smith, *Desiring the Kingdom* (Grand Rapids: Baker Academic, 2009); *Imagining the Kingdom* (Grand Rapids: Baker Academic, 2013); *Awaiting the King* (Grand Rapids: Baker Academic, 2017); Nicholas Wolterstorff, "Christology, Christian Learning, and Christian Formation: Mark Noll's *Jesus Christ and the Life of the Mind*," *Books & Culture*, September–October 2012.

[45]Smith, *Desiring the Kingdom*, 25.

[46]Jennifer M. McBride, *Radical Discipleship: A Liturgical Politics of the Gospel* (Minneapolis: Fortress, 2017), 2-5.

[47]McBride, *Radical Discipleship*, 4.

[48]McBride, *Radical Discipleship*, 4.

[49]McBride, *Radical Discipleship*, 5-6, 41-47.

book's procession through the Christian year highlights the "social and political significance of [each] liturgical season."[50]

Smith's trilogy and McBride's *Radical Discipleship* do an excellent job of explaining how liturgies relate to Christian formation as well as "social and political" transformation; however, more work is needed that considers the implications of Smith's and McBride's arguments about liturgy for the rhetoric of Christian witness.[51] That is, we need to consider not only how worship forms our identities and transforms social and political realities but also how worship forms Christians into people fit to respond to the communicative challenges of the Great Commission. Put another way, we need to extend existing conversations about the ways that Christian liturgies shape the character of individuals and society by considering how our liturgies relate to various constructions of rhetorical character, or *ēthos*.[52]

---

[50]McBride, *Radical Discipleship*, 6.

[51]Alan Noble has also highlighted the importance of the connection between worship and witness, claiming, "The church can either define its witness by its worship, aesthetics, and rites or capitulate to secular conceptions of faith as a personal lifestyle preference" (*Disruptive Witness*, 120). And Noble is correct when he later notes that "the image of worship that Smith articulates in *Desiring the Kingdom* is a powerful disruptive witness" (*Disruptive Witness*, 144; see also 132). There is, however, more to be said about the study and practice of rhetoric in light of Smith's work.

[52]This particular line of inquiry has many forerunners, one of whom is Michael G. Cartwright. In his piece "Being Sent: Witness," in *The Blackwell Companion to Christian Ethics*, ed. Stanley Hauerwas and Samuel Wells, 481-94 (Malden, MA: Blackwell, 2004), Cartwright describes "seven features of the *ethos* of witness" (484). According to Cartwright, two of these features are "keeping time" (i.e., following the Christian calendar) and "performing liturgy" (484-86). My book develops and extends Cartwright's claims by exploring how particular seasons and worship practices resonate with particular configurations of *ēthos* (and other closely related rhetorical concepts). Although Cartwright uses the term "*ethos*" throughout his piece, he does not discuss rhetoric in great detail.

Another forerunner is David Cunningham. In his book *Faithful Persuasion* (Notre Dame: University of Notre Dame Press, 1992), Cunningham—a rhetorician interested in the rhetoric of theology—asks an important question related to my inquiry: "How can theology speak with a *character* that will bring about true conversion?" (146, emphasis added). Cunningham's project explores theology and theological argument as rhetorical, and his approach is primarily theoretical. It does not, however, focus on Christian witness in light of rhetorical studies. To clarify the difference between Cunningham's project and mine, *Faithful Persuasion* theorizes about the rhetoric of theology, while I analyze acts of Christian witness rhetorically.

A third forerunner is Jaroslav Pelikan. In the epilogue to his book *Divine Rhetoric*, Pelikan maintains that rhetorical methodologies (and, in particular, Aristotle's rhetorical appeals) can help us better understand two important types of Christian instruction: theological and doctrinal discourse (which he refers to as "summa") and preaching (which he refers to as

This study comprises five interconnected case studies and a concluding chapter that attempts to weave the preceding chapters together.
Each case study explores the rhetoric of an influential Christian writer,
focusing on his or her appeals to *ēthos* or another closely related concept. This material is arranged so as to present information from the
history of rhetoric more or less chronologically. But the book's more
fundamental structure proceeds according to the church's clock. Taking a cue from McBride, my chapters track with the times and seasons
of the church year: Advent, Christmas, Epiphany, Lent, Easter, and
Pentecost. And the book also keeps time on a smaller scale. As my
titles and epigraphs suggest, each chapter is themed around a different
element of the Christian worship service: collect, creed, sermon, confession, Eucharist, and benediction.[53] This arrangement stems from my
conviction that such ways of ordering time are among the church's, and
indeed all of humanity's, greatest rhetorical achievements.

The church year is, as Phillip Pfatteicher rightly notes, a "collective
composition, shaped over many centuries, even millennia, by diverse
hands and many cultures."[54] The same is true of patterns of Christian

---

"sermon") (151-53). My book engages these two types of discourse in chapters two and three,
respectively. Pelikan's final sentence in his book hints at the notion that rhetoric can also help
us understand the relationship between these forms of Christian instruction and "prayer and
worship" (155). I seek to explore the relationship between rhetoric and worship further.

Finally, Robert E. Webber's book *God Still Speaks: A Biblical View of Christian Communication*
(Nashville: Thomas Nelson, 1980) and his Ancient-Future series serve as additional forerunners
of the current project. Though Webber does not focus on rhetoric, his work has productively
shaped the discussions about the relationship between liturgy and evangelism. In *God Still
Speaks,* he writes, "Symbolic communication in the church is a valid means of communicating
truths of the Christian faith. The reenactment of the birth of Christ, the sorrow over His death,
the joy of His resurrection, and the power of Pentecost cannot be completely nor adequately
communicated through words alone. If man is a creature whose brain is oriented towards spatial
as well as verbal communication, then *Christian communication, both within the church and
outside the church, must not neglect the symbolic, nonverbal, and ritualistic means of communication*" (147). To this I would add that Christians ought to consider ways that our verbal communication should be shaped by "the symbolic, nonverbal, and ritualistic" elements of worship.

[53]I realize that different churches order worship practices in different ways, and I don't mean to
suggest that my sequence of the order of worship is the definitive one.

[54]Phillip Pfatteicher, *Journey into the Heart of God: Living the Liturgical Year* (Oxford: Oxford University Press, 2013), 7.

worship. And these collective compositions—the church year and patterns of Christian worship—can be persuasive: they can function, to cite Augustine's adaptation of Cicero's formula, "to instruct, delight, and move" us.[55] What is more, as Smith and others have shown, the forms and practices associated with the church year and Christian worship can "constitute our character," both individually and collectively.[56] Rhetoricians refer to discourse that functions this way using the term *constitutive rhetoric* (a notion we will return to later in the book). Through their persuasive and constitutive functions, rhetorics of the church year and Christian worship orient us in particular ways toward God and one another. But even more significant for my purposes, these rhetorics orient us in particular ways toward the world, shaping the rhetoric of our witness. In other words, the rhetorics of the church year and Christian worship are not just for those inside the church but for the whole of humanity. This book, then, invites Christians to pay greater attention to the relationship between our rhetorics of worship and witness. Attending to the ways that we worship God throughout the seasons of the church year may help us respond to Paul's exhortation to season our speech (Col 4:6).[57]

My use of Paul's metaphor of seasoned speech should not be taken to mean that I think rhetoric's scope ought to be limited to matters of presentation (as Plato, Ramus, and even Augustine suggested). Practicing rhetoric is not simply about flavoring the truth with a dash of eloquence; it involves the discovery, invention, analysis, interpretation, construction, recollection, arrangement, *and* presentation of information, knowledge, and wisdom. And rhetorical activity is also not

---

[55]Pfatteicher, *Journey into the Heart of God*, 7; Augustine, *On Christian Teaching*, 117.

[56]Smith, *Desiring the Kingdom*, 80.

[57]My aim in this book is not to present an in-depth analysis of Christian liturgy; rather, I simply aim to highlight a few connections between liturgical and rhetorical practices in order to suggest that worship offers us rhetorical resources for Christian witness. For a more thorough exploration of Christian liturgy, see Pfatteicher's book.

merely about appearances. It can be profoundly true. Consider, for example, Pfatteicher's following comments about the church year, keeping in mind my remark that this way of ordering time is indeed rhetorical:

> The liturgical year is not a mere commemoration of the events of the Gospel; it is in fact the actualization of these events, their renewal upon earth. Thus the act of salvation—begun in Bethlehem, accomplished on Good Friday, vindicated on Easter Day, crowned on Ascension Day—is an ever-continuing process as its fruits are made real in the lives of those who accept this redemption. The Church's calendar, its day-by-day observance of the liturgical year, is not only a pious recollection of historic events and people. The liturgical year is not a lifeless representation of the events of the past or a bare record of a former age. It is rather Christ himself who is ever living in his Church.[58]

Therefore, though stylistic elements are included in my conception of "seasoned speech," they are far from the whole. I also use the phrase to refer to speech that resonates with the seasons of the church year as well as speech that stems from our liturgical-rhetorical traditions and, thus, has been "fitted for use" or "matured." To be clear, I am not using the phrase to suggest that speech that resonates with a particular season of the church year must only be used during that season; rather, I want to maintain that we ought to study seasonally relevant speech so that, to borrow again from Paul, we will "be ready in season and out of season" (2 Tim 4:2).

Overview

Chapter one explores how C. S. Lewis establishes goodwill in his writings through an analysis of his essays in *God in the Dock*. The chapter introduces readers to Aristotle's explanation of the ways that

---

[58]Pfatteicher, *Journey into the Heart of God*, 21. In the final sentences of this passage, Pfatteicher borrows language from an encyclical by Pope Pius XII (345).

rhetors can establish the argument from *ēthos*. Chapter two analyzes Dorothy L. Sayers's radio play *He That Should Come* and several of her other writings to make the case that Sayers utilizes what Quintilian refers to as *enargeia* to confront her audience with the audacity of the creeds. Chapter three explores Dietrich Bonhoeffer's work in light of Kenneth Burke's descriptions of identification and division. I focus on Bonhoeffer's attempts to align himself with or distance himself from various audiences and the resultant clarity or obscurity of his witness with respect to these audiences. Chapter four brings Desmond Tutu's appeals as chair of the South African Truth and Reconciliation Commission into conversation with journalist Antjie Krog's account of the TRC. In this chapter, I suggest that Krog's book *Country of My Skull* serves as an act of repentance in response to Tutu's constitutive rhetoric of *ubuntu*. Chapter five offers a reading of Marilynne Robinson's Gilead trilogy in light of premodern understandings of *ēthos*. To borrow two phrases from rhetorician Michael J. Hyde's discussion of *ēthos*, my analysis suggests that Robinson's narrative rhetoric "grants . . . *living room* to" the Christian faith, helping her readers to "feel more *at home*" with belief and some of its most difficult questions.[59]

The arc of the book's argument is to move from a discussion of individual postures of Christian witness (*ēthos* as an appeal to an individual's character) to a discussion of communal ones (*ēthos* as an appealing gathering place). In light of this trajectory, the final chapter breaks from the conventions of previous chapters. Instead of looking at the rhetorical postures of an influential individual, I bring back all of the book's figures and introduce readers to Mikhail Bakhtin's concept of heteroglossia in order to reflect on the polyvocality of Christian witness.

---

[59]Michael J. Hyde, ed., *The* Ethos *of Rhetoric* (Columbia: University of South Carolina Press, 2004), xiii.

Taken together, the chapters demonstrate that Christians can enhance the persuasiveness of our witness as individuals and create a hospitable community for wanderers and wayfarers by paying careful attention to both the rhetorical tradition and our own liturgical practices. In brief, I want to encourage church members to reflect on various aspects of the rhetorical tradition, highlight important and practical ways of establishing *ēthos* when witnessing, and bring the rhetorical facets of Christian worship into relief.

It is my hope that the rhetorics of Christian witness explored in this book will provide fodder for reflection, discussion, and perhaps even imitation.[60] In both the Western rhetorical tradition and the Christian tradition, imitation has long been viewed as a highly worthwhile practice. Ancient rhetoricians taught their students the art of rhetoric by having them imitate model texts, and many contemporary speech and writing teachers (myself included) still ask the same of their students.[61] Correspondingly, the apostle Paul encouraged the people at Corinth to model their lives on him even as he modeled his own life on the Lord Jesus, writing, "Be imitators of me, as I am of Christ" (1 Cor 11:1). And Thomas à Kempis began the first chapter of his great devotional work, *The Imitation of Christ,* by suggesting that followers of Jesus Christ ought to "imitate His life and His ways, if we truly desire to be enlightened and free of all blindness of heart."[62]

---

[60]James K. A. Smith rightly notes that Christians have long championed imitation as a means of developing virtue (*You Are What You Love: The Spiritual Power of Habit* [Grand Rapids: Brazos Press, 2016], 18). To this I would add that what is true of imitation and virtue is true of imitation and persuasive communication as well. Here I am taking a page from Walter Jost and Wendy Olmsted's introduction to *Rhetorical Invention and Religious Inquiry.* Jost and Olmsted describe the pieces in their edited collection "as rhetorical models and resources for community- and self-invention" (2).

[61]For a contemporary example of this pedagogical approach that is based in ancient rhetorical practice, see Crowley and Hawhee, *Ancient Rhetorics for Contemporary Students*, 301-24.

[62]Thomas à Kempis, *Imitation of Christ* (New York: Random House, 1998), 3. Steiner's proposed "model by which evangelical Christians can engage in civil discourse" also notes the importance of "imitating Christ" ("Reconceptualizing Christian Public Engagement," 293-95).

Practicing imitation as a rhetor, a disciple of Jesus Christ, or both does *not* mean that we simply copy what has come before us. As rhetorician Michael Leff noted, practicing imitation was not understood by ancient rhetoricians to involve "mere repetition or mechanistic reproduction of something found in an existing text."[63] Rather, it was seen as an instrument of invention, of making something new by way of remaking something old.[64] Such invention was partially a product of the rhetor's unique rhetorical situation. Existing forms had to be transformed to meet the distinctive demands of the present context.[65] Invention also resulted from other creative activities involved in the practice of imitation, including, Leff suggested, the recovery, interpretation, application, and re-embodiment of prior language use.[66] The major figures discussed here all practice rhetoric in this more dynamic sense, remaking past practices in present contexts to witness to the gospel of Jesus Christ. Their words are grounded firmly in the truth, but they have been seasoned with the salt of the saints who went before them.

May this study of their speech season your own.

---

[63]Michael C. Leff, "Hermeneutical Rhetoric," in *Rethinking Rhetorical Theory, Criticism, and Pedagogy: The Living Art of Michael C. Leff,* ed. Antonio de Velasco, John Angus Campbell, and David Henry (East Lansing: Michigan State University Press, 2016), 313.

[64]Leff, "Hermeneutical Rhetoric," 313-15.

[65]Leff, "Hermeneutical Rhetoric," 315.

[66]Leff, "Hermeneutical Rhetoric," 315. Leff wrote, "*Imitatio* functions as a hermeneutical rhetoric that circulates influence between past and present. As the embodied utterances of the past are *interpreted* for current *application*, their ideas and modes of articulation are *reembodied*, and old voices are *recovered* for use in new circumstances" (315, emphases added).

1

PREPARING THE WAY

C. S. Lewis and the Goodwill of Advent

A voice cries: "In the wilderness prepare the way of the LORD;
make straight in the desert a highway for our God."

ISAIAH 40:3

Merciful God, who sent your messengers the prophets to preach repentance
and prepare the way for our salvation: Give us grace to heed their warnings
and forsake our sins, that we may greet with joy the coming of Jesus Christ
our Redeemer; who lives and reigns with you and the Holy Spirit, one God,
now and for ever. Amen.

CONTEMPORARY COLLECT FOR THE SECOND SUNDAY OF ADVENT,
THE BOOK OF COMMON PRAYER

I have not tried to prove that the religious sayings are true, only that they are
significant: if you meet them with a certain good will, a certain readiness to
find meaning. For if they should happen to contain information about real
things, you will not get it on any other terms.

C. S. LEWIS, "THE LANGUAGE OF RELIGION"

CLIVE STAPLES LEWIS WORSHIPED at Holy Trinity Anglican
Church, a small parish church in Headington Quarry, Oxford.[1] The
stone building has a side entryway leading into the nave, which,
though not as famously snug as the church where the poet George
Herbert served as rector, is a charmingly intimate worship space. A
single row of stone columns runs parallel to the center aisle, a design

---

[1] A version of this chapter first appeared as an article in the journal *Religion & the Arts*. I am grateful to InterVarsity Press for granting the necessary permissions to the journal.

feature that Lewis took advantage of when worshiping there. He almost always sat toward the back of the nave, on the far side of one of the pillars. When I visited the church nearly eighteen years ago, I made a point of sitting as close as I could to the spot that Lewis once sat, hoping to experience worship from his chosen vantage point. I cannot recall a word from the sermon that day, but I do remember thinking that Lewis's spot was a very comfortable one. After the service ended, I rose from my seat to find Lewis's gravestone. Parishioners were still filing out of the church, and an older gentleman and I started to chat while we waited to exit the building. He mentioned that he had been going to Holy Trinity for a long time and that he had known Lewis.

"What was he like?" I asked, a bit too eagerly.

I could tell immediately from the man's amused expression that this question was not new to him, and he had a ready answer designed to poke fun at tourists who made their reverence for Lewis known. Eyes twinkling, the man replied, "He used to sit around and smoke his pipe and look for someone to set right."

There was, of course, some truth in the man's wry remark: Lewis could often be found sitting and smoking with his friends at Oxford pubs such as The Eagle and Child or The Lamb and the Flag, and he himself admitted that he was in the business of correcting misunderstandings and false assumptions about Christianity.[2] On occasion he was as argumentative and curmudgeonly as the man's comment implies.[3] But as those familiar with Lewis's writings know, the persona Lewis developed in his prose is seldom haughty or holier-than-thou.

---

[2]Christopher W. Mitchell, "Bearing the Weight of Glory," in *The Pilgrim's Guide: C. S. Lewis and the Art of Witness*, ed. David Mills (Grand Rapids: Eerdmans, 1998), 5.

[3]Lewis was, of course, not perfect. Greg M. Anderson has noted that his colleagues referred to him as a "polemicist" and observed that "he could be mean" ("A Most Potent Rhetoric: C. S. Lewis, 'Congenital Rhetorician,'" in *C. S. Lewis: Life, Works, and Legacy*, vol. 4, *Scholar, Teacher, and Public Intellectual*, ed. Bruce L. Edwards [Westport: Praeger, 2007], 211).

He shares his vast knowledge with others but wears his learning lightly, calls people to righteousness but sidesteps self-righteousness, and meets his audiences on their terms but manages to avoid even a hint of disdain. C. S. Lewis has much to teach us about how to season our speech.

Scholars and critics have long recognized Lewis's potent persuasiveness and acute audience awareness. Lewis is also routinely praised for his versatility as a writer: many have commented on the fact that he employs a wide variety of literary devices and genres to make his convictions convincing.[4] What is more, Lewis himself seems to have thought deeply about persuasive language: in his speeches and essays, he often reflects openly on how best to appeal to particular audiences.[5] However, in spite of widespread praise for Lewis's persuasiveness as well as his own interest in the topic, only a relatively small group of scholars have turned to rhetoric to understand Lewis's corpus, and many who have done so have argued that we need more scholarship exploring how Lewis's writings work rhetorically.[6]

This gap in the critical conversation may be the result of Lewis's own intellectual preferences. As Greg M. Anderson notes in a superb piece on Lewis's rhetoric, Lewis received some training on the subject from his classics teacher, Harry Wakelyn Smith (or, as

---

[4]For example, Lyle Dorsett writes that Lewis "served up age-old themes in formats suitable for everyone. Almost any topic he covered in prose can be found in his fiction and poetry as well" (introduction to *The Essential C. S. Lewis* [New York: Collier/Macmillan, 1988], 16). Jerry Root notes that Lewis "mastered multiple modes of communication" (*Lewis and a Problem of Evil* [Eugene, OR: Pickwick, 2009], xi).

[5]Examples appear in "Christian Apologetics" (89), "God in the Dock" (240-41), and "Before We Can Communicate" (256), all in *God in the Dock: Essays on Theology and Ethics*, ed. Walter Hooper (Grand Rapids: Eerdmans, 1970).

[6]In *The Rhetoric of Certitude* (Kent, OH: Kent State University Press, 2009), Tandy states that "there is a noticeable lack of critical material that analyzes in detail the rhetorical and literary qualities of Lewis's prose" (x). Likewise, in "Most Potent Rhetoric," Greg M. Anderson writes, "We are just now coming to grips with [Lewis's] rhetorical undergirding to his defense of the Christian faith" (195). And in *Branches to Heaven* (Dallas: Spence, 1998), James Como—whom Anderson also cites—proposes that we should read Lewis "as he was essentially: a wary yet energetic, ambivalent yet committed *Homo rhetoricus*" (180).

Lewis refers to him in *Surprised by Joy*, Smewgy).[7] However, though Lewis held Smewgy up as one of his two best instructors, he clearly preferred the study of dialectic to that of rhetoric.[8] According to James Como, Lewis's personal library bears witness to this fact. Como points out that works by ancient rhetors are in short supply in Lewis's collection, and he also highlights that one of Lewis's logic books contains copious notes while his copy of Aristotle's *On Rhetoric* contains none.[9] Perhaps even more telling is Gary L. Tandy's observation that none of Lewis's many writings focus exclusively on rhetoric.[10]

Lewis's own preference for dialectic over rhetoric should not, however, discourage us from an exploration of his rhetoric. As many who study his rhetoric have noted, Lewis self-identified as "an apologist and a rhetor" on one occasion and as "a born rhetorician" on another.[11] And almost all of the scholars who write about Lewis from a rhetorical perspective have called attention to the apology of rhetoric that appears in his *A Preface to* Paradise Lost.[12] Lewis writes, "I do not think (and no great civilization has ever thought) that the art of the rhetorician is necessarily vile. It is in itself noble, though of course, like most arts, it can be wickedly used."[13] Rhetoric has been dismissed repeatedly by writers throughout the subject's history, so much so that today the term is almost always used pejoratively outside of academic contexts. But as this passage indicates,

---

[7]Anderson, "Most Potent Rhetoric," 197.

[8]Anderson, "Most Potent Rhetoric," 197.

[9]Como, *Branches to Heaven*, 27. Anderson cites and counters Como's assertion, noting that, although Lewis did not annotate Aristotle's *On Rhetoric*, he *did* mark works on rhetoric by Quintilian, Hugh Blair, and I. A. Richards (among others) ("Most Potent Rhetoric," 197-98). Root, too, challenges Como, noting that "the works of the rhetoricians may not be the only means by which Lewis could have learned the canons of rhetoric" (*Lewis and a Problem of Evil*, xii).

[10]Tandy, *Rhetoric of Certitude*, 27.

[11]Quoted in Anderson, "Most Potent Rhetoric," 195, 211; Tandy, *Rhetoric of Certitude*, 27.

[12]Anderson, "Most Potent Rhetoric," 199; Como, *Branches to Heaven*, 146; Tandy, *Rhetoric of Certitude*, 28.

[13]C. S. Lewis, *Preface to* Paradise Lost (New York: Oxford University Press, 1961), 53.

Lewis knew better, probably as a result of his familiarity with the *trivium* as well as his immense knowledge of the medieval period and the Renaissance.[14]

Moreover, in spite of the fact that Lewis did not mark his copy of Aristotle's *On Rhetoric*, a few recent studies have made fruitful connections between Lewis's writings and the works of rhetoricians. Both Tandy and Anderson frame their studies of Lewis's rhetoric using Aristotle's explanation of rhetoric.[15] Benjamin Fischer and Philip C. Derbesy make a compelling case that Lewis's imitative approach is similar to Quintilian's rhetorical counsel.[16] And Jerry Root, who makes the claim that "the thing that generates Lewis's holding power is his rhetoric," draws on the work of twentieth-century rhetorician Richard M. Weaver to illuminate what Lewis is doing rhetorically in his writings.[17] As the aforementioned scholars have demonstrated and as I attempt to show in what follows, considering Lewis's works in relation to rhetorical theory can deepen our understanding of Lewis's writings and the appeal of his witness.

---

[14]Tandy, *Rhetoric of Certitude*, 28; Root, *Lewis and a Problem of Evil,* xii. Lewis's comments about rhetoric may have even been innovative in his circles (see Anderson, "Most Potent Rhetoric," 199-203). Around the middle of the twentieth century, rhetoric began to flower again in the academy, and two of the most influential books on the subject—Kenneth Burke's *A Rhetoric of Motives* and Chaïm Perelman and Lucie Olbrechts-Tyteca's *La Nouvelle Rhétorique: Traité de l' Argumentation*—were published, respectively, eight and sixteen years after Lewis's comments about rhetoric in *A Preface to* Paradise Lost. The first edition of Edward P. J. Corbett's landmark textbook, *Classical Rhetoric for the Modern Student*, did not appear until 1965, some seventeen months after Lewis's death. After reviewing what Lewis says about rhetoric in *A Preface to* Paradise Lost as well as several of Lewis's other scholarly books, Greg M. Anderson rightly remarks, "He was fifty years ahead of his time in the prominence he gave rhetoric in his historical work" ("Most Potent Rhetoric," 203). "Lewis was at the very least," Anderson writes a few pages earlier, "a grandfather to the recent rediscovery of rhetoric" (199).

[15]Tandy, *Rhetoric of Certitude*, 28-29; Anderson, "Most Potent Rhetoric," 200-201.

[16]Benjamin Fischer and Phillip C. Derbesy, "Literary Catholicity: An Alternative Reading of Influence in the Work of C. S. Lewis and G. K. Chesterton," *Religion and the Arts* 19, no. 4 (2015): 392.

[17]Root, *Lewis and a Problem of Evil* xi, xvii. Root makes a convincing case for reading Lewis's work rhetorically by drawing our attention to "Lewis's rhetorical training, in the broadest sense" as well as "the way in which his written work operates with rhetorical purposes" (xiii).

The present chapter advances existing conversations about Lewis's rhetoric through an investigation of appeals to *ēthos* in his nonfiction, with a special emphasis on the essays that appear in his collection *God in the Dock: Essays on Theology and Ethics*.[18] This particular conceptual focus is warranted in part by existing Lewis scholarship. For example, after highlighting Lewis's grasp of the rhetorical appeals of *ēthos, pathos,* and *logos,* Jerry Root adds, "Perhaps the mode most strongly evident in him is *ethos*."[19] Building on such insights, I contend that a primary way that Lewis establishes *ēthos* is by demonstrating what Aristotle referred to as *eunoia*, goodwill toward one's audience.[20] Lewis's rhetoric of goodwill—which involves addressing audiences on their own terms, adopting a

---

[18]The collection—compiled posthumously by Walter Hooper, Lewis's literary executor—was originally published in the UK as *Undeceptions: Essays on Theology and Ethics*. Though the older title may not be as catchy as the new one, it captures one of the collection's central themes more accurately. In many of the pieces, Lewis highlights faulty thinking about faith in the hopes that, once these barriers to belief are cleared away, people will come to embrace the good news of Jesus Christ.

[19]Root, *Lewis and a Problem of Evil*, xvi. Though the remainder of Root's study does not revolve around the concept of *ēthos* explicitly, he offers the following immensely useful summary of Lewis's argument from *ēthos*: "He is honest, and he displays in his work that authenticity of character that is full of genuine humility and childlike wonder. His *ethos* is exhibited when he wrestles with thorny passages in the Psalms that others tend to avoid because of their difficulty. It is seen as he announces to his readers that there is much about prayer he does not understand, or when he confesses that academic study should end in some degree of doubt. His *ethos* is equally evident by the confidence with which he presses a point that he has developed discursively, championing it with bulldog tenacity" (xvi). I return to several of these aspects of Lewis's *ēthos* in my own analysis.

[20]In what follows, I draw primarily on Aristotle to make sense of Lewis's rhetoric; however, one of my anonymous readers helpfully suggested that, given Lewis's predilection for dialectic, his work might also be understood in terms of "Platonic rhetoric." The reader suggested that Richard M. Weaver's piece on the *Phaedrus,* which offers a more charitable reading of Plato's views about rhetoric than I present in my introduction, might help me make the connection between Lewis's work and Plato's rhetoric. Based on a reading of Plato's dialogue, Weaver presents "true rhetoric" as the "intellectual love of the Good" (*The Ethics of Rhetoric* [Davis, CA: Hermagoras Press, 1985], 20, 25). Weaver suggests, moreover, that the "lover of truth" can practice rhetorical "exaggeration," noting, "The exaggeration which this [true] rhetorician employs is not caricature but *prophecy*" (19-20, emphasis added). Such observations resonate with my definition of goodwill below as well as Joel D. Heck's suggestion, which I return to later in the chapter, that Lewis was a modern-day prophet ("*Praeparatio Evangelica*," in *C. S. Lewis: Lightbearer in the Shadowlands: The Evangelistic Vision of C. S. Lewis,* ed. Angus J. L. Menuge [Wheaton: Crossway, 1997], 235). Ultimately, both Platonic and Aristotelian conceptions of rhetoric can help us understand Lewis, but here I have chosen to focus on the latter.

forthright yet humble stance, and cultivating communities of good-will, helps him achieve one of his chief aims as a writer: "preparing the way" for the coming of the Lord into people's lives.[21] In this respect, Lewis's manner of witnessing echoes one of the great themes of Advent worship, which invites Christians to prepare for the annual celebration of the birth of Christ and, at the same time, for his return at the end of time. We also hear Advent themes in Lewis's emphasis on the doctrine of the incarnation, his explanation of the concept of joy, and his conversion experience (all of which are also related to his rhetoric of goodwill). C. S. Lewis's life and rhetoric speak the language of the Advent season.

C. S. Lewis's *Ēthos*

According to Aristotle's *On Rhetoric: A Theory of Civic Discourse*, *ēthos* is one of three rhetorical appeals by which a rhetor persuades an audience.[22] *Ēthos*, the appeal from character, is Aristotle's attempt to account for the fact that a rhetor's ability to persuade is tied to who the rhetor is—or who the rhetor appears to be to an audience. The term may be used to describe both the "prior reputation" that the rhetor brings to a rhetorical situation (sometimes called *extrinsic ēthos*, because the appeal is based *outside* of the discourse at hand) as well as the character that a rhetor establishes for himself or herself as a result of the discourse (called *intrinsic ēthos*, because the appeal is constructed *within* the speech or writing).[23] While much could be

---

[21] Heck, "*Praeparatio Evangelica*," 235. This claim synthesizes the work of several scholars and sources (*The Collected Letters of C. S. Lewis*, vol. 2, ed. Walter Hooper [New York: HarperCollins, 2004], 484; Christopher W. Mitchell, "Bearing the Weight of Glory," in *The Pilgrim's Guide: C. S. Lewis and the Art of Witness*, ed. David Mills [Grand Rapids: Eerdmans, 1998], 5; Root, *Lewis and a Problem of Evil*, xvi). I return to these sources over the course of the chapter.

[22] Aristotle, *On Rhetoric* 1356a3-5. Additionally, a rhetor can persuade by appealing to the emotions or feelings of the audience (*pathos*) and through logical argumentation (*logos*).

[23] Craig R. Smith, "*Ethos* Dwells Pervasively: A Hermeneutic Reading of Aristotle on Credibility," in *The Ethos of Rhetoric*, ed. Michael J. Hyde (Columbia: University of South

said about Lewis's extrinsic *ēthos*, for the purposes of this chapter, I focus on Lewis's rhetorical artistry and explore the way he establishes intrinsic *ēthos* in his writings.[24]

An observation by Michael Ward provides a good starting place for this discussion. Ward has claimed that Lewis "keeps his own Christian persona off-stage almost entirely" in his writings.[25] This comment is not unlike observations made by Owen Barfield about Lewis's work. According to Stephen Logan, "Owen Barfield remarked that reading a poem of Lewis's produced an impression 'not of an "I say this," but of a "This is the sort of the thing a man might say."'"[26] Logan maintains that "Barfield was noticing an impulse in Lewis towards self-abnegation which, paradoxically, but in a way fully consistent with Christian teaching, became a distinctive feature of his literary personality."[27] Citing both Barfield and Logan, Benjamin Fischer and Philip C. Derbesy agree with this

---

Carolina Press, 2004), 16; Jeanne Fahnestock and Marie Secor, *A Rhetoric of Argument*, 3rd ed. (New York: McGraw-Hill, 2004), 51-52; George A. Kennedy, *Classical Rhetoric and Its Christian and Secular Tradition from Ancient to Modern Times* (Chapel Hill: University of North Carolina Press, 1980), 37n37. The dividing line between intrinsic *ēthos* and extrinsic *ēthos* is seldom clear cut: appeals to character in discourse often enhance one's reputation, and one's reputation may be referenced in discourse to strengthen one's appeals to character.

[24]Lewis's extrinsic *ēthos* developed remarkably rapidly after he became a Christian. When Lewis appeared on the cover of *Time* magazine, the story about him focused on his popularity among Christians. Citing the number of books Lewis had sold ("over a million copies of his 15 books") and the number of listeners who tuned into his radio broadcasts ("an average of 600,000"), the author of the article noted, "Any fully ordained minister or priest might envy this Christian layman his audience" ("Don v. Devil," *Time*, September 8, 1947, 65). The article also referred to Lewis as "the most popular lecturer in the University" (65), "the most influential spokesperson for Christianity in the English-speaking world" (65), and "a celebrity" (72). "I certainly never intended being a hot gospeler," Lewis was quoted as saying. "If I had only known this when I became a Christian" (72).

[25]"If he talks in the first person," Ward continues, "it is his pre-Christian self that he brings forward. Never does he give the impression that he wants the reader to copy his practice of Christianity (unlike Saint Paul); but he quite often calls up his own 'search' for Christ" ("Escape to Wallaby Wood: Lewis's Depictions of Conversion," in Menuge, ed., *C. S. Lewis: Lightbearer in the Shadowlands*, 147).

[26]Stephen Logan, "Literary Theorist," in *The Cambridge Companion to C. S. Lewis*, ed. Robert MacSwain and Michael Ward (Cambridge: Cambridge University Press, 2010), 34.

[27]Logan, "Literary Theorist," 34.

assessment, noting that Lewis's "self-abnegation is present through-out his career."[28]

I agree that Lewis does not often hold himself up as a model for other Christians to imitate and that he tends toward self-abnegation, especially when writing about faith. However, I think Ward's claim that Lewis's "Christian persona" is rarely visible goes too far, limiting our understanding of what such a persona can entail. While it may be true that Lewis seldom discusses his practice of Christianity in the first person, it does not necessarily follow that Lewis's Christian persona is hidden from view. There are many ways to establish a Christian persona (one of which is self-abnegation), and Christians may establish a Christian persona without referring to their own religious acts overtly.

One way that Lewis establishes his Christian persona is by peppering his comments about Christianity with expressions of delight.[29] His writing, as many other scholars have noted, is winsome—a word that comes to us from the Old and Middle English *wynsum* (meaning "pleasant, agreeable, [and] delightful") and includes the root *wyn* (meaning "joy").[30] Witnessing the delight and joy of others is itself often a great delight, and the deep pleasure Lewis takes in things outside himself makes many of his writings an absolute joy to read, thereby enhancing their appeal. Furthermore, such delight is

---

[28]Fischer and Derbesy, "Literary Catholicity," 391. One of Fischer and Derbesy's primary tasks in their article is to respond to commentators who critique Lewis for the "derivative voice" and "lack of originality" that accompanies such self-abnegation (390-92). They demonstrate that Lewis's imitation of other writers is actually an expression of his faith, noting, "To point out the beauty and truth that other writers have disclosed, and to shine another light upon it, is the Christian writer's vocation" (392).

[29]As Alan Jacobs rightly observes in *The Narnian: The Life and Imagination of C. S. Lewis* (San Francisco: HarperCollins, 2005), Lewis's work is characterized through and through by "an openness to delight" (xxi).

[30]Bruce L. Edwards, "A Thoroughly Converted Man: C. S. Lewis in the Public Square," in *The Pilgrim's Guide: C. S. Lewis and the Art of Witness*, ed. David Mills (Grand Rapids: Eerdmans, 1998), 27; Philip G. Ryken, "Winsome Evangelist: The Influence of C. S. Lewis," in Menuge, ed., *C. S. Lewis: Lightbearer in the Shadowlands*, 57, 62, 73. For more on the word's etymology, see the *Oxford English Dictionary*, s.v. "winsome" and "win" (Oxford: Oxford University Press, 2016).

especially appealing because of the vigor with which he expresses it. Alan Jacobs refers to this feature of Lewis's writing as *gusto* and suggests that it really only comes into view after Lewis's conversion.[31] Though Lewis seldom discusses his post-conversion life in the first person, his Christian persona is not absent in his writings; rather, it is displayed through his delight, winsomeness, and gusto.

Gary L. Tandy, who has written one of the most thorough explorations of Lewis's rhetoric to date, highlights other important features of Lewis's intrinsic *ēthos*. Tandy correctly observes that Lewis displays *humility* when writing about topics in which he does not consider himself an expert and *authority* when writing about his areas of expertise.[32] But of all of the ways Tandy describes Lewis's *ēthos*, the one most essential to his book's argument is *certitude*.[33] While Tandy's work goes a long way toward describing Lewis's intrinsic *ēthos* and, for that matter, many other rhetorical features of his writing, Tandy himself acknowledges at the conclusion of his book that there are "other rhetorical stances and stylistic mannerisms" to be explored, and he urges scholars to "shift their focus from Lewis's ideas and personality to the works themselves."[34] In what follows, then, I take up Tandy's call, highlighting another important facet of Lewis's Christian *ēthos*. His writings are, I argue, seasoned with goodwill toward his audiences. Looking at Lewis's work in light of goodwill helps us understand many features of his witness.[35]

---

[31]Jacobs, *Narnian*, 131.

[32]Tandy, *Rhetoric of Certitude*, 63, 65. Lewis typically takes a more humble stance in his theological arguments and a more authoritative stance when writing literary history and criticism. John V. Fleming also comments on the nature of the authority that Lewis establishes in his writing, rightly noting that Lewis's "tone of authority . . . never becomes the tone of the bully" ("Literary Critic," 27).

[33]Tandy, *Rhetoric of Certitude*, 63. For more on Lewis's "rhetoric of certitude," see 83-117.

[34]Tandy, *Rhetoric of Certitude*, 123-24.

[35]Like Tandy's book, the present chapter reads Lewis's nonfiction writings rhetorically, and I marshal some of the same evidence that Tandy uses in his book to support my claims; however,

A Rhetoric of Goodwill

Aristotle does not define goodwill (*eunoia*) explicitly, but his comments about the concept provide us with enough information to arrive at a working definition. In *On Rhetoric*, Aristotle claims that there are three ways to construct *ēthos* within one's discourse. One can demonstrate good sense (a persuasive speaker knows the right thing to do in particular situations); good moral character (a persuasive speaker is one who, having discovered the right thing to do in a specific situation, does not lie about it); and goodwill toward one's audience (a persuasive speaker is one who does not withhold "the best advice" about the right thing to do in a particular situation).[36] These three ways of demonstrating *ēthos* build on one another. One must have good sense in order to practice good moral character, otherwise one's honesty will result in the circulation of incorrect notions. And one must have both good sense and good moral character to practice goodwill, otherwise one's counsel will be either unintentionally incorrect or deliberately false. Thus, although Aristotle never gives us a formal definition of goodwill, we can infer from his description that goodwill involves sharing one's good sense with one's audience forthrightly.

Furthermore, Aristotle implies that there is a connection between goodwill and friendship. Shortly after he mentions goodwill, he informs readers that he will elaborate on it later, claiming that "good will and friendliness need to be described in a discussion of the

---

my conclusions about Lewis's *ēthos* are different than (though not incompatible with) Tandy's. I focus on Lewis's rhetoric of goodwill, while Tandy emphasizes his rhetoric of certitude.

[36]In *Rhetoric of Certitude*, Tandy succinctly defines *ēthos* as "ethical appeal," noting that *ēthos* is a means by which a rhetor "establishes a relationship with his audience, reveals an attitude toward his subject, and projects an image" (63). This threefold description corresponds nicely with Aristotle's suggestion that *ēthos* is demonstrated through goodwill toward one's audience, good sense about one's subject, and good moral character (*On Rhetoric* 1378a5-6). For another explanation of these aspects of *ēthos*, see Tim Muehlhoff and Richard Langer's *Winsome Persuasion* (Downers Grove, IL: InterVarsity Press [2017]), 68-75.

emotions."[37] Curiously, however, Aristotle does not return to the notion in the section of *On Rhetoric* devoted to the emotions.[38] William Fortenbaugh contends that Aristotle does not use the term again because—like Callicles and Socrates in Plato's *Gorgias*, who "treat good will and friendship interchangeably"—Aristotle views the concepts as closely related to each other.[39] To the extent that there *is* a difference between the two concepts for Aristotle, it likely has to do with the rhetor's expectations. Unpacking a relevant passage from book 8 of Aristotle's *Ethics*, Craig R. Smith notes that the difference between Aristotle's understanding of friendship and his conception of goodwill is that those who practice goodwill are not looking for its recipients to respond in kind.[40] Unlike acts of friendship, Aristotelian goodwill is a gift given solely for the benefit of another.[41]

We can round out our understanding of the concept by turning to Lewis's own work. Like Aristotle, Lewis did not write extensively about goodwill, but he does make a few comments that shed light on the nature of the concept. First, in the passage that serves as my epigraph for this chapter, Lewis suggests that goodwill involves a "readiness to find meaning."[42] In other words, practicing goodwill requires cultivating receptivity: one must be willing to listen to, and at times embrace, others' ideas.[43] Lewis's brief definition here seems especially pertinent for rhetors. One who has not been attentive to the needs of his or her audience can hardly hope to appeal to them. Secondly, in "Answers to Questions on Christianity," Lewis explains that loving

---

[37] Aristotle, *On Rhetoric* 1378a7.

[38] William W. Fortenbaugh, "Aristotle on Persuasion Through Character," *Rhetorica: A Journal of the History of Rhetoric* 10, no. 3 (1992): 210, 219; Smith, "*Ethos* Dwells Pervasively," 11.

[39] Fortenbaugh, "Aristotle on Persuasion," 219; Smith, "*Ethos* Dwells Pervasively," 11-12.

[40] Smith, "*Ethos* Dwells Pervasively," 12.

[41] Smith notes that because of this difference, "for most audiences goodwill generates more credibility than friendship" ("*Ethos* Dwells Pervasively," 12).

[42] C. S. Lewis, "The Language of Religion," in *Christian Reflections* (Grand Rapids: Eerdmans, 1967/1989), 141.

[43] Lewis, *Christian Reflections*, 141.

another involves "a steady wish for the loved person's ultimate good as far as it can be obtained."[44] The phrase raises the stakes of our discussion of goodwill. Lewis is not only interested in the current well-being of his audiences but in their ultimate well-being, which, for Lewis, is resurrection life with God. Consequently, Lewis's practice of goodwill does not involve compromising his core convictions or downplaying the seriousness of a situation to save face; rather, it involves honesty and, when necessary, a willingness to challenge his audiences.

Having defined goodwill, let us now look more closely at how Lewis practiced it. While much could be said, I focus here on the following aspects of Lewis's prose: his willingness to address his audiences on their own terms, his forthright yet humble stance, and his attempts to cultivate communities characterized by goodwill. Though Lewis scholars have touched on these aspects of his writing before, to the best of my knowledge, no one has united these aspects of Lewis's prose around Aristotelian goodwill, and it is my hope that the concept of goodwill will serve as a lens to see his writings anew.[45]

Addressing audiences on their own terms. In 1948 Lewis was asked to write an article on the challenges that Christians have to confront when sharing their faith with "modern unbelievers."[46] Those who gave Lewis this assignment must have thought that such a prompt would be perfect for him, but Lewis begins the article by highlighting

---

[44]C. S. Lewis, "Answers to Questions on Christianity," in *God in the Dock*, 49.

[45]Hooper highlights Lewis's audience awareness (preface to *God in the Dock*, 8); Thomas Lessl discusses Lewis's "attention to his audiences" ("The Legacy of C. S. Lewis and the Prospect of Religious Rhetoric," *Journal of Communication and Religion* 27, no. 1 [2004]: 129-30); Root writes that "because Lewis had a rhetorical interest in his readers, he was particularly aware of his audience" (*Lewis and a Problem of Evil*, xii); and Anderson, Cunningham, Heck, and Tandy all explore issues of audience and translation in Lewis's writings (Anderson, "Most Potent Rhetoric," 206-9; Richard Cunningham, *Faithful Persuasion: In Aid of a Rhetoric of Christian Theology* [Notre Dame: University of Notre Dame Press, 1992], 137-40; Heck, "*Praeparatio Evangelica*," 245-47; Tandy, *Rhetoric of Certitude*, 35-39). Como highlights Lewis's "regard for the reader" along with Lewis's "[h]umility and companionability" (*Branches to Heaven*, 166).

[46]Lewis, "God in the Dock," in *God in the Dock*, 240.

a problem with his assignment. There is not one kind of modern unbeliever. He writes, "The difficulties [of the task] vary as the audience varies. The audience may be of this or that nation, may be children or adults, learned or ignorant."[47] In light of this wrinkle, Lewis decides to limit his remarks by considering non-Christians of a particular nation, social class, and age group. He chooses English-speaking, working-class adults. But even among this group, the matter is not a simple one according to Lewis, since many different belief systems are represented.[48] What is more, the people Lewis is trying to write about have different intellectual abilities, different views about the value of history, and different English dialects.[49]

Lewis's observations speak to the necessity of learning about one's audience members before addressing them, and his willingness to do such legwork is an important aspect of his rhetoric of goodwill. Because he took the time to learn about his audiences, Lewis felt he could address their theological needs more effectively. Some of the clearest examples of this view appear in his "Rejoinder to Dr. Pittenger." Dr. Norman Pittenger had written a review of Lewis's work, critiquing it for the way that Lewis presented God in relation to the world. Doctrinally speaking, he faulted Lewis's presentation of the *transcendence* and *immanence* of God, suggesting that Lewis exaggerated the former while repudiating the latter.[50] Lewis responds, "I freely admit that, believing both, I have stressed the transcendence of God more than His immanence. I thought, and think, that the present situation demands this. I see around me no danger of Deism but

---

[47]Lewis, "God in the Dock," 240.

[48]Lewis, "God in the Dock," 240.

[49]Lewis, "God in the Dock," 240-42. Despite these difficulties, Lewis presses on in the piece, and when he describes the characteristics of "English Proletariat" or "the uneducated Englishman," Lewis makes some generalizations that many contemporary readers may find cringe-worthy. However, it is worth remembering that he did highlight that the category "modern unbeliever" is actually composed of many different types of people, and he has, therefore, made some strides in alerting Christians to the rhetorical complexity of their acts of witness.

[50]Lewis, "Rejoinder to Dr. Pittenger," in *God in the Dock*, 180.

much of an immoral, naive and sentimental pantheism. I have often found that it was in fact the chief obstacle to conversion."[51] Without abandoning the orthodox position that God is both wholly other than his creation and intimately involved in it, Lewis chooses to give more emphasis to one of these realities based on the needs of his audience.[52] He tries to demonstrate a care for his audience that is both theological *and* rhetorical.

Along similar lines, Lewis also practices a rhetoric of goodwill by translating theological discourse into language that is more readily understandable. Observing that doing so requires learning the vernacular of one's audience, Lewis basically recommends that the Christian rhetor ought to determine how words are being used—not surprising advice coming from someone who wrote a book called *Studies in Words*—and then translate one's message accordingly.[53] Lewis strongly believed that these acts of translation were the responsibility of all Christians and that translation was an especially important practice for future members of the clergy to learn. He stresses, "Every examination for ordinands ought to include a passage from some standard theological work for translation into the vernacular."[54]

Lewis himself was particularly good at this sort of translation, and he quickly developed a reputation for it. When his picture appeared on the cover of *Time* in 1947, the writeup on him compared his eloquence and wit to that of G. K. Chesterton and described his "special

---

[51]Lewis, "Rejoinder to Dr. Pittenger," 181.

[52]In the piece, Lewis issues a critique of Dr. Pittenger's argument that drives home the point that Lewis was indeed a rhetor. He writes, "This [example] illustrates what appears to me to be a weakness in [Dr. Pittenger's] critical method. He judges my books *in vacuo*, with no consideration of the audience to whom they were addressed or the prevalent errors they were trying to combat" (Lewis, "Rejoinder to Dr. Pittenger," 182).

[53]Lewis, "God in the Dock," 242-43. Lewis's essay "Christian Apologetics" further illustrates what the task entails, ending with a short glossary of terms used by "the uneducated Englishman" (*God in the Dock*, 96-98).

[54]Lewis, "God in the Dock," 243. Lewis repeats the point in "Christian Apologetics" (*God in the Dock*, 98-99) and "Before We Can Communicate" (*God in the Dock*, 256).

gift for dramatizing Christian dogma," which involved "putting old-fashioned truths into a modern idiom."[55] Lewis seems to have agreed with *Time*'s characterization of him, discussing his own translation efforts in ways that suggest he viewed it as an important aspect of his vocation. Having watched the theological jargon of churchmen and the passionate appeals of evangelists fail to persuade people of the truth of the gospel, he had recognized a part he could play.[56] His role was, he wrote, "simply that of a *translator*—one turning Christian doctrine, or what he believed to be such, into the vernacular, into language that unscholarly people would attend to and could understand."[57]

The metaphors Lewis uses in this discussion are particularly instructive. Lewis claims that using sophisticated language would have been ineffective because it would have given audience members the impression that he was "facing both ways" and "sitting on the fence."[58] Such imagery implies that the language writers use *places* them in relation to their audiences. When writers do not use a language that is familiar to their audiences, they often come across as outsiders; conversely, when they engage in acts of translation, they are often able to build bridges to their audiences and come alongside them. Had Lewis chosen not to translate Christian doctrine into the vernacular, he suggests that his presentation of doctrine would have made him seem two-faced, uncertain, insincere, and even deceptive; however, by translating doctrine from the language of clerics and academics into everyday language, he was better able to meet his audiences' needs—a hallmark of goodwill.[59]

---

[55]"Don v. Devil," 65.

[56]Lewis, "Rejoinder to Dr. Pittenger," 183.

[57]In his comments about Lewis's "rhetoric of translation," Anderson cites a portion of this passage as well ("Most Potent Rhetoric," 207). He connects the passage to Lewis's notion of transposition and the doctrine of the incarnation, which we will return to later in the chapter. Heck highlights the connection between Lewis's understanding of translation and incarnation as well (246).

[58]Lewis, "Rejoinder to Dr. Pittenger," 183.

[59]Lewis, "Rejoinder to Dr. Pittenger," 183.

Adopting a forthright yet humble stance. It is important to note that Lewis's rhetoric of goodwill did not involve sugarcoating Christian doctrine or ingratiating himself to his audiences. Rather, he frequently made forceful and direct calls for repentance throughout his writings, often in conjunction with warnings about the second coming of Christ.[60] Remarks from his essay "The World's Last Night" offer a particularly striking example. He writes, "The doctrine of the Second Coming teaches us that we do not and cannot know when the world drama will end. The curtain may be rung down at any moment: say, before you finished reading this paragraph."[61] Lewis's use of the second person in this passage is arresting, forcing readers to look up from the page and wonder if the end will be momentarily at hand.

Similarly arresting is the last page of *The Great Divorce*, Lewis's allegory about the fate of souls in the afterlife. In the book, Lewis (the narrator, who we later find out is dreaming) travels on a bus with other ghosts to a country between heaven and hell. There, the dead are given the choice—representing a lifetime of choices—either to turn from their sinful selves, become whole and solid creatures, and journey to the mountains of heaven or to cling to their sins and return to what for them will become hell. Accompanied for part of his journey by guide George MacDonald (a character based on one of Lewis's foremost literary influences), Lewis witnesses soul after soul make the decision, and a surprising number of them choose to take the bus back to hell. There is not, however, an endless amount of time for the ghosts to make their decisions: Lewis learns that when the sun rises, all choice will cease. At the end of the book, as he is talking with MacDonald, that is precisely what happens—and the description of the eschaton calls into question

---

[60]Practicing goodwill isn't about being, or helping others to be, "nice." In *Mere Christianity* (New York: Macmillan, 1977), Lewis writes that "we must not suppose that even if we succeeded in making everyone nice we should have saved their souls" (182).

[61]C. S. Lewis, *The Joyful Christian: 127 Readings* (New York: Touchstone, 1996), 71.

James Como's claim that he "never uses bald fear of the sort resembling the motivating horror of . . . that old divine Jonathan Edwards."[62] When the first rays of morning arrive, Lewis trembles in fear and can only manage a brief look over his shoulder. His immobility is accompanied by assaulting sights and sounds. The sunbeams are lethal arrows, and the sounds of the wood are—at least to Lewis's ears—a cacophony of noises in which the song of angels is joined by howling animals. Lewis shrieks, hides his face, and cries out, "I am caught by the morning and I am a ghost."[63] Then his head is crushed by the light of the dawn. His dream, it turns out, is a terrifying nightmare—and a wake-up call. Even though Lewis the author never explicitly asks his readers to turn from their sins, when his book's narrator falls out of the chair where he had been sleeping and wakes up, we readers know that we, too, have been called to wake up and repent.

Lewis's appeals to fear may strike some readers as heavy-handed, and others may find the ways that he talks about his audiences condescending. However, while there are certainly times in Lewis's writings when these charges stick, such moments are rare: Lewis relinquishes pride far more often than he relishes in it, and his prose seems to be characterized less by self-importance than by self-renunciation. The excerpt from *The Great Divorce* illustrates the point. While the passage is indeed a call to repent, it is Lewis himself who is at the center of the story and is most in need of repentance: the conclusion of *The Great Divorce* should be read not only as a call to repentance but also as a confession.

There is, moreover, an intellectual humility that permeates Lewis's work.[64] In "Answers to Questions on Christianity," for example, Lewis

---

[62]Como, *Branches to Heaven*, 163.

[63]Lewis, *The Great Divorce*, 125.

[64]Many scholars have commented on Lewis's attempts to position himself as a layperson in his theological writings. For more on this strategy, see Tandy's reflections on Lewis's use of the ethical appeal (*Rhetoric of Certitude*, 63-66). Tandy notes, "Besides putting his reader at ease,

admits that he knows "nothing at all" about the subject of modern industry, that he does not "know the solution" to the dehumanizing effects of factory work, and that he "may be wrong" about one of his arguments.[65] Twice he reminds his audience that he is "only a layman."[66] Elsewhere, when discussing the translation of Christian doctrine into the vernacular, Lewis is quick to note that the practice of translation has had the effect of humbling him.[67] Lewis also defends others against attacks on their intellect. He rejects the claim that the first readers of Scripture were inferior intellectually, and he is adamant that children should not be talked down to.[68] Regarding the proper conduct toward children, he also writes, "We must of course try to do them no harm: we may, under the Omnipotence, sometimes dare to hope that we may do them good. But only such good as involves treating them with respect."[69] Hoping to do others good in a respectful way—such an idea neatly encapsulates Lewis's rhetorical approach and gets at the very essence of his goodwill.

Cultivating communities of goodwill. A final aspect of Lewis's rhetoric worth noting here is his cultivation of communities of goodwill. I noted earlier that Aristotle suggests that goodwill is associated with friendship and the emotions, but he does not elaborate on the point. Even so, Aristotle's suggestion is useful for our purposes because it moves us beyond the idea that *ēthos* is tied solely to the rhetor's character. As we have seen, goodwill is as much concerned with the rhetor's audience as it is with the rhetor. It stretches its bearer toward his or her

---

Lewis's technique of emphasizing his nonprofessional status also causes the reader to feel that the man who is addressing him is honest and reliable. By admitting his weaknesses, rather than glossing over or attempting to conceal them, Lewis disarms the potential critic and establishes a path of identification with the reader" (64).

[65]Lewis, "Answers to Questions," 48-49.

[66]Lewis, "Answers to Questions," 60, 62.

[67]Lewis, "Before We Can Communicate," in *God in the Dock*, 256.

[68]Lewis, "Answers to Questions," 57; "On Stories," in *On Stories, and Other Essays on Literature,* ed. Walter Hooper (New York: Harcourt Brace Jovanovich, 1982), 41-42.

[69]Lewis, "On Stories," 41-42.

audience. When writers and speakers establish goodwill, they are not simply building up their own *ēthos* but also that of the communities of which they and their audience members are a part. Such communities exhibit characteristics of goodwill practiced by their individual members: they are distinguished by forthright yet humble conversation, attentiveness, and responsiveness to the needs and ideas of individual members, and—for Lewis and other Christians—a shared desire among members to help one another toward resurrection life. Lewis's writings reveal that he was *deeply* committed to creating and participating in these kinds of communities. In his social circles, Lewis sought to build up, in the words of Christopher Mitchell, "an atmosphere where faith could be possible—rationally and imaginatively plausible—and where it could grow and thrive."[70]

The most famous example in Lewis's life of this community building, of course, was the Inklings—a group of thinkers and writers who haunted Oxford pubs such as the Eagle and Child and discussed theology and literature over pipes and pints.[71] But Lewis's cultivation of goodwill extended beyond the Inklings. John V. Fleming suggests, for instance, that Lewis's "generosity of spirit" flowed not only to his mates but also to his critics.[72] One example of Lewis's display of generosity toward his critics appears in an exchange between Lewis, S. L. Bethell, and George Every.[73] While Lewis's comments in the

---

[70]Mitchell, "Bearing the Weight," 5-6. Similarly, Jerry Root writes, "As a rhetorician of the written word, Lewis . . . sees that community is an essential environment necessary for dialectic and the shaping of ideas, as well as shaping character" (*C. S. Lewis and a Problem of Evil*, 42). The use of words like *atmosphere* and *environment* in such comments is not unrelated to the concept of *ēthos*. We will explore the connections between *ēthos* and one's surroundings in more detail in chapter five.

[71]Highlighting the astonishingly "*social* context of his literary thought," John V. Fleming notes that "Lewis was a man of deep intellectual friendships, and he enjoyed the good fortune of having friends who were great in more sense than one, men who shared broad sympathies and imaginative powers: Owen Barfield, J. R. R. Tolkien, Charles Williams and many others" ("Literary Critic," 25).

[72]Fleming, "Literary Critic," 26.

[73]Lewis, "Christianity and Culture," in *Christian Reflections*, 12-36.

exchange represent "an early step in his spiritual pilgrimage" (according to Walter Hooper), they showcase Lewis's goodwill prominently.[74] Lewis is forthright about his disagreements with Bethell and Every, and he also admits his omissions and seeks points of agreement with them, especially in his "Peace Proposals for Brother Every and Mr. Bethell."[75] Lewis also extended goodwill to his students: he showed them compassion and met them where they were.[76] The care Lewis showed to student Kenneth Tyran when Tyran was facing personal difficulties is a particularly notable example.[77] Alan Jacobs, who offers a detailed and moving account of Lewis's interactions with Tyran in *The Narnian,* observes that Lewis "knew the difference that he could make in the lives of his pupils by sheer kindness."[78] Furthermore, Lewis extended goodwill far and wide through his remarkable letter-writing practices.[79] At the height of his career, Lewis devoted an incredible amount of time and energy to personal correspondence, sharing the rhetoric of goodwill with one audience member at a time.

Lewis was particularly adamant that members of Christian communities demonstrate goodwill toward one another. Only in such an environment would non-Christians find the church an attractive and hospitable place to reside. For that reason, in his writings for non-Christians, Lewis almost always chose to focus his energies on highlighting shared beliefs among all Christians as opposed to disagreements.[80] "The discussion of . . . disputed points," he writes at the beginning of *Mere Christianity,* "has no tendency at all to bring an

---

[74]Hooper, preface to *Christian Reflections,* xii.
[75]Lewis, "Christianity and Culture," in *Christian Reflections,* 27-36
[76]Jacobs, *Narnian,* 311.
[77]Jacobs, *Narnian,* 309-14.
[78]Jacobs, *Narnian,* 311.
[79]Jacobs, *Narnian,* 223-26.
[80]Lewis, *Mere Christianity,* 6; Menuge, "God's Chosen Instrument: The Temper of an Apostle," 128-29; Hooper, preface to *Christian Reflections,* xi.

outsider into the Christian fold. So long as we write and talk about them we are much more likely to deter him from entering any Christian communion than to draw him into our own."[81] As Walter Hooper has noted, Lewis's correspondence with Rev. Edward T. Dell illustrates the point.[82]

In the final year of Lewis's life, Dell wrote to Lewis, asking if he would write a review of Bishop John A.T. Robinson's book *Honest to God*. Lewis had already written a charitable response to an article-length summary of Robinson's book that had appeared in *The Observer*, in which he downplayed the theological differences between the two men.[83] But the book went too far. Robinson claimed that the Bible's truth is mythological in nature, and he maintained that Christians should abandon the "unashamedly supranaturalistic" position of Scripture and reconceptualize God as "the ground of our being."[84] Robinson's argument called into question several tenets of orthodox Christianity, including the idea of the incarnation. And as if these attacks on orthodoxy were not enough to incite a response from Lewis, Robinson also took several shots at Lewis throughout the book. However, while Lewis would have had much to criticize about *Honest to God*, he declined Dell's offer to review the book.[85] In his response to Dell's inquiry, he wrote, "I'd rather keep off Bishop Robinson's book. I should find it hard to write of such a man with charity, nor do I want to increase his publicity."[86] When Dell persisted, trying to entice Lewis by noting that he would receive monetary compensation for writing the review,[87] Lewis replied as follows:

---

[81]Lewis, *Mere Christianity*, 6.
[82]Hooper, preface to *Christian Reflections*, xi.
[83]Lewis, "Must Our Image of God Go," in *God in the Dock*, 184-85.
[84]John A. T. Robinson, *Honest to God* (Philadelphia: Westminster, 1963), 32-33, 29.
[85]*The Collected Letters of C. S. Lewis*, vol. 3, ed. Walter Hooper (New York: HarperCollins, 2007), 1422.
[86]*Collected Letters*, vol. 3, 1422.
[87]*Collected Letters*, vol. 3, 1424n53.

I'm afraid I must stick to my position. Even if I wanted to abandon it—and I don't—I could hardly do so now that you have mentioned the fee! What would you yourself think of me if I did? There will be implicit answers to some of Robinson's nonsense in parts of a book on prayer which I've just finished, and I can "do my bit" much better that way.

A great deal of my utility has depended on my having kept out of all dog-fights between professing schools of "Christian" thought. I'd sooner preserve that abstinence to the end. I wd. like to oblige you personally, if I could, but I don't feel this is a way in which I can. Forgive me.[88]

For Lewis, responding to Robinson would have come at the expense of Christian charity and might have been disastrous for those outside of the faith; therefore, such a response—though theologically justified—had to be avoided. Lewis was interviewed about a week after he sent his reply to Dell, and the interviewer asked him about *Honest to God*. Lewis simply remarked, "I prefer being honest to being 'honest to God,'" and he left it at that.[89]

Though Lewis was adamant about cultivating goodwill among Christians, he was also interested in building communities of goodwill that were not exclusively Christian. He was, for example, an active member of the Oxford Socratic Club, a group of Christians and atheists who came together regularly to debate matters of belief and unbelief. It was a community in which participants attempted to value the arguments of one another: each side, Lewis noted in a piece about the club, hoped to hear "the best" of what the other side had to offer and to present the most compelling cases for their own positions.[90] Comparing the club's interactions to those in the Socratic dialogues, Lewis wrote, "At the very least we helped to civilize one another; sometimes we ventured to hope that if our Athenian patron were allowed to be

---

[88]*Collected Letters*, vol. 3, 1424.
[89]Lewis, "Cross-Examination," in *God in the Dock*, 260.
[90]Lewis, "The Founding of the Oxford Socratic Club," in *God in the Dock*, 127.

present, unseen, at our meetings he might not have found the atmosphere wholly alien."[91]

Lewis's willingness to dialogue openly with non-Christians about matters of faith seems to have made some Christians uneasy. To those Christians who viewed the Oxford Socratic Club's proceedings as irreverent, Lewis offered the following defense: "Christianity is not merely what a man does with his solitude. It is not even what God does with His solitude. It tells of God descending into the coarse publicity of history and there enacting what can—and must—be talked about."[92] In other words, at the heart of Lewis's participation in the Oxford Socratic Club—and, for that matter, at the heart of many of his expressions of goodwill—was the coming of the Word into the world.

An Advent Witness

In reading Lewis's writing over the years, I have come to believe that many aspects of his work—including his rhetoric of goodwill—exemplify ways of witnessing that Christians are invited to adopt during the first season of the church year. C. S. Lewis demonstrates what it means to be an Advent witness.[93] Derived from the Latin word meaning "to come," Advent is the season of the church year in which the people of God await the celebration of the first coming of Christ at Christmas and, simultaneously, prepare for his second coming at the end of time. During Advent, churches often read about Mary, the mother of Jesus, and John the Baptist, and these two figures show Christians the postures that are to characterize the

---

[91] Lewis, "Founding," 127.

[92] Lewis, "Founding," 128.

[93] When I claim that Lewis is an Advent witness, I am not saying that that is all that his witness entails. Nevertheless, I do believe that facets of C. S. Lewis's approach to Christian witness clearly resonate with many of the postures that Christians are called to embrace in Advent. (At least one other person has noticed this connection. Heidi Haverkamp's devotional *Advent in Narnia: Reflections for the Season* makes connections between the Advent season and *The Lion, the Witch, and the Wardrobe*.)

season.[94] Following after Mary, our liturgies invite us to wait with a kind of joyful longing for the birthday celebration of the one who brings justice and peace. And taking a cue from John the Baptist's cry in the wilderness, our liturgies call us to engage in acts of self-examination and repentance, reminding us that, in Lewis's words, "the Author will have something to say to each of us on the part that each of us has played" when he comes again.[95]

There are several noteworthy connections between Advent and Lewis's rhetoric of goodwill. One of Advent's primary emphases—the coming of God to the human race in the incarnation—provides the basis for Lewis's rhetorical approach.[96] Calling the incarnation "the very centre of Christianity," Lewis argues that the doctrine "illuminate[s] the whole of the rest of the manuscript," and he refers to it throughout his corpus.[97] He uses it to describe the "vicarious-ness" of the natural world, to articulate the relationship between "natural love" and charity, and to explain the nature of miracles.[98] More important for my purposes, however, the doctrine of the incarnation seems to have offered Lewis a theological rationale for his recommendations regarding audience awareness, translation, and debate with non-Christians.[99] In a piece on translating Scripture,

---

[94]Jennifer M. McBride offers an excellent account of the "social and political significance" of Mary and John the Baptist in the "Advent" chapter of her book (*Radical Discipleship* [Minneapolis: Fortress, 2017], 6, 25-41).

[95]Lewis, *Joyful Christian*, 71.

[96]For more on Lewis's rhetoric and the Incarnation, see Tandy, *Rhetoric of Certitude*, 31, and Anderson, "Most Potent Rhetoric," 207-9.

[97]Lewis, "The Grand Miracle," in *God in the Dock*, 82, 85-86.

[98]Lewis, "Grand Miracle," 85; Lewis, *Four Loves*, 133-34; Lewis, *Miracles: How God Intervenes in Nature and Human Affairs* (New York: Macmillan, 1978), 108.

[99]Lewis, "Modern Translations of the Bible," in *God in the Dock*, 230; Lewis, "Founding," 128; Anderson, "Most Potent Rhetoric," 206-9; Heck, "*Praeparatio Evangelica*," 245-47; Francis S. Rossow, "Old Wine in New Wineskins," in Menuge, ed., *C. S. Lewis: Lightbearer in the Shadowlands*, 275-76. Communication scholar Kenneth R. Chase challenges the notion that Christian rhetoricians should use the doctrine of the incarnation as an analogy for rhetorical practices such as adapting one's message to one's audience ("Christian Rhetorical Theory: A New (Re)Turn," *Journal of Communication and Religion* 36, no. 1 [2013]: 30-34). According to Chase, this "incarnation-as-adaptation view" implies that, in the incarnation of Jesus Christ, "God plays a

he reminds us that the New Testament was written in the "utilitarian, commercial and administrative language" of "'basic' Greek."[100] Then he writes, "Does this shock us? It ought not to, except as the Incarnation itself ought to shock us. The same divine humility which decreed that God should become a baby at a peasant-woman's breast, and later an arrested field-preacher in the hands of the Roman police, decreed also that He should be preached in a vulgar, prosaic, and unliterary language."[101] We Christians, Lewis's corpus would seem to suggest, are to imitate such divine humility in our own language use. God's condescension to us in taking on flesh involves a kind of translation from God to God-man, offering us a Word that we are able to hear and understand—and Christians can imitate our Lord (in a limited way, of course) by addressing the needs of our audiences.

---

role, or wears a mask, in order to connect with the human race"—which is a form of the heresy known as modalism (32). Modalism, Chase explains, "is seeing Father, Son, and Spirit as expressions of the one God who differentially adapts to the human condition at different historical moments. Modalism sacrifices the plurality of God's triune persons in the task of maintaining God's oneness" (31-32). The incarnation-as-adaptation view also reinforces the longstanding divide between truth and persuasion (34). That is not to say that the incarnation is not relevant to rhetorical practice; in fact, it requires that we see Christ's truth and his persuasion as "inseparable" (34, 37). Chase writes, "The doctrine of the incarnation directs us to the profound observation that Christ lived truth within and through human culture. . . . Thus, the suasory practices of Christ's discourse are an inseparable feature of his revelation" (34). "In Christ," Chase notes, "truth is embodied persuasion" (35). I find myself persuaded by Chase's argument; however, I do not think we need to rush to reject Lewis's comments connecting the incarnation with audience adaptation and translation, in part because Lewis is quick to note that adaptation and translation influence speaker and audience alike. For Lewis, acts of adaptation and translation are less about dressing up truth in a particular guise and more about obedience to the truth, and this view seems fairly consistent with the position that Chase ultimately recommends when he writes, "I am advocating an altered relationship among speaker, message, and audience. Christian rhetors are redemptively constituted within particular cultures and communities, being as much influenced by the messages they construct (and perhaps more so) as the audiences to whom the messages are directed. This is a fully immersive view of the rhetor-audience relationship, one that emphasizes the inclusive appeals of truth's suasory potency. Audiences are not so much 'adapted to' as they are 'participating with' the rhetors' own formative processes; rhetors are not so much the masters of the messages as they are mastered by the messages" (41). Lewis often exemplified this sort of rhetorical practice.

[100]Lewis, "Modern Translations," 230.

[101]Lewis, "Modern Translations," 230. Rossow includes a quotation from this passage of "Modern Translations of the Bible" as well ("Old Wine," 276).

As Joel D. Heck has observed, Lewis's rhetoric also shares similarities with the message of John the Baptist, a prominent figure in Advent liturgies.[102] John served to "prepare the way of the Lord" and "make his paths straight"—and, in a similar way, Lewis's rhetoric serves to prepare people for the coming of the Lord into their lives (Mt 3:3).[103] In an oft-cited letter to his friend Sister Penelope, Lewis describes his own role in precisely this way, noting, "Mine are *praeparatio evangelica* rather than *evangelium*."[104] Also like John the Baptist, Lewis witnesses to Christ with both humility and conviction. As we have seen, Lewis admits when he does not know something and is quick to point out his own finitude, but he is not timid about urging audiences to repent. Finally, Lewis's calls to repentance are, like John's, often tied to claims about the imminent advent of Christ and warnings of future judgment: the eschaton is, as the above excerpts from "The World's Last Night" and *The Great Divorce* suggest, an event that appears in several places in his corpus. To borrow a quotation from theologian Jennifer M. McBride, in Lewis's writings "the Advent message resounds: Wake up! Be alert!"[105]

---

[102]Though Heck describes Lewis as a John-the-Baptist figure, he does not link Lewis's rhetoric to the Advent season to the best of my knowledge (*"Praeparatio Evangelica,"* 235).

[103]Heck also includes such passages in his piece, which come from Isaiah 40:3 (*"Praeparatio Evangelica,"* 243).

[104]*Collected Letters of C. S. Lewis*, vol. 2, 484. Heck—who has done an excellent job tracing the notion of *praeparatio evangelica* throughout Lewis's writings (*"Praeparatio Evangelica,"* 235-37)—unpacks the idea as follows: "C. S. Lewis used the Latin term *praeparatio evangelica*, 'evangelical preparation,' or better, 'preparation for the Evangel, the Gospel,' to describe his role in the cause of evangelism. The term suggests that he did not see his role as that of an evangelist. His role was a preparatory role. He was a John the Baptist, a forerunner, a twentieth-century Elijah, preparing the way for those who would proclaim the Gospel—the priests and vicars and curates, in short, the evangelists" (235). Christopher Mitchell described Lewis's "preparatory" approach this way: "Lewis saw himself not so much as a reaper of souls, but as one who prepares the soil, sows the seed, and weeds out what hinders growth. His job, as he understood it, was on the one hand to seek to break down the intellectual prejudices to Christianity by detecting and exposing the fallacies of current objections to belief in such a way as to make faith in Christianity intellectually plausible, and on the other to prepare the mind and imagination to receive the Christian vision" ("Bearing the Weight," 5).

[105]McBride, *Radical Discipleship*, 57. In his emphasis on judgment and eschatology, Lewis's witness is very much in tune with the church's long-standing understanding of the Advent season (McBride, *Radical Discipleship*, 26).

"The Psalms" is one essay in which Lewis writes as a John the Baptist-like figure and weaves together several Advent themes, including the exaltation of the humble, the promise of judgment, and the call to repentance. In the relevant section of the essay, Lewis unpacks Psalm 109, praising its final verse because it sides with the lowly and in doing so "anticipates the character of the *Magnificat*"— another of the Advent season's primary readings.[106] Lewis goes on to note that the psalm's conclusion "will commend itself even to a modern unbeliever of *good will*; he may call it wishful thinking, but he will respect the wish."[107] So far, so good. But then Lewis highlights a problem. The remainder of the psalm is a song of pure hatred.[108] "What good can we find in reading such stuff?" he asks, seemingly rhetorically.[109] Instead of leaving it at that, though, Lewis answers his own question. While the Psalms are indeed filled with startling expressions of hatred, they also convey a profound longing for things being put to rights, a message which, Lewis claims, is purified by God and eventually transformed into Mary's song. In a characteristically compelling passage, he writes, "There is . . . mixed with the hatred in the psalmists, a spark which should be fanned, not trodden out. That spark God saw and fanned, till it burns clear in the *Magnificat*. The cry for 'judgement' was to be heard."[110] Lewis then warns that this judgment may ultimately be directed at *us*, inviting us to examine the ways we have harmed others.[111] As he so often does, Lewis turns our judgments back on us. Instead of judging Scripture, we are judged by it—and we stand in need of repentance. This Advent-appropriate message hinges on goodwill: Lewis

---

[106]Lewis, *Christian Reflections*, 117.
[107]Lewis, *Christian Reflections*, 117-18, emphasis added.
[108]Lewis, *Christian Reflections*, 118.
[109]Lewis, *Christian Reflections*, 118.
[110]Lewis, *Christian Reflections*, 122.
[111]Lewis, *Christian Reflections*, 119.

highlights the psalmist's goodwill and models goodwill through his response to the psalmist's words.

A final connection between Lewis's rhetoric of goodwill and Advent is his emphasis on joy. The communities of goodwill that Lewis cultivated were certainly sources of joy for their participants, and—as others have noted—Lewis's writings were composed in ways that kindle joy and delight in readers. Such joy, at least according to Lewis's own descriptions of it, is a thoroughly Advent-like notion. He presents it as an incredibly strong (and even painful) "longing" that cannot be satisfied on this side of glory.[112] As a young boy, Lewis experienced the longing when he encountered his brother's toy garden, Beatrix Potter's story *Squirrel Nutkin*, and the death of Balder from the *Saga of King Olaf*.[113] The experience was, in Lewis's own words, like "Milton's 'enormous bliss' of Eden (giving the full, ancient meaning to 'enormous')"—a desire of "almost sickening intensity [for] something never to be described."[114] Although he could not satisfy the longing, Lewis spent his early years chasing after this feeling of feelings. Eventually Lewis realized that chasing after joy should not be his end goal. The experience "was valuable only as a pointer to something other and outer"—a truth beyond oneself.[115] Like the Advent season and the figure of John the Baptist, joy is a pointer to future life with God. Though there is now a period of waiting, God himself is coming to meet his people: the White Witch's grip on creation is breaking, the snow is melting, and Christmas is near. As Father Christmas exclaims in *The Lion, the Witch and the Wardrobe*, "Aslan is on the move."[116]

---

[112]Lewis, *Surprised by Joy: The Shape of My Early Life* (New York: Harcourt Brace & Company, 1955), 7, 16-17.

[113]Lewis, *Surprised by Joy*, 7, 16-17.

[114]Lewis, *Surprised by Joy*, 16, 17.

[115]Lewis, *Surprised by Joy*, 238, 220. Jerry Root explains, "Lewis found that desire, properly followed, may lead to God. It is not a thing to be suppressed or denied, only rightly guided" ("Tools Inadequate and Incomplete: C. S. Lewis and the Great Religions," in *The Pilgrim's Guide: C. S. Lewis and the Art of Witness*, ed. David Mills [Grand Rapids: Eerdmans, 1998], 230).

[116]Lewis, *The Lion, the Witch and the Wardrobe* (New York: HarperCollins, 2001), 159.

December 25, 1931

Much of C. S. Lewis's rhetoric is tied to his own faith journey, and his rhetoric of goodwill is no exception. Though Lewis's conversion story is a well-known one, it is worth highlighting that his testimony hinges upon an Advent posture (the deep longing he experienced as a young child) and also includes a John the Baptist–like figure—George Mac-Donald, whose book *Phantastes*, Lewis famously wrote, baptized his imagination.[117] It also turns on several expressions of goodwill, which are most evident in the account of Lewis's famous walk with J. R. R. Tolkien and Hugo Dyson on the grounds of Magdalen College on September 19, 1931. As Humphrey Carpenter tells the story, during the walk Tolkien engaged Lewis about matters of faith by translating doctrine into a subject they both understood and adored—mythology.[118] When Lewis claimed that myths were "lies and therefore worthless, even though breathed through silver," Tolkien disagreed.[119] Mythmakers, Tolkien suggested, are not liars: they draw their ideas from God and imitate God's acts of creation through their stories.[120] God is, in other words, the ultimate mythmaker, but—unlike the stories of human mythmakers—God's story is historical fact, and the characters involved are actual people.[121] By witnessing in a way that

---

[117]Lewis, *Surprised by Joy*, 7, 16-17, 78; Lewis, introduction to George MacDonald, *Phantastes: A Faerie Romance* (Grand Rapids: Eerdmans, 2000), xi. The connection between Lewis, MacDonald, and Advent may run even deeper. Extending Boyd Hilton's claims about the shift in nineteenth-century Britain from an emphasis on the atonement to an emphasis on the incarnation, Timothy Larsen makes a compelling case that George MacDonald's work typifies what Hilton refers to as "the Age of the Incarnation" (*George MacDonald in the Age of Miracles: Incarnation, Doubt, and Reenchantment* [Downers Grove, IL: IVP Academic, 2018], 12-13). Given Lewis's respect for MacDonald, I think a persuasive argument could be made that situates Lewis's writings on the incarnation in relation to Hilton's thesis and Larsen's claims about MacDonald (James E. Beitler, "Response to 'George MacDonald in the Age of the Incarnation,'" in *George MacDonald in the Age of Miracles: Incarnation, Doubt, and Reenchantment*, by Timothy Larsen [Downers Grove, IL: IVP Academic, 2018], 39).

[118]Humphrey Carpenter, *The Inklings: C. S. Lewis, J. R. R. Tolkien, Charles Williams, and Their Friends* (Boston: Houghton Mifflin, 1979), 42-43.

[119]Carpenter, *Inklings*, 43.

[120]Carpenter, *Inklings*, 43.

[121]Carpenter, *Inklings*, 43

spoke to Lewis's love of mythology, Tolkien himself adopted a posture of goodwill in relation to his friend, which would serve as an excellent model for Lewis to imitate after he became a Christian.

But Tolkien did not simply model goodwill for Lewis; he presented him with an argument about divine activity that served as the foundation for Lewis's own rhetoric of goodwill. Nearly fifteen years after his walk with Tolkien and Dyson, Lewis delivered a paper at the Oxford Socratic Club that connected Tolkien's argument about myth to the notion of *evangelical preparation*. He suggested that mythological accounts "may well be a *preparatio evangelica*, a divine hinting in poetic and ritual form at the same central truth which was later focused and (so to speak) historicised in the Incarnation."[122] With Tolkien's help, Lewis had come to view mythology as a pointer to "something—indeed, *someone*—else."[123] Much like the sensations of joy that Lewis had experienced as a boy, mythology served as *a divine expression of goodwill* that pointed to Jesus Christ and prepared humans for his coming.[124] In light of these conceptions of joy and mythology, it is little wonder that Lewis developed a rhetoric of goodwill in relation to his audiences.[125] An imitation of God's means of

---

[122]Lewis, "Religion Without Dogma?," in *God in the Dock*, 132. The spelling of *preparatio evangelica* in this piece differs from the spelling that appears in Lewis's letter to Sister Penelope.

[123]Douglas T. Hyatt, "Joy, the Call of God in Man: A Critical Appraisal of Lewis's Argument from Desire," in Menuge, ed., *C. S. Lewis: Lightbearer in the Shadowlands*, 307. Hyatt's quotation here is in reference to joy, not mythology.

[124]I am not the first to discuss divine communication in relation to *eunoia*. Jaroslav Pelikan suggests that Aristotle's notion of *eunoia* helps us understand Luther's reading of the Sermon on the Mount (*Divine Rhetoric: The Sermon on the Mount as Message and as Model in Augustine, Chrysostom and Luther* [Crestwood, NY: St. Vladimir's Seminary Press, 2000], 111-15).

[125]Lewis found pointers to Christianity in Paganism as well as in joy and in mythology. In "A Christmas Sermon for Pagans," a recently discovered article from a December 1946 issue of *The Strand Magazine*, Lewis suggests that "pre-Christian" people are closer to belief in Christianity than "post-Christian" people because the former are "sick and know it" (i.e., they are aware of their own sinfulness) while the latter are "sick and don't know it" (*Journal of the Marion E. Wade Center* 34 [2017]: 47, 50). As such, Lewis contends that Paganism better prepares the way for Christian belief, writing, "It looks to me, neighbours, as though we shall have to set about becoming true Pagans if only as a preliminary to becoming Christians" (49). Toward the end of the article, Lewis turns us once again to the incarnation, claiming that Christianity "adds a

engaging with humans, Lewis's rhetoric pointed to and prepared his audiences for the advent of the Word.[126]

After his walk with J. R. R. Tolkien and Hugo Dyson, C. S. Lewis eventually converted to Christianity, and on Christmas Day of that same year he made his way to church.[127] While it is possible that he did "sit around and smoke his pipe" later that day, we cannot be certain of it. We can be reasonably sure, however, that someone was "set right"—Lewis himself. On December 25, 1931, Lewis did something that he had not done in a very long while. According to Humphrey Carpenter's account, "He made his Communion for the first time since childhood days."[128] And it is a good bet that Lewis also heard someone read the angels' words from the second chapter of the Gospel of Luke: "Glory to God in the highest, and on earth peace, goodwill toward men" (Luke 2:14 KJV).

---

wonder of which Paganism has not distinctly heard—that the Mighty One has come down to help us, to remove our guilt, to reconcile us" (50).

[126]In his piece "*Praeparatio Evangelica*," Joel D. Heck accurately describes Lewis as a "pre-evangelist and evangelist, proponent of the natural Law, smuggler of theology, author and apologist, storyteller and baptizer of imaginations, twentieth-century Elijah and preparer for the Gospel, Incarnationist" (253).

[127]Carpenter, *Inklings*, 46.

[128]Carpenter, *Inklings*, 46.

2

PROFESSING THE CREEDS

Dorothy L. Sayers and the Energy of Christmastide

And in the same region there were shepherds out in the field, keeping watch over their flock by night. And an angel of the Lord appeared to them, and the glory of the Lord shone around them, and they were filled with great fear. And the angel said to them, "Fear not, for behold, I bring you good news of great joy that will be for all the people."

LUKE 2:8-10

We believe in one Lord Jesus Christ,
the only Son of God,
eternally begotten of the Father,
God from God, Light from Light,
true God from true God,
begotten, not made,
of one Being with the Father;
through him all things were made.
For us and for our salvation he came down from heaven,
was incarnate from the Holy Spirit and the Virgin Mary
and was made man.

NICENE CREED

It is really the Nativity Play that made me write. I am so glad you did it. I have seen and read many stories of the Nativity, but never one that impressed me as that did. I probably have a very typical outlook on religion, lazy, semi-agnostic, willing to believe if someone could convince me, regarding the Church of England as the best of a rather unsatisfactory batch of creeds. I had a casually intellectual interest in religions, but it seldom survived inside a church. I think I never felt really strongly until Christmas Night. I knew

the story was beautiful and I loved the literature and music surrounding it,
but the people themselves never seemed alive. On Sunday they were real for
the first time.

RESPONSE TO DOROTHY L. SAYERS'S RADIO PLAY
HE THAT SHOULD COME

DOROTHY L. SAYERS'S PLAY *The Zeal of Thy House* depicts the story
of William of Sens, the architect who was hired to rebuild Canterbury
Cathedral's choir after a fire destroyed it in 1174. Sayers's William is an
excellent but prideful craftsman, and his hubris grows as the cathedral
ascends heavenward, culminating in his blasphemous declaration,
"This church is mine / And none but I, not even God, can build it."[1]
Judgment comes swiftly for William after he makes these remarks to
his lover, Ursula. As he stands on the scaffolding to help put the keystone of the choir's great arch in place, one of the ropes fails, and
William falls more than fifty feet. He is, quite literally, brought low,
and humility (a word that comes from the Latin words *humilis* and
humus, meaning "low" and "ground," respectively) eventually follows.
Back broken and physically unable to finish his work, he is told the
story of the God-man's condescension.[2] Only then does William
stoop before God spiritually, confessing, "O, I have sinned. The eldest
sin of all / Pride. . . . Wipe out my name from men / But not my work;
to other men the glory / And to Thy Name alone."[3]

The story is haunting, in part, because the stage itself is haunted.
Collapsing the divide between the natural and the supernatural,
Sayers's play shows audience members the spiritual forces at work
in William's story. Four imposing angels and a young cherub watch

---

[1]Dorothy Sayers, *The Zeal of Thy House* (Eugene, OR: Wipf & Stock, 2011), 90.
[2]William receives the following message: "So, when God came to test of mortal time / In nature
of a man whom time supplants, / He made no reservation of Himself / Nor of the godlike stamp
that franked His gold, / But in good time let time supplant Him too" (Sayers, *Zeal*, 124).
[3]Sayers, *Zeal*, 125.

the architect's conceit grow, and when William finally makes claims about his own divinity, these "angels in the architecture" intervene. As William leaves the stage to help insert the keystone into the great arch, the archangel Michael draws his sword and follows him off-stage. We are a long way from an *ēthos* of goodwill at this point; in fact, what comes next has the trappings of a contemporary horror movie. Two cantors chant verses about the consequences of failing to rely on God in one's endeavors, a choir begins singing about the Lord's judgment, and—like the camera angles of many horror flicks—the scene does not permit audience members to witness the action. Instead, we are forced to watch and listen to the crowd as they themselves watch William's ascent, which takes place offstage. Sayers is a master playwright when it comes to using the voices of the crowd to set the mood, and here she creates suspense by delaying the main event.[4] Voices from the crowd inform us that, just as the builders are about to place the keystone, they stop to wait for William. We hear that William is "half-way up" and then that he is "just getting to the top of the scaffolding." Finally somebody shouts, "Get ready to cheer, boys"—and we wait in anticipation of the crowd's reaction.

Another trope of horror is to grant otherworldly vision or prophetic insight to children ("I see dead people," Haley Joel Osment's character tells Bruce Willis's character in *The Sixth Sense*), and Sayers grants this insight to a young boy, who—according to the stage directions—"*shrilly*" cries out, "Oh, look! look at the angel—the terrible angel!"[5] When the crowd questions him, he cries out again, "High on the scaffold, with the drawn sword in his hand!"[6] "Mother of God!" Ursula screams, crumpling to the ground as she sees William fall. Then the crowd erupts not in cheers but in chaos.

---

[4]Sayers, *Zeal*, 92.
[5]Sayers, *Zeal*, 93.
[6]Sayers, *Zeal*, 93.

First performed in the Chapter House of Canterbury Cathedral for the 1937 Canterbury Festival, the play must have been especially haunting to its initial audiences. Setting the action of the play in the very church where audience members had gathered would have charged the performance venue with meaning, its walls and roof signifying judgment. Despite, or perhaps because of, this haunting message, the play was well received. Of all the reviews about the play, a remark by the Society of the Sacred Mission's Father Herbert Kelly seems to me to best capture Sayers's accomplishment. Kelly praises Sayers for her ability to "state the vital force of a Christian faith in God and His Christ, not in the abstract fashion which is all we theologians can teach, but in a *living, pictorial fashion* which common people can follow."[7] As *The Zeal of Thy House* illustrates and other examples from this chapter will show, Sayers's Christian witness involved depicting hard truths realistically: her dramas conveyed "the vital force" of the gospel to her audiences.

A Context in Need of Creed and Calling

In a lecture Sayers gave in 1940 (which eventually became the great essay "Creed or Chaos?"), she described what she saw as one of the fundamental barriers to Christian witness in England. Christian dogma—the body of statements that the church holds to be true and necessary for salvation—was widely thought to be "irrelevant" to most people's lives.[8] Sayers contended that this view was completely mistaken. And she leveled blame for this mistake primarily at clergymen, who, she suggested here and elsewhere, had undermined the

---

[7]Quoted in Barbara Reynolds, *Dorothy L. Sayers: Her Life and Soul* (New York: St. Martin's, 1993), 287, emphasis added. Christine A. Colón quotes Kelly as well (*Writing for the Masses: Dorothy L. Sayers and the Victorian Literary Tradition* [New York: Routledge, 2018], 164).

[8]Dorothy Sayers, "Creed or Chaos?," in *Creed or Chaos? Why Christians Must Choose Either Dogma or Disaster (Or, Why It Really Does Matter What You Believe)* (Manchester, NH: Sophia Institute, 1999), 48.

relevance of dogma in at least three ways: by failing to share it with their audiences, explaining it incorrectly, and neglecting to translate it into the vernacular.[9]

The first of these three failures—the failure simply to share creedal statements—absolutely infuriated Sayers. In February of 1943, she wrote to Rev. Dr. James W. Welch, the BBC's Director of Religious Broadcasting, lamenting the fact that a Christian newsletter she had recently received in the mail was anything but Christian, reducing the crucifixion of Christ to "a little mild theism."[10] Later in the same letter, she took issue with a priest whom she heard on the radio dismissing the importance of the creeds by claiming that "it wasn't necessary to remain in the shallows worrying about the details—one should go for the deep things and have faith in God."[11] But how, Sayers wondered, could one do so without *any* reference to Christ? "I could only conclude," she wryly observed, "that He was one of the superfluous details to be swept up with the rest of the rubbish." The solution to this problem for Sayers was straightforward: archbishops needed to charge ministers to deliver sermons on the incarnation and the crucifixion each and every day for the next year. Absent that reform, Sayers seems to have had some less judicious solutions in mind. Regarding the priest on the radio, she threatened (only half-jokingly), "If I could have hit that padre last night with a brick, I would have thrown it."[12] Notwithstanding the souls of English Christians, it seems that the life and livelihood of at least one clergyman hung in the balance.

The second ministerial failure—flawed explanations of dogmatic statements—was as detrimental as the first in undermining the relevance of Christian dogma. Sayers illustrates the problem by exploring

---

[9]Sayers, "Creed or Chaos?," 50-51.

[10]Sayers, "Letter to James Welch, 11 February 1943," in *The Christ of the Creeds and Other Broadcast Messages to the British People during World War II* (West Sussex: Dorothy L. Sayers Society, 2008), 72.

[11]Sayers, "Letter to James Welch," 73.

[12]Sayers, "Letter to James Welch," 73-74.

misrepresentations of what she refers to as the "central dogma" of Christianity: the incarnation.[13] For Sayers, preaching that does not acknowledge both the distinctly human nature and distinctly divine nature of the one person of Jesus Christ (a doctrine that theologians refer to as Christ's hypostatic union) renders the doctrine and, thus, all of Christianity completely inconsequential. If Christianity is going to matter to the world, its doctrines must actually be professed "rightly."[14]

While preaching dogma and preaching it rightly are both necessary to dogma's relevance, they are not sufficient. A third ministerial failure Sayers criticized involved neglecting to take one's audience into account—neglecting, in other words, to view Christian witness rhetorically. Much like C. S. Lewis, Sayers believed that ministers rendered dogma irrelevant when they failed to translate it into the vernacular. "If the 'average man' is going to be interested in Christ at all," she wrote, "it is the dogma what will provide the interest. The trouble is that in nine cases out of ten, he has never been offered the dogma. What he has been offered is a set of technical theological terms that nobody has taken the trouble to translate into language relevant to ordinary life."[15]

These failures of Christian witness—silence, distortion, and cant from the pulpit—not only exasperated Sayers as a Christian but also offended her sensibilities as an artist. In her letter to Welch, she literally underlined the point, bemoaning, "[T]hey've got the most terrific story in the world and *they don't tell it*."[16] Later, in her introduction to *The Man Born to Be King*, she publicly reprimanded Christians for a related error: "Not Herod, not Caiaphas, not Pilate, not Judas

---

[13]Sayers, "Creed or Chaos?," 50-51.
[14]Sayers, "Creed or Chaos?," 51.
[15]Sayers, "Creed or Chaos?," 51.
[16]Sayers, "Letter to James Welch," 72. She continues, "Let me tell you, good Christian people, an honest writer would be ashamed to treat a nursery tale as you have treated the greatest drama in history" (30).

ever contrived to fasten upon Jesus Christ the reproach of insipidity; that final indignity was left for pious hands to inflict. To make of His story something that could neither startle, nor shock, nor terrify, nor excite, nor inspire a living soul is to crucify the Son of God afresh."[17] For Sayers, the failure to preach and perform the truths of Christianity was not simply a failure of discipleship; it was also a failure of aesthetic judgment, rendering an inherently captivating narrative utterly *taste*less.

Many evangelists during Sayers's lifetime addressed the problem of the perceived irrelevance of dogma by encouraging people to make a personal commitment of faith. Sayers found this approach unpalatable. She was, as John Thurmer put it, a "reluctant evangelist."[18] However, though Sayers didn't identify with the evangelical movement, her writings made Christian truths relevant in other ways. While evangelicals sought to make Christianity relevant by focusing

---

[17]Sayers, *The Man Born to Be King: A Play-Cycle on the Life of our Lord and Savior JESUS CHRIST* (Grand Rapids: Eerdmans, 1979), 30.

[18]James Brabazon's biography of Sayers includes a letter from her to John Wren-Lewis, dated April 16, 1954, in which she expresses her discomfort with certain types of evangelism. "One day," Sayers writes in reference to *The Zeal of Thy House*, "I was asked to write a play for Canterbury . . . I liked the story, which could be so handled as to deal the 'proper truth' of the artist— a thing on which I was then particularly keen . . . so I wrote the thing and enjoyed doing it. . . . I never, so help me God, wanted to get entangled in religious apologetic, or to bear witness for Christ, or to proclaim my faith to the world, or anything of that kind" (quoted in James Brabazon, *Dorothy L. Sayers: A Biography* [New York: Charles Scribner's Sons, 1981], 165). Brabazon goes on to remark that, after Sayers got more famous as a Christian writer, she "did her best to depersonalize the whole thing by scrupulously sticking to a restatement of Church doctrine, and refusing to be drawn at any time into 'what Christ means to me' or any other form of personal avowal" (166). Furthermore, in her piece "Playwrights Are Not Evangelists" (*World Theatre* 5 [1955–1956]: 61-66), Sayers claims that "evangelisation is not the proper concern of the playwright" and that church leaders should not ask it of them (62). This is not to say that Christian playwrights cannot witness; however, the artist's first priority should be to produce good work, and his or her witness may be—as we saw in the case of C. S. Lewis—more about preparation for conversion than conversion itself. It is the job of clergy to build on this preparation. Sayers writes, "[Clergy] can, and indeed must, follow up such opportunities [for conversion] as the play affords. A drama (or any other work of art) will not by itself make anybody a Christian. . . . It is especially for the clergy to see that the springs of awareness released by a dramatic presentation—and it *can* release them—are directed into the right channels, and not suffered to spread and stagnate into a morass of undisciplined sentiment" (64). Laura Simmons offers a nice summary of Sayers's views on this topic in *Creed Without Chaos: Exploring Theology in the Writings of Dorothy L. Sayers* (Grand Rapids: Baker, 2005), esp. 133-34, 141-42.

on the individual's personal commitment, Sayers went in the opposite direction, emphasizing Christianity's public aspects. The church
makes Christianity relevant, Sayers implied repeatedly and consis-
tently throughout her writings, through the public *professions* of
its members.

Such a claim holds true for two different meanings of the word
profession. Christians make their faith relevant by *professing* Christian
dogma accurately and understandably, and by serving society in and
through their *professional* occupations. Christianity, in other words,
is cultivated through creed and calling. Throughout her career as a
Christian writer, Sayers embraced both calling and creed zealously,
and her work deserves our careful attention in part because of the
ways that she weaves these two professions together in her own life.[19]

One of the primary ways that Sayers married calling and creed in
her own life was by dramatizing dogma. She used performance to
present Christian belief.[20] Whether it was the Chapter House of

---

[19]Note that these two public professions do not preclude the notion that faith has personal dimensions. Nor do they suggest that practicing creed and calling will look identical for all Christians.
How one demonstrates allegiance to the church's doctrine and the professional standards of one's
own guild may play itself out in different ways depending on one's context and vocation. However, Sayers's emphases remind us that Christian witness is always much more than an interac-
tion between a Christian and a non-Christian; witness is always a corporate action, the ministry
of the church of Jesus Christ in and for the communities of the world.

[20]The dramatization of Scripture and dogma—one of Sayers's primary means of bearing witness
in the world—is the central metaphor of Kevin Vanhoozer's canonical-linguistic approach to
theology. Much like Sayers, Vanhoozer claims that the "gospel . . . is intrinsically dramatic," and
his theological approach draws on the language of the theater to help Christians understand
how they can bear witness to Scripture in the world (*The Drama of Doctrine: A Canonical Linguistic Approach to Christian Theology* [Louisville: Westminster John Knox, 2005], xi). He suggests that witnessing involves learning how to perform our parts in the great gospel drama and,
like the best method actors, "becoming integrated persons whose characters coincide with their
roles" (366, 373). Also like Sayers, Vanhoozer builds upon the doctrine of the incarnation: "The
canonical-linguistic approach to theology has as its goal the training of competent and truthful
witnesses who can themselves incarnate, in a variety of situations, the wisdom of Christ gleaned
from indwelling canonical practices and their ecclesial continuations" (25). Celebrating doctrine as "the reward that faith finds at the end of its search for the meaning of the apostolic
testimony to what God was doing in the event of Jesus Christ," Vanhoozer presents doctrine as
the direction we players receive from our director, the Holy Spirit. He writes, "Doctrine is a
guide for the church's scripted yet spirited gospel performances. . . . The drama of doctrine
consists in the Spirit's directing the church rightly to participate in the evangelical action by

Canterbury Cathedral or the recording studios of the BBC, the stage was at one and the same time Sayers's workplace and her pulpit—a public space where she could redress the drubbing dogma had received from "pious hands." However, though Sayers knew that dramatizing dogma could be a powerful means of revealing the relevance of Christianity to her contemporaries, she was also well aware that one could easily do the thing poorly. In her introduction to *The Man Born to Be King,* she suggested that though Christian dramatists should see dogma as the building blocks of their craft, they also needed to guard carefully against professing Christian doctrines at the expense of effective storytelling, since bad art "is useless for any purpose whatsoever—even for edification—because it is a lie, and the devil is the father of all such."[21] To dramatize dogma in a way that would be persuasive, it was absolutely crucial that the dramatist's commitment to craft be just as resolute as his or her commitment to the creeds, if not more so. Sayers contends that "it is the business of the dramatist not to subordinate the drama to the theology, but to approach the job of truth-telling from its own end, and trust the theology to emerge undistorted from the dramatic presentation of the story."[22] This brings us to the question that will occupy our attention for much of the rest of the chapter: how, exactly, did Sayers "approach the job of truth-telling" as a dramatist?

Quintilian on *Enargeia*

Sayers's technique in her plays is not unlike a rhetorical strategy championed by the Roman rhetorician Quintilian, and an exploration

---

performing its authoritative script" (102). Though Vanhoozer only cites Sayers a handful of times in his book, *The Drama of Doctrine* is arguably the best theological account of what Sayers is up to vocationally. Sayers's work literally exemplifies the metaphor that Vanhoozer uses to explain his approach.

[21] Sayers, introduction to *The Man Born to Be King,* 14, 15. For more on this point, see Sayers's piece "Playwrights are not Evangelists" (64).

[22] Sayers, introduction to *The Man Born to Be King,* 14.

of Sayers's practice in light of Quintilian's theory is instructive.[23] In book six of the first volume of the monumental *Institutio oratoria*, Quintilian addresses ways that a speaker might sway the opinions of judges, "molding and transforming [their minds], as it were, to that disposition which we wish them to assume."[24] Though at this point in the *Institutio oratoria* Quintilian is writing primarily about delivering speeches in courts of law, his discussion of the concept of *enargeia* helps us understand what Sayers's drama is doing in rhetorical terms.

After noting that the concept is akin to Cicero's notions of "illustration" and "evidentness," Quintilian writes that *enargeia* "seems not so much to narrate as to exhibit."[25] He then adds that "our feelings will be moved not less strongly than if we were actually present at the affairs of which we are speaking."[26] *Enargeia* involves depicting an event so vividly that the one who speaks and, thus, one's audience feel as they would if they were really there, experiencing the moment.[27] Such vivid depiction is clearly connected to the emotional appeals of *pathos*, but it also is related to *ēthos*. Swaying a judge through *enargeia* hinges primarily upon *the speaker's* imaginative ability to experience the emotions that one present at the scene of the crime would have

---

[23]Sayers is not typically described as a rhetor; however, she was an excellent one, who championed the study of rhetoric herself. In her well-known piece "The Lost Tools of Learning," Sayers proposes that the educational system for children ages 9 to 16 be rebuilt around the trivium: grammar, dialectic, and rhetoric (in *A Matter of Eternity: Selections from the Writings of Dorothy L. Sayers* [Grand Rapids: Eerdmans, 1973], 119-20, 131).

[24]Quintillian, *Institutio oratoria* 6.2.1, in *Quintilian's Institutes of Oratory*, ed. Lee Honeycutt, trans. John Selby Watson, http://rhetoric.byu.edu/Primary%20Texts/Quintilian.htm.

[25]Quintillian, *Institutio oratoria* 6.2.32.

[26]Quintillian, *Institutio oratoria* 6.2.32.

[27]Quintilian was not the first or only critic to discuss *enargeia*. As classicist Andrew Ford notes, "The Greek critics adopted this word to describe poetry that puts its incidents clearly before the audience's eyes. Aristotle says the poet can achieve vividness by composing with his plot 'placed squarely before his eyes,' and he finds it especially keen in drama, even when read and not performed. Longinus connects it with the poet's powers of visualization, *phantasia* (*On the Sublime* 15, 26)" (*Homer: The Poetry of the Past* [Ithaca: Cornell University Press, 1992], 54). Aristotle's associations of *enargeia* with drama are particularly relevant for my purposes in this chapter, since I explore Sayers's dramatic works in light of the concept.

felt.[28] Quintilian writes, "The chief requisite . . . for moving the feelings of others, is, as far as I can judge, that we ourselves be moved; for the assumption of grief, and anger, and indignation, will be often ridiculous, if we adapt merely our words and looks, and not our minds, to those passions."[29] There is, in other words, a kind of rhetorical honesty to the technique. The speaker does not try to conjure up feelings in the audience that are not true to the speaker's own feelings.

Movement—and, in particular, the movement of the feelings of one's audience—is also central to Quintilian's description of *enargeia*. While the metaphor of movement was not new to Quintilian, his account of the technique puts a special emphasis on the persuasive force involved in moving one's audience. He frames his discussion of *enargeia* by noting that rhetors who "can *seize the attention* of the judge, and *lead him* to whatever frame of mind he desires, *forcing him* to weep or feel angry as their words influence him, are but rarely to be found. But it is this *power* that is supreme in [legal] causes; it is this that makes eloquence effective."[30] About these lines from the *Institutio oratoria,* communication scholar Michele Kennerly calls attention to Quintilian's word choices, rightly observing, "Quintilian casts vivid visualization in violent terms without severing it from eloquence. . . . *Verbum*—the Latin *logos*—is a dominator that does not so much *move* a listener as snatch, throw over the shoulder, and run off with one."[31]

---

[28]Quintilian did not, moreover, consider *ēthos* and *pathos* to be qualitatively different types of appeal. For him, *ēthos* and *pathos* are both emotions, though the latter are more intense than the former. Communication scholar Richard A. Katula describes Quintilian's use of these terms as follows: "Pathos is the 'affectus' while ethos refers, for want of a better term, to moral behavior or qualities of character that one displays. Pathos describes the stronger and sometimes 'darker' emotions, ethos the milder" ("Quintilian on the Art of Emotional Appeal," *Rhetoric Review* 22, no. 1 [2003]: 8). For Quintilian, then, the difference between *ēthos* and *pathos* is less a difference in kind than one of degree. An argument from *pathos* is a more forceful argument from *ēthos*.
[29]Quintillian, *Institutio oratoria* 6.2.26.
[30]Quintillian, *Institutio oratoria* 6.2.3-4, emphases added; also quoted in Michele Kennerly, "Getting Carried Away: How Rhetorical Transport Gets Judgment Going," *Rhetoric Society Quarterly* 40, no. 3 (2010): 274. Kennerly uses a different translation than I do; however, I've followed her lead and highlighted relevant words from the passage.
[31]Kennerly, "Getting Carried Away," 274.

Through vivid depiction, speakers seize judges and carry them off to the scene of the crime.

An alternative way to conceptualize the movement—or "rhetorical transport," as Kennerly nicely describes it—that occurs through *enargeia* is as a transposition of the past into the present. *Enargeia* involves depicting an event so realistically that the event, along with the mood and atmosphere surrounding it, seems present to audience members. Looked at from this direction, *enargeia* is a *haunting* experience: the strategy disturbs the present with the spirit of the past through the activation of the imagination and emotions.

At times the vividness of *enargeia* may be too much to take, similar to an encounter with the divine. The comparison is particularly apt not only because this chapter focuses on the Christmas season and the doctrine of the incarnation but also because of Homer's use of a related term, *enargēs*, in *The Iliad*. Translator Alice Oswald explains that "Hera, in book 20 of the Iliad, says: 'When gods appear in their actual forms [*enargēs*] they are hard to bear.'"[32] Based in part on Hera's remark, Oswald defines *enargeia* as "bright unbearable reality," and her remarkable version of *The Iliad* aims to convey this feature of Homer's poem to English readers.[33] Notably for my purposes, Oswald likens her translation process to "lift[ing] the roof off a church in order to remember what you're worshipping."[34] *Enargeia* seems a particularly fitting rhetorical technique for bearing witness to Immanuel, "God is with us."

Enargeia in Sayers's Work

Visualization was a crucial aspect of Sayers's writing process. She relied heavily on her imagination (as well as actual sketches) to see elements

---

[32]Alice Oswald, "The Unbearable Brightness of Speaking," *The New Statesman*, October 17, 2011. I am grateful to Richard H. Gibson for introducing me to Oswald's work and her reflections on *enargeia*.

[33]Alice Oswald, *Memorial: A Version of Homer's* Iliad (New York: W.W. Norton, 2011), ix.

[34]Oswald, *Memorial*, ix.

of her stories and their settings. In his biography about Sayers, James Brabazon speaks to this point, specifically mentioning the care Sayers took to visualize Fenchurch St. Paul, the setting for her greatest mystery novel, *The Nine Tailors*.[35] Sayers drew maps of the village, and she asked an architect to help her with sketches of one of the novel's most important set pieces—the parish church.[36] Such attention to the visual details of the novel's setting provides evidence of what literary scholar Crystal Downing has called Sayers's "architectural imagination," which involved not only visualizing her stories' settings but also writing in different settings. Sayers organized her writing life by carrying out her various writing tasks in different spaces in her home.[37] "This sensitivity to the poetics of space," Downing contends, "enabled Sayers to conceptualize three-dimensional settings for her novels, a skill which helped her to envision the architectural and geographical intricacies of Dante's Hell and Purgatory."[38] Given Sayers attention to such intricacies, it is little wonder that some of the most detailed schematics of Dante's universe—those of Charles Wilfred Scott-Giles—accompany Sayers's translation of *The Divine Comedy*.[39] What I want to suggest is that Sayers's reliance on image and imagination in her writing process was also an important feature of her rhetorical approach: many of Sayers's works rely on *enargeia,* and her comments about her writing imply that vivid depiction was important to her.

Here we will focus on examples of *enargeia* present in Sayers's radio play *He That Should Come.* In *The Zeal of Thy House,* Sayers

---

[35]Sayers, *The Nine Tailors* (New York: Harcourt Brace, 1934), 150.

[36]These sketches, along with Sayers's descriptions in *The Nine Tailors,* were vivid enough to inspire architect David Collins to create a "Virtual Tour of the Parish Church of Fenchurch, St. Paul" in 2011.

[37]Doing so involved "associating each [writing project] with its space of containment" (Crystal Downing, *Writing Performances: The Stages of Dorothy L. Sayers* [New York: Palgrave Macmillan, 2004], 67, 70). It is worth noting that this approach to writing is not unlike a placed-based technique of memorization taught by some ancient rhetoricians.

[38]Downing, *Writing Performances,* 70.

[39]Barbara Reynolds, "Fifty Years On: Dorothy L. Sayers and Dante," *VII* 13 (1996): 6.

had been able to use visual elements of stagecraft—props, lighting, costumes—to tell her story; however, when she turned to the medium of radio in 1938, she had to rely more heavily on vivid depiction to shape the *visiones* of her audiences members, in ways not unlike the orators that Quintilian addressed in the *Institutio oratoria*.[40] In what follows, we will see how she vividly depicts the nativity, staging "haunts" that were intended to make her audience members feel as they would if they were actually present at Jesus's birth. We will also hear from Sayers about her dramatic techniques. Like Quintilian, Sayers does not shy away from using the language of trauma to describe what she is up to: she claims that she wants her dramatic depictions to "shock" audiences, spurring them away from the popular opinion that Christian dogma—and, more specifically, the doctrine of the incarnation of Jesus Christ—is irrelevant and shepherding them toward the manger and, simultaneously, the cross.[41] Sayers's witness has a sharp edge, bringing Jesus's claim that he has "not come to bring peace, but a sword" to the stage (Mt 10:34).

Sayers on realism. Sayers's own comments about her work imply that one of her primary goals as a dramatist was to move audience members through vivid depiction. Though Sayers did not use Quintilian's term *enargeia* in reference to her work, she did emphasize that her plays were intended to be realistic portrayals of the gospel. Her standard response to fan mail about her nativity play *He That Should Come* called attention to this aim. She told admirers that the work "was rather an experiment to produce this traditional play in so realistic a manner, and it is, therefore, particularly helpful to be told that

---

[40]Christine A. Colón rightly observes that *He That Should Come* offered Sayers "the opportunity not only to practice crafting a play for the medium of radio but also to start thinking about how to make the stories in the Bible real and powerful to a listening audience" (*Writing for the Masses: Dorothy L. Sayers and the Victorian Literary Tradition* [New York: Routledge, 2018], 164-165).

[41]Sayers, introduction to *The Man Born to Be King*, 17.

people liked it."[42] To accomplish this sort of realism, it was absolutely imperative for Sayers that one's characters *not* possess the hindsight we now possess about the gospel story. As Sayers notes in her introduction to *The Man Born to Be King,* when reading and retelling the gospel, we tend to impart the knowledge of nearly two thousand years of church history and tradition—including the knowledge that Jesus is God incarnate—to the people who interacted with and crucified Jesus.[43] Doing so allows us to demonize those who killed him and distance ourselves from them. Put another way, giving biblical figures too much awareness has the effect of flattening them: they become the two-dimensional, motionless caricatures that still haunt some Sunday school flannel boards—not "people painfully like us" but "'sacred personages,' standing about in symbolic attitudes, and self-consciously awaiting the fulfillment of prophecies."[44] Audiences are unlikely to identify with such caricatures, rendering the gospel less realistic and less relevant to them.[45]

Sayers discusses other storytelling blunders as well. Using biblical characters to moralize or safeguard our own beliefs about good taste also distances audiences from the gospel.[46] And overly sentimental dramatizations compound these errors. In a letter written to Reverend T. A. Agins, Sayers describes sentimental nativity plays as "a device of the devil." The sentimentality of such plays distorts the truth of the gospel; it is, moreover, not true to the genre's tradition. "Cheap sentiment," Sayers continues in her letter to Agins, "is the most damnable thing in the world, and the last thing you will ever find in a

---

[42]Sayers, "Letter to Mrs. F. Bayley," *He That Should Come* Archive, box 1, folder 4, The Marion E. Wade Center, Wheaton College, Wheaton, IL. Numerous letters from the Marion E. Wade Center's *He That Should Come* Archive contain this response or one very similar to it (see box 1, folders 4-5).

[43]Sayers, introduction to *The Man Born to Be King,* 15-16.

[44]Sayers, introduction to *The Man Born to Be King,* 16.

[45]For more on the realism of *The Man Born to Be King,* see Christine A. Colón's *Writing for the Masses* (197-202). In her analysis of the plays' characters, Colón shows how Sayers "helps listeners imagine them as real people rather than stained-glass saints" (198-199).

[46]Sayers, introduction to *The Man Born to Be King,* 15-16.

mediaeval mystery. Broad comedy, vulgar horse-play, a singular boldness of intimacy, crudeness and a happy freedom of theology you get
frequently in the Middle Ages; but sentimental twaddle, never."[47]
Note the contrast that Sayers draws here. She describes sentiment as
"cheap" and "twaddle," whereas the medieval plays are "broad," characterized by "boldness" and "happy freedom." We tend to define sentimentality in art in terms of excess—too much tenderness, for
example—but the excesses of sentimentality always push other things
to the side, making it just as accurate to speak of sentimentality in
terms of deficiency, as Sayers does here. Much like flat characterization, sentimentality in Christian art renders the biblical narrative less
complete and less accurate—and, therefore, less relevant.

What *is* imperative in establishing realism, Sayers notes, is that dramatists "present . . . the events and people as they appeared to themselves at the time."[48] They must represent the historical, social, political, and religious contexts of first-century Judea as accurately as
possible and represent biblical characters in ways that are true to that
setting.[49] Sayers suggests that concrete language is to be preferred
over abstractions when representing context and character in this
manner, and specific details are better than generalities.[50] "*Ecce homo*,"
the Vulgate's translation of Pilate's words when he presented Jesus to
the angry mob before the crucifixion, is one of her guiding principles
as a dramatist.[51] More specifically, Sayers suggests that those who
want to write about the events of Scripture must not simply discuss
"Man-in-general and God-in-His-thusness"; they must also depict
"God-in-His-thisness, and *this* Man, *this* person, of a reasonable soul

---

[47]Sayers, "Letter to Rev. T. A. Agins," *He That Should Come* Archive, box 1, folder 4, The Marion
E. Wade Center, Wheaton College, Wheaton, IL.
[48]Sayers, introduction to *The Man Born to Be King*, 15.
[49]Sayers, introduction to *The Man Born to Be King*, 15-17.
[50]Sayers, introduction to *The Man Born to Be King*, 15.
[51]Sayers, introduction to *The Man Born to Be King*, 15; John 19:5.

and human flesh subsisting, who walked and talked *then* and *there,* surrounded, not by human types, but by *those* individual people."[52] To borrow from the linguist's lexicon, one must fix the meaning of indexical language—those words that can point to *any* person, place, thing, or time—to *particular* persons, places, and things. What Sayers advocates for is a kind of vivid description that allows us to behold the man Jesus Christ.

To the best of my knowledge, Sayers's attempts at verisimilitude involve a commitment to the cultural contexts of biblical figures in all areas, save one: language. She argues that plays should be depicted in contemporary, everyday language—a rhetorical choice that helps the dramatist to move audience members. Sayers writes, "Tear off the disguise of the Jacobean idiom, go back to the homely and vigorous Greek of Mark or John, translate it into its current English counterpart, and there every man may see his own *face. We* played the parts in that tragedy, nineteen and a half centuries since, and perhaps are playing them to-day."[53] By vividly depicting the past using the vernacular, the dramatist is more easily able to reposition audience members, forcing them to see themselves as characters on the stage and, ultimately, as participants in the biblical narrative. When we look into the mirror that Sayers sets before us, we are meant to see ourselves as Herod, Pilate, the holier-than-thou Pharisee, the know-it-all Greek gentleman, and—perhaps most terrifying of all—part of the angry crowd, feverishly shouting, "Crucify! Crucify! Crucify!"[54]

The convergence of the gospel's historical, social, political, and religious contexts with the audience's linguistic context is not necessarily a pleasant experience for playgoers, nor does Sayers intend it

---

[52]Sayers, introduction to *The Man Born to Be King*, 15.
[53]Sayers, introduction to *The Man Born to Be King*, 17.
[54]Sayers, *The Man Born to Be King*, 277.

to be. Calling to mind for us Quintilian's description of *enargeia* and especially its associations with a measure of violence, Sayers wants not only to *move* her audiences but also to *confront* and *disturb* them, for it is only by doing so that one will be able to cut through the present age's thick spirit of decorum and reveal the force and relevance of the gospel.[55] She writes, "If you show people [the 'sordid business' of crucifixion], they are shocked. So they should be. If that does not shock them, nothing can. If the mere representation of it has an air of irreverence, what is to be said about the deed? It is curious that people who are filled with horrified indignation whenever a cat kills a sparrow can hear that story of the killing of God told Sunday after Sunday and not experience any shock at all."[56] Sayers wants her vivid depiction of the gospel to scare the hell out of us (quite literally) and to instill in us a proper and holy fear of the Lord. And one of Sayers's best examples of this move comes from what may seem to us to be a very unlikely place—the inn and manger at Bethlehem.

Vivid depiction in He That Should Come. Sayers bookends her play *He That Should Come* with scenes of the Magi. In the opening scene, the three wise men gaze into a crystal, and the audience is led to believe that they, along with the audience members themselves, are witnessing the story of Christ's nativity. Much like the angels in *The Zeal of Thy House,* the wise men haunt the narrative, charging the events with significance: we learn through this framing device that Christ and his kingdom are characterized by innocence, vulnerability, and humility.[57] But even more important for our purposes, Sayers

---

[55]"The question is," Sayers wonders, "are we at this time sufficiently disturbed by this extremely disturbing story?" (introduction to *The Man Born to Be King*, 19).

[56]Sayers, introduction to *The Man Born to Be King*, 17. Christine A. Colón notes that Sayers "crafts her plays both to shock her listeners out of their complacency and to help them recognize the story's connections to their own lives" (*Writing for the Masses,* 197).

[57]Sayers, *He That Should Come*, 36, 100.

uses this frame to ignite the imagination—or, as Quintilian would put it, to invite *visiones,* those "images by which the representations of absent objects are so distinctly represented to the mind that we seem to see them with our eyes and to have them before us."[58] Sayers's Magi point us to Bethlehem and the play's main action as follows:

> Caspar: Gather the rays of the Star in the crystal.
> Melchior: Look, and see the shape of things afar off.
> Balthazar: Listen, and hear the shadow speak in the crystal.
> *[A murmur of movements and voices behind the tableaux curtains or gauzes.]*
> Caspar: See! the light stirs and blurs to a pale cloud in the crystal—
> Melchior: Like an opal, with green fire darting and parting at the core!
> Balthazar: Look and listen! the life of the world is born in the heart of the crystal.[59]

The language Sayers uses here calls to mind the New Testament's use of the Greek word *idou,* meaning "Behold!" or "Look!" Greek lexicons suggest that the word *idou* is used to direct the reader's attention, signaling something important that is usually outside of oneself.[60] While Sayers's opening lines certainly do this rhetorical work, note how *undefined* the objects we are called to attend to are: we are listening to shadows, trying to discern distant shapes, and watching "stirs and blurs" of starlight resolve into a "pale cloud" and then into dancing, viridescent flames. This entire passage has an indexical character but lacks a clear referent, calling our mind's eye to open and then forcing it to strain in attempt to see more clearly. By activating our imagination in this way, Sayers readies us for the vivid description that will follow.

---

[58]Quintilian, *Institutio oratoria* 6.2.29.

[59]Sayers, *He That Should Come,* 39-40.

[60]Frederick William Danker, *The Concise Greek-English Lexicon of the New Testament* (Chicago: University of Chicago Press, 2009), 173-74; Spiros Zodhiates, ed., *The Complete Word Study Dictionary: New Testament* (Chattanooga, TN: AMG, 1992), 756.

But as we peer with our mind's eye toward the inn at Bethlehem, the scene does not immediately come into focus. Allowing the obscurities with which she began the play to linger for a few moments longer, Sayers presents listeners with a cacophony of the voices of those at the inn.[61] Like the exchange among the Magi, this hubbub is mirrored at the end of the play, and this frame within a frame further activates our imagination for the *enargeia* that is to come.[62] It also immediately challenges some of our most cherished commonplaces about the scene at Bethlehem. Thanks in no small part to sentimental Christmas cards and some of our most beloved carols, Christians are accustomed to imagining the place where the Christ child arrived as a city of tranquility. In our typical *visiones* of the scene, the stars drift quietly over a quaint town that lies in complete stillness, and—though the cows may be lowing softly in the stable out back—the infant king sleeps soundlessly in his mother's gentle arms. Such images are not entirely false. Silence serves as a metaphor for the sacredness of Christ's nativity, heralding the Messiah at a volume befitting his way of peace. However, by emphasizing the spiritual significance of the nativity over a realistic portrayal, we risk losing Christ's humanity in his divinity, moving us away from what the creeds tell us about him and making the story less real and relevant to us. Sayers aims to move us in the other direction by depicting Bethlehem as the overcrowded and chaotic place it must have been at census time.

As the various voices vie for attention, the first thing listeners are invited to imagine is a very diverse crowd at the inn. In the *dramatis personae* at the beginning of the play, Sayers specifies the types of voices that are needed for each part, and her specifications (e.g., the inn's landlord should be a "husky-voiced person" and the landlady should have "a shrill voice") would have produced a clamor of

---

[61]Sayers, *He That Should Come*, 41-42.
[62]Sayers, *He That Should Come*, 99.

different ages, genders, ethnicities, occupations, social classes, and—of particular importance in light of the play's medium—tone and timbre.[63] As the play unfolds and Sayers slowly enhances the resolution of the scene, her listeners would have begun to hear the jumble of voices resolve into a diverse array of characters, all speaking in a colloquial and familiar way. The dialogue would have sounded familiar to Sayers's listeners not only because of her use of colloquial language but also because of the variety of viewpoints present at the inn. Over the course of the play, social and economic issues—such as taxation, public works projects, the relationship between religions and the state, the value of the arts—are debated by a religiously tolerant Roman centurion, a *laissez faire*-minded merchant, a legalistic Pharisee, a more liberal Jewish gentleman (who today might be described as a practitioner of Reform or Progressive Judaism), a scholarly Greek gentleman, and three humble—and, the landlady suspects, drunk—shepherds.

From a rhetorical point of view, one might think that the familiar atmosphere that Sayers creates would be a comfortable one for her audience members to inhabit, but in this case the play's atmosphere grows increasingly uncomfortable precisely *because* it is familiar. Even as we begin to feel at home in the world of the play (and perhaps even begin to "see" our own faces mirrored in one or more of the characters), the characters begin talking about the Messiah. And as conversations about Christ so often are, these discussions are deeply troubling because they shine a light on the characters' sinfulness—and ours. When finally the angels announce the birth of the Messiah in Sayers's telling of the story, we learn just how far many of the characters (and indeed many of us) are from the manger and the Christ child.

---

[63]Sayers, *He That Should Come*, 32.

The Pharisee reveals himself to be farthest away. His Messiah will come in battle to save the Israelites from other nations, who ultimately have no hope.[64] When the Pharisee is asked if he believes that salvation will be extended from Jew to Gentile, he answers, "Certainly not. It is blasphemous and ridiculous. He will set his foot upon the necks of the nations, and the heathen will be cast into outer darkness with wailing and gnashing of teeth."[65] And with that, the Pharisee declares he is going outdoors to get away from the racket at the inn. He is nowhere to be found when the angelic hymn begins. One character asks where he is, and another replies, "Oh, he cast himself into outer darkness some time ago."[66] The Pharisee's judgmental and presumptuous attitude about others, Sayers shows us, has distanced him to such an extent that he is physically unable to encounter the Christ.

Though the merchant, Greek gentleman, and centurion remain in the inn during Christ's birth, they are too far away spiritually to hear and understand the significance of the angels' good news. The merchant is a coward, so fearful of his own safety that when the other characters start discussing the Messiah, he nervously pleads for them to stop.[67] The Greek gentleman, meanwhile, maintains an objective distance from religion that prevents him from being moved by the gospel. Regarding his relationship to Christ, he says, "I like to get the reactions of the common people to all these academic questions."[68] Later, after the Pharisee issues his judgment on "the heathen" and makes his exit, the Greek gentleman issues a (self-) judgment of his own: "What a very dogmatic person! It must be marvellous to feel so positive about everything. I never feel certain

---

[64]Sayers, *He That Should Come*, 61, 66, 70.
[65]Sayers, *He That Should Come*, 85.
[66]Sayers, *He That Should Come*, 95.
[67]Sayers, *He That Should Come*, 70.
[68]Sayers, *He That Should Come*, 75.

of anything."[69] And the centurion so identifies with the state's position on "religious toleration" that he has grown completely deaf to the claims that the gospel makes upon other religions and on him as an individual.[70]

When the angels begin to sing, neither the centurion nor the Greek gentleman (nor, we assume, the merchant) can hear _anything_.[71] In fact, aside from the holy family, the only characters who hear the heavenly hosts herald Christ's birth are the Jewish gentleman—who can only perceive it indistinctly—and the shepherds, whose testimonies are quickly dismissed as the raving words of drunk men.[72]

In showing us these characters, _He That Should Come_ pulls back from the view of the manger depicted by our cards, carols, and crèches to reveal all of the _outsiders_ created by the angels' announcement of the incarnate God. Sayers's manger scene separates the sheep and the goats from one another, forcing us to consider what our own proximity to the manger would be. As we have already seen, in Quintilian's description of _enargeia_, audience members are carried away (almost violently) through the use of vivid depiction, and Sayers's use of depiction functions in a similar manner. Her Christmas story begins by moving us (with the Magi) toward the inn at Bethlehem, but then, as soon as we get close to those at the inn, she reminds us how far away from the manger we actually are. Sayers's Christmas vision is not polite, sentimental, or calm; it is positively _unsettling_.

Even more unsettling is the fact that Christ's future haunts the manger scene in Sayers's depiction of the story. She has the shepherds and not the Magi bring gifts to the Christ child, and their pastoral

---

[69]Sayers, _He That Should Come_, 85.
[70]Sayers, _He That Should Come_, 70.
[71]Sayers, _He That Should Come_, 96.
[72]Sayers, _He That Should Come_, 97.

presents—a fleece, a staff, and "a twist of flowing thorn"—foretell Christ's role as the shepherd king and the sacrificial lamb.[73] Speaking for her son (and prefiguring his own words from the cross), Sayers's Mary replies, "My Son shall remember you all when He comes into His Kingdom."[74] And with that, the listening audience realizes precisely where Sayers has taken us: we have been transported from the inn at Bethlehem to Jerusalem's Golgotha. To drive the point home, Sayers reveals the identity of the Jewish gentleman: Joseph of Arimathea.[75] Sayers's Christmas message—which has already taken us from the Magi's otherworldly vision to the inn to the manger to the cross—has now carried us to the grave, confronting us with the depths of God's incarnation.

***Responses to* He That Should Come.** The play took some listeners to places where they did not want to go—especially at Christmas. Shortly after Sayers's radio play aired on the radio, she received a letter from a Mrs. E. Day who, as we can infer from reading Sayers's response, seems to have criticized the radio play for its crude depiction of the nativity.[76] Sayers answered most of the letters she received about *He That Should Come* with the brief standard reply noted above, but she wrote a lengthy response to Day defending her approach in the play:

> First of all: you speak of the condescension of God; but forgive me for saying that it is impossible to measure that condescension unless one realises that He was born, not into an allegory, or a devotional tableau, or a Christmas card, with everybody behaving beautifully; but into this confused, coarse, and indifferent world, where people quarrel and swear, and

---

[73]Sayers, *He That Should Come*, 99.

[74]Sayers, *He That Should Come*, 99.

[75]According to Scripture, after Jesus died on the cross, Joseph of Arimathea reclaimed Christ's broken body from its despisers and, with Nicodemus, buried the body in what was to be Joseph's very own resting place (Jn 19:38-42; Mt 27:59). Sayers's Joseph of Arimathea promises Mary to give Jesus a "rich gift" should they meet again (Sayers, *He That Should Come*, 99).

[76]Sayers, "Letter to E. Day," *He That Should Come* Archive, box 1, folder 4, The Marion E. Wade Center, Wheaton College, Wheaton, IL.

make vulgar jokes and spit on the floor. He was a real person, born in blood and pain like any other child, and dying in blood and pain, like the commonest thief that was ever strung up on the gallows. Why should we suppose that the Heavenly Hosts made easy His passage into the world? [T]hey did not ease His passage out of it. If things had been made easy for Him, He would not have been wholly Man. We may shrink from the brutal facts of life, but He did not; and that is the measure of His strength and our weakness.[77]

Sayers's defense of *He That Should Come* highlights her deep commitment to the church's affirmations that God became human. If our retellings of the gospel are to be true to Scripture and the creeds, it is crucial that we present Jesus as fully human, bloodied and wounded both in his death *and* his birth. She also teaches us here that, if we are to understand the incarnation rightly, how we depict the world is as important as how we depict the Word. If our artistic attempts at Christian witness sentimentalize, sanctify, or sterilize Christ's earthly surroundings instead of depicting them realistically, we keep God in his heaven, separate from the world. It is only when we swaddle the Christ child in the tatters of a sinful world that we are able to begin to grasp the magnitude of God's humility.

Sayers received many favorable responses to *He That Should Come* as well, many of which she records almost word-for-word in her lengthy response to Day.[78] Reading through the letter, I was struck by how many admirers of the play commented specifically on its vividness. One listener remarked that Sayers told the tale "so vividly" that it "made [her] realize 'where all past years are' – here with us today."[79] Another described her family's experience listening to the play as follows:

---

[77]Sayers, "Letter to E. Day."
[78]Sayers, "Letter to E. Day." Sayers's reproductions of the quotations are true to the words of the original letters, although Sayers sometimes adds underlining for emphasis.
[79]Sayers, "Letter to E. Day."

We quickly felt the wild[,] unruly, unfriendly atmosphere of the inn and as the play progressed and we followed each sidelight on the environment of the little Family the whole scene became amazingly vivid, and the people "came alive".

None of us realised before how much we had just *accepted* the story without properly visualising it. It gave us a new vision of it all and the tiny infant's cry brought home to us as never before the *real* humanity of Jesus.[80]

At least two listeners contrasted the potency of play with that of sermonic discourse. Calling the play "enthralling," one wrote that the play "must do far more good than many dry-as-dust sermons," and the other noted, "It said just what so many priests try to say in their pulpits *but* said it effectively. It made the Christmas story live."[81] The praise Sayers received for the vividness and liveliness of *He That Should Come* was, moreover, often accompanied by descriptions of imaginative "transport," not unlike those that Quintilian claimed would be caused by *enargeia*. "Your Nativity Play is just over," a fan remarked, "and I've seldom heard anything so simply and deeply moving. For the first time it was possible to 'place' the Story against a 'real' background, without 'groping' with one's imagination. For much blind groping, especially for the everyday details of long-past times, rather tends to prevent one from yielding fully to [the] atmosphere."[82] Sayers concluded her letter to Day with the following note of praise from a listener: "I can't help writing to tell you how very much I enjoyed your Nativity Play. It was quite wonderful, and nothing except the Midnight Mass itself seemed to take me straight back through all

---

[80]Sayers, "Letter to E. Day." James Brabazon's and Barbara Reynolds's biographies of Sayers also contain versions of this response, which, Brabazon records, appeared in the play's promotional materials (Brabazon, *Dorothy L. Sayers: A Biography* [New York: Charles Scribner's Sons, 1981], 171-172, 292; Reynolds, *Dorothy L. Sayers: Her Life and Soul* [New York: St. Martin's Press, 1993], 290).

[81]Sayers, "Letter to E. Day."

[82]Sayers, "Letter to E. Day." According to Brabazon's book (*Dorothy L. Sayers,* 172, 292), a version of this quotation also appeared in the promotional materials for the play.

the ages, to the 'Cave' at Bethlehem, as your play did. It just made Christmas seem present here and now."[83]

Enargeia and Energy

Enargeia is not simply one of Sayers's preferred rhetorical techniques. I want to suggest that it is also related to an important aspect of her Trinitarian understanding of human creativity—the concept of Energy. In her book *The Mind of the Maker*, Sayers suggests that works of human creativity are analogous to the Trinity because each one consists of three, consubstantial expressions: an Idea, analogous to the Father; Energy, analogous to the Son; and Power, analogous to the Holy Spirit.[84] Because Idea, Energy, and Power are all expressions of the same creative concept, they are one.[85] But like the three persons of the Trinity, they are also distinct from one another. Idea is the creative concept that develops in the artist's mind, Energy involves the materialization of that concept in the world, and Power consists of the effects of the concept's materialization on the author and his or her audiences.[86]

In light of her Trinitarian analogy, it is not surprising that Sayers uses christological language to elaborate on Energy's meaning. She draws most heavily on the doctrine of the incarnation, the notion that

---

[83]Sayers, "Letter to E. Day."

[84]Sayers, *Mind of the Maker* (San Francisco: HarperCollins, 1987), 37-38. Sayers first introduced these three concepts in the concluding lines of *The Zeal of Thy House*, the play with which I began this chapter. In *Zeal of Thy House's* final moments, the archangel Michael proclaims the Trinitarian nature of creative acts (130-31).

[85]Sayers, *Mind of the Maker*, 41.

[86]Sayers, *Mind of the Maker*, 38-41. Neither Christians nor rhetoricians (nor Christian rhetoricians) will likely find themselves agreeing with all of Sayers's points about creative work. As a writing teacher, for example, I am not persuaded by Sayers's claim that the "creative act . . . does not depend for its fulfillment upon its manifestation in a material creation" (42). Sayers's attempt here to be true to God's oneness by suggesting that the Idea is fulfilled irrespective of its materialization does not account for the invention and discovery—i.e., the *new* creation—that occurs through processes of drafting and revision (Energy) as well as through collaboration and audience feedback (Power). Nevertheless, her attempt to speak to members of her profession without compromising her commitment to the creeds of the church is laudable.

God, the Word, "became flesh and dwelled among us" (Jn 1:14). Sayers frames her main chapter on Energy with a passage from St. Augustine's *On the Trinity*, in which he presents human communication in christological and incarnational terms. Augustine notes that, after we have "conceived" of "the true knowledge of things" in our minds, "we beget it from within" by "apply[ing] to the word . . . the ministry of the voice or of some bodily sign."[87] Elsewhere in the book, Sayers suggests that it is Energy that brings about the Creative Idea in the physical world—in space, time, and matter.[88] The Idea is bounded by locality, temporality, and materiality: limits that Christ imposed upon himself when he condescended to humans by taking on flesh.[89] Such Energy is not, moreover, exercised disinterestedly. Sayers writes, "To [Energy] belongs everything that can be included under the word 'passion,'" and she goes on to observe that the Idea's materialization is "the urgent desire of the creative mind."[90] The theological language is again unmistakable. Here, at the center of Sayers's theory of the artist's work, we can hear the echoes of language about the one who, in his great love for his creation, took on human flesh and suffered death on a cross.[91]

Sayers's concept of Energy is not, of course, identical to Quintilian's *enargeia*, but the concepts do have much in common. Like *enargeia*, Energy makes one's Ideas visible to oneself and others. What is more,

---

[87]Sayers, *Mind of the Maker*, 47.

[88]"The incarnation of the Energy," she writes, "stands wholly within the space-time frame: it is written by a material pen and printed by a material machine upon material paper; the words were produced as a succession of events succeeding one another in time . . . the *body* of the Energy is a created thing, strictly limited by time and space, and subject to any accident that may befall matter" (Sayers, *Mind of the Maker*, 114).

[89]Here Energy is analogous to the kenotic activity of Jesus Christ, who, as the apostle Paul writes in his glorious hymn in Philippians, "did not count equality with God a thing to be grasped, but emptied himself, by taking the form of a servant, being born in the likeness of men" (Phil 2:6-7).

[90]Sayers, *Mind of the Maker*, 40, 42.

[91]One of my anonymous readers helpfully noted that, for Sayers, Energy is not always material and temporal but, like the Son's "eternal generation" from the Father, can also be "pre-incarnate." While Sayers emphasizes incarnational Energy in *The Mind of the Maker*, the point is well taken. I also appreciate the reader's additional remark that my own emphasis on incarnational Energy is fitting, given my chapter's focus.

Sayers specifically mentions the role that the imagination plays in bringing an Idea into the world when she describes Energy. The relevant passage explores how writers create fictional characters—a subject that Sayers was well qualified to speak on by the time she wrote *The Mind of the Maker*.[92] "When making a character," Sayers notes, "[the writer] in a manner separates and incarnates a part of his own living mind."[93] She goes on to describe how the writer must envision what it would be like for this one part of his identity to govern his entire being and behavior, and then he must work to flesh this out in a character.[94] This process of character creation—the process of imagining an attribute of oneself to permeate one's entire being and then representing that new creation on the page—is, according to Sayers, absolutely essential for making characters believable.[95] Absent this, characters become "mere dummies," about which Sayers writes, "the Energy is not incarnate; they do not, as we say, 'come to life,' and as a result of the failure of the Energy to create, no Power flows out upon or from them."[96] Put in rhetorical terms, characters that are not a product of this imaginative and incarnational process will not be persuasive to audiences, and—if the process does not happen, even in the case of a single minor character—the persuasiveness of the whole work will suffer. Here Energy sounds very much like *enargeia* indeed.

What follows in Sayers's description of the Energy of character creation is an illustration of the process that bears a striking similarity

---

[92]Sayers had written over a dozen detective novels and many more short stories by that point.

[93]Sayers, *Mind of the Maker*, 51.

[94]Sayers, *Mind of the Maker*, 51, 53.

[95]As I have shown, Sayers's *He That Should Come* presents us with a diverse cast of characters, contributing to the work's rhetorical power by encouraging us to consider our own proximity to the Christ child. Sayers's description of the Energy of character creation in *The Mind of the Maker* implies that she knew what she was doing rhetorically in *He That Should Come*. After describing how writers create characters, Sayers suggests that, if a work is to be effective, characters cannot all be the same; rather, the writer must "incarnate" (to use Sayers's language) different aspects of his or her identity in different characters. Without such "diversity," Sayers notes, "the wholeness is destroyed and the Power diminished" (Sayers, *Mind of the Maker*, 53).

[96]Sayers, *Mind of the Maker*, 54.

to Quintilian's writings on *enargeia*. Quoting Chesterton, Sayers writes the following:

> [The writer] recognizes in himself a powerful emotion—let us say, jealousy. His activity then takes this form: Supposing this emotion were to become so strong as to dominate my whole personality, how should I feel and how should I behave? In imagination he becomes the jealous person and thinks and feels within that frame of experience, so that the jealousy of Othello is the true creative expression of the jealousy of Shakespeare. He follows out, in fact, the detective system employed by Chesterton's "Father Brown": "I mean that I really did see myself, and my real self, committing the murders. . . . I mean that I thought and thought about how a man might come to be like that, until I realised that I really *was* like that, in everything except actual final consent to the action."[97]

Compare this passage to Quintilian's illustration of *enargeia* in action:

> I make a complaint that a man has been murdered; shall I not bring before my eyes everything that is likely to have happened when the murder occurred? Shall not the assassin suddenly sally forth? Shall not the other tremble, cry out, supplicate or flee? Shall I not behold the one striking, the other falling? Shall not the blood, and paleness, and last gasp of the expiring victim present itself fully to my mental view?[98]

It is noteworthy that both Sayers (drawing on Chesterton) and Quintilian write about visualizing the scene of a crime with the help of the imagination. Energy and *enargeia* are both used to help us understand, to *see*, vice and violence with greater clarity. But it is also interesting to note the difference between the illustrations. For Quintilian the imagined assassin "sall[ies] forth," and the imaginer stands detached from both victim and perpetrator. But Father Brown puts himself in the murderer's shoes, which, as Sayers well knows, is

---

[97]Sayers, *Mind of the Maker*, 51-52.
[98]Quintillian, *Institutio oratoria* 6.2.31

precisely where Christians need to place themselves. The difference is an important one. Whereas Quintilian described the powers of vivid visualization in the *Institutio oratoria* as a means of moving a judge to rule on the fate of another in a court of law, Sayers used vivid visualization in *He That Should Come* to confront audience members with the brutal reality of the incarnation and bring about their own self-judgment. Sayers seems to intend her "rhetorical transport" to set us on a crash course with the "firstborn of all creation" (Col 1.15)—who plummeted with a velocity so swift and sure that, should our paths collide, we will be brought low.

A Witness of Christmastide

The aspects of Sayers's writing that I have been exploring in this chapter demonstrate what it means to be a witness of Christmastide.[99] Her writings' content (the humiliation of William of Sens and the birth of Christ), rhetorical techniques (*enargeia*), and theoretical underpinnings (Energy) all confront us with the reality of the incarnation.[100] But Sayers also takes us one step further. Her theory of human creativity suggests that the work of *all* artists, Christian and non-Christian alike, points us to the incarnation of Jesus Christ.[101] This is

---

[99]Like the writings of all the figures I consider in this book, Sayers's work resonates with *many* different days and seasons of the Christian year. As should be clear from the previous discussion, both *The Zeal of Thy House* and *He That Should Come* have strong Advent and Lenten undertones, and—as we will see in the final chapter—Sayers has much to teach us about the rhetorical witness of Pentecost.

[100]As we have seen throughout this chapter and especially through our exploration of Energy, Sayers's writings frequently remind us of Christ's role as maker. And the Christmas season is an ideal time to witness by proclaiming Christ as maker because the incarnation involves the continuation of Christ's creative activity. Moreover, as Timothy Larsen reminds us in his book *George MacDonald in the Age of Miracles: Incarnation, Doubt, and Reenchantment* (Downers Grove, IL: InterVarsity Press, 2018), "[T]he Christmas season was a traditional time to tell ghost stories" (32). It is arguably the case that Sayers's penchant for mystery—as well as the sort of horror I described concerning *The Zeal of Thy House*—offers another link between her work and Christmas.

[101]Furthermore, all creative work points us to the Trinity: Idea, Energy, and Power are a "Trinity in Unity" that bears witness to the Godhead who made all things (Sayers, *Mind of the Maker*, 37-42, 227).

the case irrespective of the beliefs or identity of the artist, the nature of the creative process or the content of the work, or the effects of the finished work on the artist or the audience.[102] If Sayers is right on these points, then artists who are staunch atheists betray their own arguments when they practice their craft: there is an inherent inconsistency between what they say in their art and the activity that brings such art about. Christian artists, moreover, are freed from worry about whether their work is sufficiently Christian. They can focus in their work on being true to their craft, confident that devotion to their vocation will bear witness to the God who made the world into which he was born.[103]

---

[102]While the doctrines of the Trinity and incarnation certainly provide Sayers with the language to explain Energy as a *theoretical concept,* she repeatedly implies that Energy *in practice* is simply the artist at work at his or her craft. In the case of the writer, Energy is "the writing of the book," which includes the emotions, decisions, actions, struggles, and accomplishments that bring the book as a physical object into being (Sayers, *Mind of the Maker,* 40). And such work need not involve, and often *should not* involve, explicitly Christian processes or goals. As I noted earlier in the chapter, Sayers believed that a crucial aspect of Christian witness simply involves practicing one's vocation. In her piece "Why Work?" she writes, "Let the Church remember this: that every maker and worker is called to serve God *in* his profession or trade—not outside it. The Apostles complained rightly when they said it was not meet they should leave the word of God and serve tables; their vocation was to preach the word. But the person whose vocation it is to prepare the meals beautifully might with equal justice protest: It is not meet for us to leave the service of our tables to preach the word" (Sayers, *Mind of the Maker,* 140). Sayers likewise maintained that the Christian artist should not witness by evangelizing or preaching (i.e., in a manner detached from his or her calling) but rather by practicing his or her craft well. On this point, she affirms the words of the Catholic philosopher Jacques Maritain: "If you want to produce Christian work, be a Christian, and try to make a work of beauty into which you have put your heart; do not adopt a Christian pose" (quoted in "Why Work?," in *Letters to a Diminished Church: Passionate Arguments for the Relevance of Christianity* [Nashville: Thomas Nelson, 2004], 140). For more on Sayers's views on work and vocation, see Christine Fletcher's "Vocation in Work: Dorothy L. Sayers and Economic Issues" (*VII* 26 [2009]: 53-80) and William H. Harrison's "Loving the Creation, Loving the Creator: Dorothy L. Sayers's Theology of Work" (*Anglican Theological Review* 86, no. 2 [2004]: 239-57).

[103]This view of Christian witness is, of course, also tied to the doctrine of the *imago Dei,* which Sayers discusses in the second chapter of *The Mind of the Maker.* Theologians have long discussed what the Bible means in Gen 1:26-27 when it claims that humans are created in God's image, suggesting, to highlight just a few common interpretations, that the phrase refers to human rationality, our use of language, or our ability to create. Sayers's view is most similar to the third of these interpretations: "Had the author of *Genesis* anything particular in his mind when he wrote [that God created man in His own image]? It is observable that in the passage leading up to the statement about man, he has given no detailed information about God. Looking at man, he sees in him something essentially divine, but when we turn back to see what he

On a day in mid-December of 1957, Sayers traveled to London to purchase a few Christmas gifts.[104] Upon returning home from her outing, she developed a blood clot and died suddenly. Her memorial service, held nine days after the Feast of the Epiphany, included a panegyric penned by C. S. Lewis.[105] Lewis wrote of Sayers's commitment to her craft as well as her rejection of the pride that often dogs artists.[106] Then he made a remark that brings together many threads of my argument: "The architect in *The Zeal of Thy House* is at the outset the incarnation of—and therefore doubtless the *Catharsis* from—a possible Dorothy whom the actual Dorothy Sayers was offering for mortification. His disinterested zeal for the work itself has her full sympathy. But she knew that, without grace, it is a dangerous virtue."[107] Within the space of a few lines, Lewis had managed to touch on Sayers's devotion to work as a form of witness, allude to

---

says about the original upon which the 'image' of God was modeled, we find only the single assertion, 'God created.' The characteristic common to God and man is apparently that: the desire and the ability to make things" (*Mind of the Maker*, 22). While this particular reading of the doctrine of *imago Dei* is not new to Sayers, she gives it a fresh spin. Her arguments in *The Mind of the Maker* imply that God is not only imaged in the artist's being, desires, abilities, or ideas; rather, God is imaged through the three expressions of a creative work—Idea, Energy, and Power. The view that being created in God's image means that we ourselves are creators has continued to receive much attention among Christian writers in recent years, helping to fuel renewed Christian engagement with culture and the arts. See, for example, Andy Crouch's *Culture Making: Recovering Our Creative Calling* (Downers Grove, IL: InterVarsity Press, 2008) and N. T. Wright's *Surprised by Hope: Rethinking Heaven, the Resurrection, and the Mission of the Church* (New York: HarperCollins, 2008).

[104]C. S. Lewis, *The Collected Letters of C. S. Lewis*, vol. 3, ed. Walter Hooper (New York: HarperCollins, 2007), 908.

[105]Walter Hooper, "Introduction" to C. S. Lewis, *On Stories, and Other Essays on Literature*, ed. Walter Hooper (New York: Harcourt Brace, 1982), xx. Lewis and Sayers counted one another as friends. In a letter to the editor that appeared in the literary magazine *Encounter* in 1963, Lewis noted that Sayers "was the first person of importance who ever wrote me a fan-letter" (Lewis, *Collected Letters*, vol. 3, 1400). He continued, "I liked her, originally, because she liked me; later, for the extraordinary zest and edge of her conversation—as I like a high wind" (1400). And when, in an interview with Sherwood Eliot Wirt, Lewis was asked which Christian writers he found to be helpful, he mentioned Sayers by name (Lewis, "Cross-Examination," in *God in the Dock: Essays on Theology and Ethics*, ed. Walter Hooper [Grand Rapids: Eerdmans, 1970], 260).

[106]C. S. Lewis, "A Panegyric for Dorothy L. Sayers," in *On Stories, and Other Essays on Literature*, ed. Walter Hooper (New York: Harcourt Brace, 1982), 92.

[107]Lewis, "Panegyric," 92.

incarnational Energy and character creation, and praise her emphasis on the virtue of humility.

Lewis devoted the last paragraphs of his panegyric to Sayers's translation of *The Divine Comedy*, and it is a fitting way to conclude this chapter as well. Sayers discovered Dante's poem when she was fifty-one years old.[108] She had read Charles Williams's book *The Figure of Beatrice* the previous year (and at that time had committed herself to reading Dante), but—as Barbara Reynolds notes—it took the privacy afforded by an air raid to bring it about.[109] Sayers found much to treasure in Dante, but one thing she particularly appreciated—which is perhaps unsurprising given her "architectural imagination" and her own use of *enargeia*—was his "affirmation of images."[110] Two weeks after she started, she wrote a letter to Charles Williams describing the opening cantos of the *Purgatorio* as "a sort of miracle . . . limpid and lovely and clean and enchanting, like one of those Italian pictures—or in fact like the real Italy, only more so."[111] Five years later, her translation of the *Inferno* appeared. And five years after that, Sayers's *Introductory Papers on Dante* was published, followed by her own translation of the *Purgatorio*. It was quite a decade.

At one point in her *Introductory Papers on Dante*, Sayers comments on the following lines from *Paradiso*, in which Beatrice explains to Dante the pilgrim why God created the universe: "Not that He might acquire any gain for Himself, for that cannot be; but in order that His splendor. . . . might, shining back to Him, declare '*I am*,' therefore in His eternity, beyond all time, beyond all limitation, according to His good pleasure, the Eternal Love unfolded Himself into new loves."[112] About these lines Sayers writes, "The image here,

---

[108]Reynolds, "Fifty Years On," 3.

[109]Reynolds, "Fifty Years On," 3.

[110]Crystal Downing, "The Orthodoxology of Dorothy L. Sayers," *VII* 22 (2005): 39.

[111]Reynolds, *Passionate*, 21.

[112]Barbara Reynolds, *The Passionate Intellect: Dorothy L. Sayers' Encounter with Dante* (Kent, OH: Kent State University Press, 1989), 47.

as throughout the *Paradiso,* is the familiar one of light; God is the light: the derived radiance of the creature is the *splendore,* the splendour. The right end of every creature is to shine back to God with that splendour, and to be able to say, thus shining (*risplendendo*); "I am—*subsisto.*"[113] "The true end of the creature," she adds a bit later, "is that it should reflect, each in its own way and to its capacity great or small, some tiny facet of the infinite variety comprised within the unity of the One."[114]

Throughout this chapter, we have been focusing on the Christian witness of artists; however, in this passage, Sayers broadens our view, highlighting how all creatures witness to God. What these more general comments about witness share with Sayers's rhetorical practice of *enargeia* and her theory of creative Energy is an emphasis on *making visible* "some tiny facet of the infinite variety" of the one God.

Sayers's comments about Dante also remind us that God alone is the source of our light. And with that, we must turn from the rhetoric of Christmastide to that of Epiphany, the feast celebrating Christ's offer of salvation to all of the nations. He is, in the words of Simeon when he held the young Jesus in his arms, "a light for revelation to the Gentiles, and for glory to your people Israel" (Lk 2:32). Sayers's wise men urge us in this direction in the closing lines of *He That Should Come*:

> Caspar: Up and to horse! Make haste! for the Star has moved on before us.
> And the east is pale with the dawn. We must ride by faith.
> Melchior: Following the light invisible.
> Balthazar: Following the Star.[115]

These lines reveal a strange truth about the Epiphany star and, thus, about God's light. Its rays are not always outwardly visible, requiring

---

[113]Sayers, *Introductory Papers on Dante* (Eugene, OR: Wipf & Stock, 1954), 47-48.
[114]Sayers, *Introductory Papers on Dante*, 48.
[115]Sayers, *He That Should Come*, 100.

that we, to fuse Caspar's final words in the play with a phrase of the apostle Paul's, "ride by faith, not by sight" (2 Cor 5:7). Here Sayers suggests to us that, if our speech is to be seasoned by Epiphany, we actually need to move beyond the discussion of vivid depiction. Let us follow the star.

3

PREACHING THE WORD

Dietrich Bonhoeffer and Epiphanic Identification

Where is the one who is wise? Where is the scribe? Where is the debater of this age? Has not God made foolish the wisdom of the world? For since, in the wisdom of God, the world did not know God through wisdom, it pleased God through the folly of what we preach to save those who believe. For Jews demand signs and Greeks seek wisdom, but we preach Christ crucified, a stumbling block to Jews and folly to Gentiles, but to those who are called, both Jews and Greeks, Christ the power of God and the wisdom of God. For the foolishness of God is wiser than men, and the weakness of God is stronger than men.

1 CORINTHIANS 1:20-25

When a preacher opens the Bible and interprets the word of God, a mystery takes place, a miracle: the grace of God, who comes down from heaven into our midst and speaks to us, knocks on our door, asks questions, warns us, puts pressure on us, alarms us, threatens us, and makes us joyful again and free and sure. When the Holy Scriptures are brought to life in a church, the Holy Spirit comes down from the eternal throne, into our hearts, while the busy world outside sees nothing and knows nothing about it—that God could actually be found here. Out there they are all running after the latest sensations, the excitements of evening in the big city, never knowing that the real sensation, something infinitely more exciting, is happening in here: here, where eternity and time meet, where the immortal God receives mortal human beings, through the holy Word, and cares for them, where human souls can taste the starkest terrors of despair and the ultimate depths of God's eternity.

DIETRICH BONHOEFFER, "AMBASSADORS FOR CHRIST"

The glory of Jesus is hidden in his humility and is perceived only in faith.

DIETRICH BONHOEFFER, "EPIPHANY: A THEOLOGICAL REFLECTION"

IN JANUARY OF 1940, Dietrich Bonhoeffer penned theological reflections on Epiphany for pastors in the Confessing Church, highlighting
the paradox at the heart of the feast. Jesus Christ manifests his
greatness through his humility, simultaneously revealing himself to
those with eyes of faith and concealing himself from those without
the eyes to see.[1] "The glory of Jesus," Bonhoeffer reminds the pastors,
"is hidden in his humility and is perceived only in faith."[2] As we shall
see in this chapter, this feature of the God-man's revelation to the
world plays a key role in Bonhoeffer's theology and helps us understand his views about Christian witness. It is, I should also note, a
feature of Bonhoeffer's thought well-captured by the title of Charles
Marsh's superb biography of the German pastor-theologian:
Strange Glory.[3]

Marsh takes his title from Bonhoeffer's well-known sermon
"Ambassadors for Christ," delivered in October of 1933, nearly seven
years before his Epiphany reflections appeared. In that message, Bonhoeffer preached that God's glory appeals to us—attempting "to win
our hearts," in Bonhoeffer's terms—in and through poverty.[4] Bonhoeffer also suggested a connection between God's hidden glory and the
genre of the sermon, alerting us to the fact that preaching both reveals
and conceals the Word. For those inside the church, when a pastor
preaches, God "comes down from heaven into our midst and speaks
to us"; however, "the busy world outside"—driven by other desires—
"sees nothing and knows nothing about it."[5] To restate Bonhoeffer's

---

[1]Dietrich Bonhoeffer, "*Epiphany:* A Theological Reflection," in *Dietrich Bonhoeffer Works,
Volume 15: Theological Education Underground: 1937-1940,* ed. Victoria J. Barnett, trans. Victoria
J. Barnett et al. (Minneapolis: Fortress, 2012), 537.
[2]Bonhoeffer, "*Epiphany*," 537.
[3]Charles Marsh, *Strange Glory: A Life of Dietrich Bonhoeffer* (New York: Alfred A. Knopf, 2014).
Marsh's book was instrumental in helping me understand Bonhoeffer's thought, and I rely on his
excellent scholarship at many points throughout this chapter.
[4]Bonhoeffer, "Ambassadors for Christ," in *Collected Sermons,* ed. Isabel Best, trans. Douglas
W. Scott et al. (Minneapolis: Fortress, 2012), 92.
[5]Bonhoeffer, "Ambassadors," 90.

remarks here using my own vocabulary, God's rhetorical action during the sermon is a kind of divine *pathetic* appeal, an attempt to persuade us by speaking to our hearts and emotions. But as Bonhoeffer's other writings on the topic make clear, such an appeal will strike many listeners as pathetic in the pejorative sense of that term: even if they *do* pause from their hustle and bustle to listen to the Word, a message about God's humiliation will sound contemptible apart from faith.

Bonhoeffer's "Ambassadors for Christ" and his Epiphany reflections were not the abstract musings of a scholar detached from the world; rather, they were the *cri de coeur* of a pastor-theologian who faced a theological and political crisis in his country that demanded that Christian witness involve not only public proclamation but also humiliation, hiddenness, and—ultimately for Bonhoeffer—execution as one numbered among his country's traitors. In response to Adolf Hitler's plans to Nazify, and eventually nullify, the church in Germany, Bonhoeffer would speak out strongly on many occasions and, near the end of his life, try to rebuild Christian ethics from the ground up. But he also devoted much of his energy during the 1930s and early '40s to building underground Christian communities. Drawing support from a growing ecumenical movement, his family and friends, and likeminded German Christians, Bonhoeffer ran an illegal seminary at Finkenwalde from 1935 to 1937, training future pastors in the ideas and practices of Christian orthodoxy while trying to avoid the gaze of the Nazi state apparatus. Unlike other German seminaries of the time, being a student at Finkenwalde Seminary not only included studying theology and homiletics but also involved practicing "spiritual disciplines" in community.[6] Marsh notes that "students soon understood that 'they were not there simply to learn new techniques

---

[6]Marsh, *Strange Glory*, 235.

of preaching and instruction' but as initiates in a new manner of being Christian. Dissent and resistance, they were taught, required spiritual nourishment: prayer, Bible study, and meditation on the essential matters to expand the moral imagination."[7] Put in the terms of the present work, Finkenwalde taught students that the rhetoric of one's public witness ought to grow out of a season of Christian "life together"—a time of fellowship devoted to learning, discipleship, and worship.

As readers may have noticed by this point, I begin each of the five main chapters of this book in a church setting. Each introduction calls attention to a place of worship in order to reinforce my claim that our rhetorics of witness ought to be grounded in the worshiping body of Christ. Though some may not consider Finkenwalde seminary to be a church in the strictest sense of the term, I have chosen it as the place of worship with which to begin this chapter.

For some readers, the choice to highlight an underground seminary at the beginning of a chapter on the Epiphany may seem strange. *Epiphany*, after all, comes from the Greek word for "reveal" and shares etymological connections with the words for "appearance," "give light (to)," "shine (on)," and "glorious."[8] But as Bonhoeffer's own reflections on Epiphany remind us, concealment and revelation always accompany each other—and only those with the eyes of faith are able to see. In this respect, Finkenwalde is a fitting ecclesiastical manifestation of the message of Epiphany: there the gospel was preached not with the backing of worldly power but in the humiliation and hiddenness of the crucified Christ—"a stumbling block to Jews and folly to Gentiles" (1 Cor 1:23).[9]

---

[7]Marsh, *Strange Glory*, 231-32.

[8]*Greek New Testament*, 4th rev. ed., ed. Barbara Aland et al. (Stuttgart: Deutsche Bibelgesellschaft, 1998), 71.

[9]Put another way, the seminary represents the need, at various times throughout church history, for Christian witness to involve an emphasis on preparation for witness through private

Other readers—especially those familiar with recent scholarship on Bonhoeffer's public witness—may have a different concern. They may wonder why my discussion of Bonhoeffer appears in this chapter and not in the next one (which explores rhetorical postures associated with repentance and the Lenten season). In her wonderful book *The Church for the World: A Theology of Public Witness*, theologian Jennifer McBride draws on Dietrich Bonhoeffer's writings to make the case that the church's witness must involve a posture of "confession of sin unto repentance."[10] Ronald C. Arnett, too, points to confession as a key aspect of Bonhoeffer's religious communication. According to Arnett, confession is "the initial communicative move that permits Bonhoeffer to meet a troubled world in need of dialogue."[11] While I agree with McBride and Arnett about the centrality of repentance and confession to Bonhoeffer's witness, my aim in this chapter is to extend their arguments by highlighting a different, though not unrelated, aspect of Bonhoeffer's public stance. More specifically, I focus on Bonhoeffer's rhetorical attempts to align himself with or distance himself from various individuals and groups—as well as God—and the resultant clarity or obscurity of his witness with respect to his audiences.[12] I aim to show, in short, that Bonhoeffer's public witness, which simultaneously reveals and conceals, has much to teach us about seasoning our rhetorical practices with the "strange glory" of Epiphany.

---

worship and catechesis. For an argument about how such a Christian theopolitical stance might be relevant to the contemporary American context, see Rod Dreher's *The Benedict Option: A Strategy for Christians in a Post-Christian Nation* (New York: Penguin Random House, 2017).

[10] Jennifer M. McBride, *The Church for the World: A Theology of Public Witness* (Oxford: Oxford University Press, 2012), 16.

[11] Ronald Arnett, *Dialogic Confession: Bonhoeffer's Rhetoric of Responsibility* (Carbondale: Southern Illinois University Press, 2005), 66.

[12] Building upon Eberhard Bethge's observations, Paul L. Lehmann writes, "Bonhoeffer's contribution to a world come of age is his restless and open-ended search for ever new language and evermore concrete ways of keeping the *identity* of a Christian in the world and the *identification* of a Christian with the world together" ("Faith and Worldliness in Bonhoeffer's Thought," in *Bonhoeffer in a World Come of Age*, ed. Peter Vorkink II [Philadelphia: Fortress Press, 1968], 40, emphases added). This chapter aims to elaborate on Lehmann's claim.

Considering Bonhoeffer's work from a rhetorical perspective follows the lead of other scholars of rhetoric and communication. To give just three examples, Arnett describes Bonhoeffer as a "twentieth-century Isocrates" with much to say to religious rhetors and theorists interested in communicative ethics; Ned O'Gorman notes that Bonhoeffer offers a conceptualization of rhetoric "as the ethical approach to communication"; and Matthew Boedy argues that Bonhoeffer's understanding of responsibility helps provide "a bridge between ethics and invention" for scholars and teachers working in the field of technical communication.[13] The present chapter extends these scholars' views about Bonhoeffer's significance as a rhetor and rhetorician. To understand this significance, it is helpful to consider Bonhoeffer's witness in light of Kenneth Burke's concepts of identification and division.

Kenneth Burke on Identification and Division

At the same time that Bonhoeffer was taking a stand against the evils of Hitler's Germany from within the country's borders, American critic Kenneth Burke was attacking it from without. In 1939, Burke—who is often regarded as one of the twentieth century's most influential rhetoricians—wrote a now-famous piece analyzing *Mein Kampf*. Burke begins "The Rhetoric of Hitler's 'Battle'" by arguing that though *Mein Kampf* infuriates and disgusts, American critics should not simply dismiss the book.[14] Rather, they should study it vigilantly

---

[13] Arnett, *Dialogic Confession*, 7, 98, 200-201; Ned O'Gorman, "'Telling the Truth': Dietrich Bonhoeffer's Rhetorical Discourse Ethic," *The Journal of Communication and Religion* 28, no. 2 (2005): 225; Matthew Boedy, "From Deliberation to Responsibility: Ethics, Invention, and Bonhoeffer in Technical Communication," *Technical Communication Quarterly* 26, no. 2 (2017): 117-18. For additional examples, see *The Journal of Communication and Rhetoric* 28, no. 2 (2005). Thank you to Matthew Boedy for sending me a link to his article, "Bonhoeffer's Performative Sensibilities in His Earliest Work." The article—which makes the case that Bonhoeffer's argument in *Act and Being* is a "rhetorical performance" with stylistic significance—pointed me to O'Gorman's piece ("Bonhoeffer's Performative Sensibilities in His Earliest Work," *The Heythrop Journal* 53 [2012]: 991, 992).

[14] Kenneth Burke, "The Rhetoric of Hitler's 'Battle,'" in *The Philosophy of Literary Form: Studies in Symbolic Action*, 3rd ed. (Berkeley: University of California Press, 1973), 191.

in the hopes of protecting the American people from the "'medicine' this medicine-man has concocted." The so-called medicine Burke refers to here is the rhetorical activity that was instrumental in bringing about unity in Germany—a unity that Burke describes as "sinister."[15]

Corrupting and parodying religious concepts, Hitler's rhetorical strategy involved pitting the Rome-like capital of Munich against a diabolical portrayal of the Jew. Burke suggests that such an approach was effective because both the "unifying center" of Munich and the Jewish enemy were *visible* to the nation. Germans could look to Munich in prayerful reverence and look at "the visible, point-to-able form" of the Jew in disgust.[16] Within this rhetorical geography, Hitler positioned himself at Munich's center, presenting his "inner voice" as the sole authority of the Aryan nation and demanding "the total identification between leader and people." Such identification was reinforced by silencing diverse voices and opinions. To enforce the silencing of this "parliamentary babel," Hitler and the Nazis inflicted both verbal and physical wounds on dissenters and those who were different. Burke points out that Hitler, in addition to utilizing "the projection device" of "scapegoating" and "the sloganizing repetitiousness of standard advertising technique," intentionally baited his audiences and then had those who dissented assaulted. He employed, in short, a variety of tactics to ensure that the state's voice was monotone and unified.[17] In a powerful paragraph that effectively summarizes and amplifies his points, Burke writes,

> Hitler's inner voice, equals leader-people identification, equals unity,
> equals Reich, equals the mecca Munich, equals plow, equals sword, equals

---

[15]Burke also refers to Hitler's rhetorical medicine as "snakeoil" and "crude magic" ("Rhetoric of Hitler's 'Battle,'" 192).

[16]Later in the piece, Burke reinforces the point about the rhetorical power of the visibility of the enemy, noting, "'The enemy' was something you could see" ("Rhetoric of Hitler's 'Battle,'" 205).

[17]Burke, "Rhetoric of Hitler's 'Battle,'" 192-95, 201-3, 207, 212-13, 218-19.

work, equals war, equals army as midrib, equals responsibility (the personal responsibility of the absolute ruler), equals sacrifice, equals the theory of "German democracy" (the free popular choice of the leader, who then accepts the responsibility, and demands absolute obedience in exchange for his sacrifice), equals love (with the masses as feminine), equals idealism, equals obedience to nature, equals race, nation.[18]

Burke's analysis of Hitler's rhetoric is instructive for our present purposes in three ways. First, it gives us a sense of the existing rhetorical formations with which Bonhoeffer and other likeminded German Christians had to contend as they sought to proclaim the gospel faithfully in their country. Second, Burke's comments about the place of "visible" and "point-to-able" proofs in Hitler's rhetoric provide us with a contrast that allows us to understand Bonhoeffer's rhetoric with greater clarity—especially as it relates to the hidden glory that is central to the Epiphany message. Third, and most important, Burke's piece serves as an introduction to this chapter's central rhetorical concept: identification. We will take this last point first, exploring the other two as the chapter unfolds.

As we have seen, "The Rhetoric of Hitler's 'Battle'" explores rhetoric's potential to unify and, in doing so, lays the groundwork for understanding Burke's concept of identification.[19] Despite the fact that Burke's analysis focuses on Hitler's rhetoric, he does not present identification as inherently immoral.[20] In fact, according to rhetorician Gregory Clark, Burke developed the notion of identification as a *response* to the horrors of twentieth-century warfare.[21] Clark writes

---

[18]Burke, "Rhetoric of Hitler's 'Battle,'" 207.

[19]Burke expert Ross Wolin notes that, despite the fact that the word does not appear much throughout the essay, identification—especially "as a mechanism for the creation and cohesion of a social body"—is central to it (*The Rhetorical Imagination of Kenneth Burke* [Columbia: University of South Carolina Press, 2001], 179).

[20]Burke, "Rhetoric of Hitler's 'Battle,'" 219-20.

[21]Gregory Clark, *Rhetorical Landscapes in America: Variations on a Theme from Kenneth Burke* (Columbia: University of South Carolina Press, 2004), 70.

that "one way of reading his work is as a lifelong project of articulating a communicative method that would enable people to do better than that—to move themselves, as he would put it in his epigraph for *A Grammar of Motives,* toward 'the purification of war.'"[22]

What, then, is identification? For Burke, identification includes all of the ways in which speakers and writers align themselves with, or are aligned with, their audiences. Identification involves turning the "I" of one's discourse into a "we" by conveying shared beliefs, values, actions, emotions, judgments, ideas, contexts, and discourses.[23] One helpful, if somewhat simplified, way to understand the concept is noted by Jeanne Fahnestock and Marie Secor in their textbook *The Rhetoric of Argument.* They describe identification as a fusion of *ēthos* and *pathos*, establishing a rhetor's representativeness in relation to his or her audience.[24] Fahnestock and Secor explain that "audience members find themselves looking into a mirror, hearing their own interests and beliefs expressed powerfully—or perhaps they hear interests and beliefs they did not know they had until they heard them expressed by their representative."

But there is more to Burke's identification than just pronoun usage and representativeness. Part of what makes the concept innovative is that this sort of rhetorical activity is ubiquitous, occurring whether rhetors and audiences are conscious of it or not. Incorporating and then going beyond Aristotle's presentation of rhetoric (and, with it, much of the Western rhetorical tradition), Burke famously distinguishes conscious appeals from unconscious appeals, noting, "If I had to sum up in one word the difference between the 'old' rhetoric and

---

[22]Clark, Rhetorical Landscapes in America, 70.

[23]George Cheney, *Rhetoric in an Organizational Society: Managing Multiple Identities* (Columbia: University of South Carolina Press, 1991), ix-x; see also James E. Beitler, *Remaking Transitional Justice in the United States: The Rhetorical Authorization of the Greensboro Truth and Reconciliation Commission* (New York: Springer, 2013), 97-98.

[24]Jeanne Fahnestock and Marie Secor, *A Rhetoric of Argument*, 3rd ed. (New York: McGraw-Hill, 2004), 55.

the 'new,' . . . I would reduce it to this: The key term for the 'old' rhetoric was 'persuasion,' and its stress was upon deliberate design. The key term for the 'new' rhetoric would be 'identification,' which can include a partially unconscious factor in appeal." In presenting identification as rhetoric's conceptual cornerstone, Burke enlarges the field of study for rhetoricians and offers new insights about human communication for rhetors.[25]

When a speaker or writer brings about identification with an audience, a community is formed, which Burke evocatively describes using the theological term *consubstantiality*.[26] Consubstantiality is "a type of mixed ontological state in which people are . . . part of a community of shared interests while remaining autonomous individuals."[27] The unity that occurs through identification is not, in other words, complete oneness. "Identification is compensatory to division," Burke writes. "If men were not apart from one another, there would be no need for the rhetorician to proclaim their unity. If men were wholly and truly of one substance, absolute communication would be of

---

[25]Burke, "Rhetoric of Hitler's 'Battle,'" 203; Burke, *A Rhetoric of Motives*, 2nd ed. (Berkeley: University of California Press, 1969), 46; Clark, *Rhetorical Landscapes*, 7-8; Wolin, *Rhetorical Imagination*, 183. Symbols are an important aspect of this expanded subject matter of rhetoric. Burke notes that language itself functions "*as a symbolic means of inducing cooperation in beings that by nature respond to symbols*" (Burke, *Rhetoric of Motives*, 43)—and while these cooperation-inducing linguistic symbols certainly include speech and writing, they also involve communicative elements such as "gesture, tonality, order, image, attitude, [and] idea" (55). Gregory Clark neatly summarizes the point: "Anything that prompts social cooperation by presenting to people symbols of collectivity with which they can each identify themselves is rhetorical" (*Rhetorical Landscapes*, 5). Though we may talk about the various communicative elements as though they are distinct from one another, the elements are, in terms of their rhetorical effects, more than the sum of their parts, with each element implicated in the effects of the others. Take, for example, the relationship between a speech's style and its logic—an issue we will return to later in the chapter when considering Bonhoeffer's preaching. "Many people today," Ross Wolin rightly observes, "continue to think of style as either mere aesthetic embellishment or as an aesthetic element that imbues communication with a kind of magical propagandistic power—in both cases, part of an emotional realm distinct from reason and opposed to it" (*Rhetorical Imagination*, 189). But for Burke, Wolin continues, "style is at one with the thought basic to a persuasive message" (190).

[26]Burke, *Rhetoric of Motives*, 21.

[27]James Jasinski, *Sourcebook on Rhetoric: Key Concepts in Contemporary Rhetorical Studies* (Thousand Oaks, CA: Sage, 2001), 306.

man's very essence."[28] Burke's main point here—that identification and division are interrelated and both present in all human communication—will be important to my argument in the pages that follow.[29] We will consider how Dietrich Bonhoeffer's rhetoric involves identification and division between himself and the German church, the ecumenical movement, and God. Our main focus will be on the span of time that Bonhoeffer himself considers in his famous essay "After Ten Years," the turbulent decade between 1933 and 1943.

Bonhoeffer and Identification

"Where Jew and German stand together": Identification with Jewish Christians. The years leading up to 1933 had involved dramatic shifts in identification for Bonhoeffer. In his 1927 dissertation *Sanctorum Communio* and his 1929 lecture "Basic Questions of a Christian Ethic," Bonhoeffer had aligned his vision of the church community and his ethical framework with the German state and, in Charles Marsh's words, "the Christianity of the Germanic warrior tradition."[30] But over the next few years, Bonhoeffer's views began to change.[31] His own privilege helped precipitate these new perspectives: coming from a wealthy German family, Bonhoeffer was able to travel extensively outside his home country. As he witnessed Christian worship and struggles for racial justice in the United States, for example, he began to change the way he viewed the church in relation to the German

---

[28]Burke, *Rhetoric of Motives*, 22.

[29]For more on this point, see Wolin, *Rhetorical Imagination*, 180. Wolin writes, for example, that "like substance, [Burkean] identification implies that X is simultaneously X and not-X. At one point, Burke says that identification and division are compensatory; at another he says that they are ironic counterparts. I tend to think that they are but different modes of presentation of a single idea" (180).

[30]Marsh, *Strange Glory*, 58-59, 84-85. *Sanctorum Communio* is arguably Bonhoeffer's own exploration of identification. It is an account written from a more theologically and ecclesiastically grounded position than Burke's.

[31]One of the many strengths of Marsh's biography is the way he charts this theological (and, as we will see, rhetorical) shift, noting that Bonhoeffer would come to disagree with the nationalistic sentiments of both of his early pieces (Marsh, *Strange Glory*, 59, 84-85).

state.[32] The gospel, Bonhoeffer came to realize in the years leading up to 1933, was good news that heralded from elsewhere.[33] In subsequent years, Bonhoeffer would use his writing to weave a rhetorical webbing, establishing ties with actors outside of the German state apparatus. Though these ties seemed to be fragile when considered in light of the destructive power of the Nazis, they proved to be durable, especially when viewed with the eyes of faith.

In 1933, when Hitler's government began enforcing the Führer principle (which basically declared that Hitler's will was the will of Germany) and the Aryan paragraph (which barred Jews from belonging to German churches), Bonhoeffer responded with rhetorical countermeasures that aimed to re-identify German Christians with those whom Hitler had displaced—Jewish Christians and, along with them, Jesus Christ himself.[34] One of his most famous pieces from this period is his essay "The Church and the Jewish Question."

Bonhoeffer spends the first two-thirds of the essay carefully delineating the proper relationship between the church and the state, seemingly attempting to anticipate objections of those who might see his argument as overstepping the bounds of the church's political authority. Having done so, Bonhoeffer contends that it is the German state that risks acting outside of its limits by exerting "too much law and

---

[32]Marsh, *Strange Glory*, 114-20, 126-35. Writing on the influence of the Harlem Renaissance on Bonhoeffer, Professor of Christian Ethics Reggie L. Williams notes, "The Harlem Renaissance community provided Bonhoeffer with a unique perspective on the racial divide within American Christianity by allowing him to see the distortion that occurs with Christianity when it becomes blended with oppressive power structures" ("Dietrich Bonhoeffer, the Harlem Renaissance and the Black Christ," in *Bonhoeffer, Christ and Culture*, ed. Keith L. Johnson and Timothy Larsen [Downers Grove, IL: InterVarsity Press, 2013], 62). At the end of his piece, Williams writes, "Bonhoeffer's *identification* with the resistance model of Christ who knew and accepted suffering in America placed him in solidarity with the outcast and the marginalized in Germany" (72, emphasis added).

[33]Marsh writes, "In his trial sermon of 1930, he struck a different note: gospel-joy reaches into human experience from a 'distant, unknown land,' one far removed from the manly Germanic piety of 'work and duty and seriousness and nothing else.' The abiding joy and strange light of Christ is a light whose source lies always and everywhere in another country" (*Strange Glory*, 97).

[34]Marsh, *Strange Glory*, 159-60, 164-68.

order" through "the obligatory exclusion of baptized Jews from our Christian congregations or a ban on missions to the Jews."[35] The piece's rhetorical power lies partially in Bonhoeffer's seemingly restrained tone, which leads, in measured argumentative steps, to bold claims and stark choices for German churchgoers. He warns that forcing baptized Jews out of the congregation "would always mean a genuine church schism . . . because it would make racial uniformity a church law to be fulfilled as a requirement for fellowship in the church."[36] In rhetorical terms, identification and division along racial lines undermines the essence of the church itself, which finds its unity through allegiance to Christ alone. Bonhoeffer writes, "It is the task of Christian preaching to say: here is the church, where Jew and German stand together under the Word of God; here is *the proof* whether a church is still the church or not."[37] In the context of Hitler's Germany, the gospel-based identification of Jewish Christians and German Christians provides some of the clearest evidence of the church's vitality, and it is also, to play on this translation's use of the word *proof*, where the church's rhetorical appeal must lie, whether German Christians find that to be persuasive or not. Bonhoeffer then draws a line in the sand: "If someone feels unable to continue in church fellowship with Christians of Jewish origin, nothing can prevent him from leaving this church fellowship. But it must be made clear to him, with ultimate seriousness, that he is turning his back on the place where the church of Christ stands."[38]

---

[35]Bonhoeffer, "The Church and the Jewish Question," in *Dietrich Bonhoeffer Works, Volume 12: Berlin: 1932-1933*, ed. Larry L. Rasmussen, trans. Isabel Best and David Higgins (Minneapolis: Fortress, 2009), 365.

[36]Bonhoeffer, "The Church and the Jewish Question," 369.

[37]Bonhoeffer, "The Church and the Jewish Question," in *Dietrich Bonhoeffer: Witness to Jesus Christ*, ed. John de Gruchy (Minneapolis: Fortress, 1991), 130, emphasis added. Throughout this chapter, I have primarily been using translations from the remarkable multivolume resource *Dietrich Bonhoeffer Works*; however, the translation I use here, which appears in an anthology of Bonhoeffer's writings edited by John de Gruchy, nicely foregrounds the rhetorical language of "proof" and the genre of preaching, which I return to later in the chapter.

[38]Bonhoeffer, "The Church and the Jewish Question," 370.

Though "The Church and the Jewish Question" did not address the problems of anti-Semitism outside of the church, the essay was a far cry from the nationalism of *Sanctorum Communio*, and as the decade wore on, Bonhoeffer would distance himself from the state more and more. He forged other connections, building outward from his attempts to establish rhetorical identification within German congregations.

Marsh's biography points us toward any number of relationships that rhetoricians could explore. Many case studies could be produced by analyzing, to give just a few examples, Bonhoeffer's correspondence with likeminded Christian friends and family members, his debates with signers of the Barmen Declaration and members of the Confessing Church, his engagement with Englishman George Bell and other participants of the ecumenical movement, and his lectures to and worship with his seminary students (and, through them, his connections with the monastics of the past).[39] Bonhoeffer also sought alliances outside the church. He corresponded with, and even considered traveling to visit, Mahatma Gandhi—and he also found himself uniting with champions of Enlightenment values, many of whom had not been allies with Christians in past decades.[40] In the end, as the situation in Germany grew increasingly dire, Bonhoeffer would align himself with conspirators plotting to kill Hitler—an attempt at identification that

---

[39]Theologian Robert J. Dean accurately summarizes one of the main aims of these connections, noting "Bonhoeffer's work during his time in London (1933-1935), at Finkenwalde (1935-1937), and with the collective pastorates (1937-1940), can be understood as his attempt to fortify a church capable of being such a limit to the omnivorous Nazi state" (*For the Life of the World: Jesus Christ and the Church in the Theologies of Dietrich Bonhoeffer and Stanley Hauerwas* [Eugene, OR: Pickwick, 2016], 159).

[40]In Larry Rasmussen's contribution to *The Cambridge Companion to Dietrich Bonhoeffer,* he notes, "Fascist vitalism, with its slogan of 'Blood and Soil' (*Blut und Boden*), may seem the utter opposite of the Enlightenment's transcendent, cosmopolitan principles. In crucial ways it was, and Bonhoeffer testifies to the Confessing Church's unexpected experience of protecting Enlightenment values against Nazi tribalism" ("The Ethics of Responsible Action," in *The Cambridge Companion to Dietrich Bonhoeffer* [Cambridge: Cambridge University Press, 2006], 211).

would eventually result in execution, the ultimate separation from the state.[41]

While almost all of these interactions involve noteworthy acts of identification and division, the remainder of the chapter focuses on these concepts in relation to Bonhoeffer's Christology, homiletics, and ecclesiology.

"The likeness of sinful flesh": Identification and the christological incognito. From May to July of 1933, around the same time that Bonhoeffer was writing "The Church and the Jewish Question," he was also delivering a lecture series on Christology at the University of Berlin.[42] Divided into sections on "the present Christ" and "the historical Christ," the lectures are extensive, highlighting Christ's form as Word, sacrament, and church community; his place at the center of existence, history, and nature; and Bonhoeffer's views about what he calls negative Christology and positive Christology—that is, heretical and orthodox views about Jesus. What is noteworthy about the lectures for our purposes is that, even as Bonhoeffer was responding publicly to the Führer principle and the Aryan paragraph, he was laying the christological groundwork for a less-conspicuous form of Christian witness—one that was, to borrow Bonhoeffer's own words about Jesus Christ, "incognito."[43]

Central to Bonhoeffer's concept of the christological incognito is 1 Corinthians 1:22-23. The apostle Paul, after having contrasted the wisdom of God with that of the world and noting that God's salvation comes through that which the world deems foolish, writes, "For Jews demand signs and Greeks seek wisdom, but we preach Christ crucified,

---

[41]For Marsh's discussions of these events, see *Strange Glory*, 200, 204-5, 213, 220-25, 231, 267-68, 338-40, 343-45, 375-76.

[42]Bonhoeffer, *Christ the Center* (New York: Harper & Row, 1978), 15. Very few of Bonhoeffer's own lecture materials remain, but many of his comments survive through his students' notes, most notably those of Gerhard Riemer ("Lectures on Christology [Student Notes]," in *Dietrich Bonhoeffer Works, Volume 12*).

[43]Bonhoeffer, "Lectures on Christology (Student Notes)," 300, 309-10, 356.

a stumbling block to Jews and folly to Gentiles." According to Bonhoeffer, the "stumbling block" that Paul refers to here "has its place not in the doctrine of God's taking human form [the incarnation] but rather in the doctrine of the God-human's humiliation."[44] Citing Romans 8:3, Bonhoeffer suggests that this humiliation involves Jesus Christ's appearance to humans in "the likeness of sinful flesh" from his birth to his crucifixion.[45] In his humiliation, his assumption of the likeness of sinful flesh, and his dying a sinner's death, the God-human is concealed from the world. The transcribed notes of Bonhoeffer's lecture record the following remarks: "The God-human who is present in time and space is veiled in the ['likeness of flesh'] (Rom. 8:3). The presence of Christ is a veiled presence. But it is not God veiled in the human being; instead, the whole God-human is hidden."[46] Here again we have the concealing revelation that characterizes the Epiphany message.

Thus, even as Bonhoeffer holds an orthodox position on the hypostatic union, for him the proper focus of Christology has less to do with *the identity of Christ* as fully God and fully man than it has to do with *how Christ identifies himself* as a sinner.[47] Bonhoeffer then makes the following justifiably famous remarks:

> How is Jesus's particular way of existing as the Humiliated One expressed? In that he has taken on sinful flesh. The conditions for his humiliation are set by the curse, the fall of Adam. In being humiliated, Christ, the God-human, enters of his own free will into the world of sin and death.

---

[44]Bonhoeffer, "Lectures on Christology (Student Notes)," 314.

[45]Bonhoeffer, "Lectures on Christology (Student Notes)," 313, 356. The stumbling block Paul refers to is not, in other words, God's act of becoming human but rather it is the presentation of Christ—who is both fully God and fully man—as the sinful, condemned one ("Lectures on Christology [Student Notes]," 313-14, 355).

[46]Bonhoeffer, "Lectures on Christology (Student Notes)," 356, 313.

[47]Bonhoeffer, "Lectures on Christology (Student Notes)," 319-20. Bonhoeffer writes, "Christology is primarily asking, not about the possible union of divinity with humanity, but rather about the hiddenness of the God-human who is present in his humiliated state. God is revealed in the flesh but hidden in the stumbling block ("Lectures on Christology [Student Notes]," 319-20).

He enters there in such a way as to conceal himself [there], so that he is no longer recognizable visibly as the God-human. He comes among us humans not in ["Godly form"] but rather incognito, as a beggar among beggars, an outcast among outcasts; he comes among sinners as the one without sin, but also as a sinner among sinners. This is the central problem for all Christology.[48]

It is helpful to compare what Bonhoeffer implies here about Christ's appearance to humans with what Burke writes about Hitler's rhetorical approach.[49] Recall that, according to Burke, Hitler's identification with Germany hinged on the visibility of his enemy. He provided a "point-to-able form" that he and his followers could separate themselves from.[50] In this rhetorical respect, Hitler was indeed a kind of the antichrist.[51] He revealed his so-called glory to humanity by distancing himself from the so-called evil ones, whereas Bonhoeffer's Christ hid himself among humanity by identifying himself with the evil ones—by becoming one of us.

Paradoxically, through Christ's identification with humans in our sinfulness, he simultaneously separates himself—Bonhoeffer uses the language of being "veiled" to indicate this rhetorical division—from all of humanity.[52] For Bonhoeffer, no one can stomach the likeness of a "sinner"-God apart from the gift of faith. (For those with power, wealth, privilege, and self-righteousness, this Christ is acutely unappealing; for the world's beggars, outcasts, and sinners, the rhetorical division, while still present, may not be quite as sharp.) It is, moreover,

---

[48]Bonhoeffer, "Lectures on Christology (Student Notes)," 356.

[49]Marsh makes a similar comparison. In his discussion of the Christology lectures, which includes excerpts from the same passage that I cite above, Marsh writes: "With the swastika replacing the cross in the 'great and glorious holy storm of present-day Volk happenings,' Bonhoeffer was drawn to the Christ who sojourns in the world as a beggar among beggars" (*Strange Glory*, 172).

[50]Burke, *Rhetoric of Motives*, 194.

[51]According to Marsh, Bonhoeffer began referring to Hitler in this way at this point in his life (*Strange Glory*, 160).

[52]Bonhoeffer, "Lectures on Christology (Student Notes)," 356. For more on the Christological incognito, see Marsh (*Strange Glory*, 118, 172) and McBride (*Church for the World*, 67-81).

precisely because of the God-man's hiddenness that faith can exist *at all*: "The form of the stumbling block is the form that makes possible all our faith in Christ. . . . Only when I give up having visible confirmation do I believe in God."[53] Here again, Burke's analysis of Hitler's rhetoric is instructive, highlighting just how immense the barrier to this sort of belief was for many Germans. For at the same time that Hitler was drawing Germany's gaze toward a city shining with promise and away from a figure caricatured as grotesque and revolting, Bonhoeffer was noting that faith demands a turn in the exactly opposite direction—from Munich to the Jew.

There are significant ramifications for public witness here as well. The God-man's approach to identification and division reveals how the church itself may be called to show itself to the world. "With the humiliated Christ," Bonhoeffer writes, "his church must also be humiliated."[54] On this point, Bonhoeffer is quick to warn that the church must avoid pride in its humiliation, and he is also careful to note that such humiliation is not the only form of the church's witness, being neither a "law" nor "a principle for the church to follow."[55] But in spite of Bonhoeffer's caveats, there are few descriptions of Christian witness that characterize Bonhoeffer's own life and witness better than the concept of the christological incognito. As we have seen,

---

[53]Bonhoeffer, "Lectures on Christology (Student Notes)," 358.

[54]Bonhoeffer, "Lectures on Christology (Student Notes)," 360. Jennifer McBride echoes this point in her book on Bonhoeffer and Christian witness, writing, "For Bonhoeffer, in order to witness faithfully to Christ, the church must mirror Jesus' own public presence" (*Church for the World*, 187). A few pages later, McBride commends one organization's approach to Christian witness for "tak[ing] the form of the Christological incognito through the informal partnerships it has with all the various groups serving the lower-income population" (189). Along similar lines, theologian George Kalantzis—citing Bonhoeffer's claim that "Christians should take a stronger stand in favor of the weak rather than considering the possible right of the strong"—implies that Christ's way of relating to us is, at least in part, ours for the world: "Though one might argue that Bonhoeffer's admonition was hued by the German experience of the 1930s, his hermeneutical premise is neither localized nor idiosyncratic. It stands as a diachronic *first principle*" ("A Witness to the Nations: Early Christianity and Narratives of Power," in *Christian Political Witness*, ed. George Kalantzis and Gregory W. Lee [Downers Grove, IL: InterVarsity Press, 2014], 90-91).

[55]Bonhoeffer, "Lectures on Christology (Student Notes)," 360.

Bonhoeffer certainly embodied the concept through his defense of Jewish Christians and his willingness to direct a hidden seminary. But he attempted to hide himself away rhetorically in other ways as well. To illustrate that point, we must now turn to his lectures on preaching.

"Preacher be quiet": Identification and the sermon. During the period from 1935 to 1937, Bonhoeffer delivered lectures on homiletics to his seminary students at Finkenwalde and also facilitated workshop-style sessions on sermon composition.[56] Once again, Bonhoeffer's instruction is known to us thanks to his dutiful students. Though the notes are not quite as complete as Gerhard Riemer's reconstruction of the Christology lectures, Bonhoeffer's thoughts on the office of preaching are clear. Warning of the perils of "self-observation," Bonhoeffer suggests that the preacher ought to serve as an unobtrusive pointer, so that one's audience might hear the Word of God and not the preacher speaking to them.[57] Doing so involves rhetorical self-restraint or (more appropriately, given the discussion above) a kind of rhetoric of self-hiddenness in which the speaker's posture is more objective and more dependent on the biblical text than on one's own personality, identity, motivations, or goals.[58]

To be clear, Bonhoeffer himself would not have described sermonic language in terms of a *rhetoric* of self-hiddenness. Viewing the scope

---

[56]Bonhoeffer, "Practical Exercises in Homiletics" and "Lectures on Homiletics," in *Dietrich Bonhoeffer Works, Volume 14: Theological Education at Finkenwalde: 1935-1937*, ed. H. Gaylon Barker and Mark S. Brocker, trans. Douglas W. Stott (Minneapolis: Fortress, 2013), 341, 487. For more on Bonhoeffer's homiletics, see Dietrich Bonhoeffer and Clyde E. Fant, *Worldly Preaching: Lectures on Homiletics*, rev. ed. (New York: Crossroad, 1991). Fant discusses Bonhoeffer's preaching in relation to the church (42-49), the dialectic between "Christian identity" and "identification with the world" (62, 71, 75), the arcane disciplines (74-81), Christology (30, 85-88), and more. For a more detailed account of the context in which Bonhoeffer sought to proclaim the gospel, see Dean G. Stroud's introduction to *Preaching in Hitler's Shadow: Sermons of Resistance in the Third Reich* (Grand Rapids: Eerdmans, 2013), 3-48.

[57]Bonhoeffer claimed, "Whenever *we* preach Christ, it can be done only by way of an outstretched finger, but important that he is present" (Bonhoeffer, "Lectures on Homiletics," 516).

[58]Bonhoeffer rejects what Ronald Arnett refers to as "communicative excess" (*Dialogic Confession*, 191).

of rhetoric in a more limited way than I present it in this project, he actually distinguishes the rhetorical from the sermonic at one point in his lectures; however, despite such claims, Bonhoeffer does not suggest that sermonic language ought to be unpersuasive.[59] He implies instead that the sermon's persuasiveness comes not from the preacher but from the Word. Rhetorically speaking, the speaker must get out of the way. Here again, Bonhoeffer's language is distinct from that of the Führer.[60]

More generally speaking, Bonhoeffer wants to distinguish sermons from other speeches—and, by implication, preachers from other orators. The orator invests language with motivations and aims and "vitality," aligning himself or herself with the words of the speech.[61] We might say that he or she takes a stand—or, better yet, a stance—in and through the utterance. Sermons, however, are different. They should convey God's Word and purposes, not those of the speaker. Bonhoeffer describes the sermonic utterance as "speaking without any intention."[62] What follows next in the lecture notes is one of Bonhoeffer's most Burkean remarks, recast to account for the theological significance of the sermon: "In normal speech," Bonhoeffer notes, "everything depends on our *identifying* with our own words. In speaking the word of God, by contrast, everything depends on the *distance*

---

[59]He notes, "There is a sermon language that is different from literary language [and] rhetorical [language]" (Bonhoeffer, "Practical Exercises in Homiletics," 342).

[60]Marsh writes, "Bonhoeffer did not shy away from offering his own sermons as exemplars of the genre. Preaching meant proclaiming the Word in the clear and measured exposition of scripture. His own idiom, he felt, had evolved to the point of banishing every trace of rhetorical manipulation. With the calculated deceit of Hitler's histrionics saturating the airwaves, truth's answer demanded simplicity" (*Strange Glory*, 233). Eric Metaxas makes a similar point (*Bonhoeffer: Pastor, Martyr, Prophet, Spy* [Nashville: Thomas Nelson, 2010], 140). Commenting on Bonhoeffer's famous radio address in which he criticized the Führer Principle, Metaxas notes that "the speech itself, in its construction and its delivery, was everything a ranting Hitler speech was not. . . . Bonhoeffer hated to draw attention to himself or to use his personality to influence or to win converts to his way of thinking" (*Bonhoeffer*, 140).

[61]Bonhoeffer, "Lectures on Homiletics," 504.

[62]Bonhoeffer continues, "In the most real sense, God is the subject of this speaking not we ourselves" (Bonhoeffer, "Lectures on Homiletics," 504).

becoming visible."[63] Employing rhetorical division from the Word instead of rhetorical identification with it, the preacher is better able to convey *God's* stance.

Though Bonhoeffer does not state it outright, this presentation of the preacher's division from God's intentions and purposes in the sermon contains the echoes of the idea of the christological incognito. Bonhoeffer notes that the "difference between our own speech and God's word" is that "with our speech, we try to *conceal* our own evil," and "we are not in the truth" (emphasis added). In contrast, Bonhoeffer implies that when preaching, preachers must reveal their own distance from the truth—not unlike the way that Christ reveals himself "in the likeness of sinful flesh." In short, preachers ought to attempt to hide the self-righteous part of themselves away during their sermons, resulting, quite possibly, in their own humiliation.

How else ought preachers to hide themselves away when delivering sermons? For one thing, Bonhoeffer claims that "what [the sermon proclamation] must *emphasize* is *not its proximity to the* Volk *but its alien character in the world*."[64] Given the context in which Bonhoeffer was writing and his previous reflections on the relationship between the church and the state, it is not surprising that he speaks of a necessary separation from one's ethnicity and nationality.[65] Using the sermon to identify with people along such lines only undermines the efficacy of the church's witness.

Also problematic is preachers' recognition of their own achievements and abilities. That is, preachers must not only hide who they *are* but also what they *have done* and *can do*. The sermon, Bonhoeffer

---

[63]I have added the emphasis to *identifying* here, but *distance* is already italicized in *Dietrich Bonhoeffer Works*.

[64]Bonhoeffer, "Lectures on Homiletics," 492.

[65]Bonhoeffer, "Lectures on Homiletics," 491-92.

emphatically remarks, is "not a defense of my own accomplishment!" And defending one's accomplishment can involve showing off rhetorically. Several comments about rhetoric appear in the lecture notes. Bonhoeffer makes clear that, to ensure that the sermon is not about himself but rather to and for the church, he eschews the use of such language: "In my sermon I avoid all devices, pathos, rhetoric, didacticism, begging, unctuousness, pushiness, [and] extolling [of] the message."[66] Sermons should also not be "flowery," nor should their language be "poetic, descriptive, [or] extravagant."[67] Such stylistic choices were probably problematic for Bonhoeffer not only because they call attention to the speaker but also because of their associations with artifice. Bonhoeffer rejects the use of the vernacular in the sermon for similar reasons. Unlike C. S. Lewis, who championed the idea that seminarians should practice translating theological doctrine into everyday speech, Bonhoeffer implies that doing so is another form of deceit.[68] The preacher should not employ "jargon" or "consciously popularizing language, similar to street language, deriving from a *false understanding of naturalness*."[69] Establishing rhetorical identification with an audience through an artificial style—be it high or low, grand or plain—has no place in discourse that needs to be "in the truth."[70]

---

[66]Bonhoeffer, "Lectures on Homiletics," 491.

[67]Bonhoeffer, "Practical Exercises in Homiletics," 342; "Lectures on Homiletics," 506.

[68]Bonhoeffer seems to reject preaching in the vernacular as much as Lewis insists upon it. Bonhoeffer's point about the necessity of truthful speech is well taken; however, I find myself agreeing more with Lewis's position: addressing one's audience on their terms need not be false. That said, the more important point may be what Lewis and Bonhoeffer agree upon here. Both want the Word of God to be proclaimed clearly and effectively. And how Christians do that—i.e., whether we follow Bonhoeffer's advice or Lewis's (or somebody else's for that matter)—may depend on the particular rhetorical situation in which we find ourselves.

[69]Bonhoeffer, "Practical Exercises in Homiletics," 342; "Lectures on Homiletics," 507.

[70]For similar reasons, Bonhoeffer was wary about incorporating stories into sermons, though he did not reject their use entirely. The key, here again, has to do with veracity: "If you do employ stories," he noted to his students, "then above all they must be true" (Bonhoeffer, "Lectures on Homiletics," 498).

Along with these guidelines about what preachers *should not* do if they are to conceal themselves while preaching, Bonhoeffer offers several suggestions about how one *should* proceed, and all of his suggestions flow from his conviction that the sermon's purpose is "that the *text* come through."[71] The Word must speak. To that end, the sermon should be rigorously focused on the biblical witness, with the "exposition of Scripture" being one of the preacher's most important duties.[72] Possessing an "[u]nqualified confidence in the text" that deemphasizes the role of both speaker and audience, the preacher ought to ask, "Not: What should *I* say to the *congregation*, but rather: What is the *text* itself saying?"[73]

Bonhoeffer's insistence "that the *text* come through" shapes his rhetorical recommendations for pastors, and he presents us with two different ways that the preacher can let the Word speak through the sermon—two ways that he holds in tension with one another throughout his lectures. On the one hand, preachers may use transparent language to convey the meaning of the biblical text. Bonhoeffer advocates for a restrained use of words, engagement with Scripture's figures of speech in place of one's own, simple and straightforward sentences, a comprehensible organizational schema,[74] and a serious tone and objective stance.[75] Bonhoeffer has some great one-liners on these points. Telling his students not to use "superlatives, exclamations, [and] appeals" in their sermons because these moves create "a false identity with the word," Bonhoeffer declares, "The word of God is itself the

---

[71]Bonhoeffer, "Practical Exercises in Homiletics," 342.

[72]Bonhoeffer, "Practical Exercises in Homiletics," 342; "Lectures on Homiletics," 491.

[73]Bonhoeffer, "Lectures on Homiletics," 499, emphasis added.

[74]Ironically, the lecture notes register Bonhoeffer's intensity about the need for clear organization, using italics as well as single and even double exclamation points: "*Paragraphs!* Introduction! Conclusion! Homily not a mosaic!!"

[75]Bonhoeffer, "Practical Exercises in Homiletics," 342; "Lectures on Homiletics," 491, 505, 507.

exclamation point that we do not need to add."[76] Students should also avoid "senseless screaming to wake the congregation up."[77] "When speaking about the trumpets of the Last Judgment," he says, "[there is] no need to suggest that we ourselves are those trumpets."[78] The suggestion underlying these colorful recommendations is that, through the use of such transparent language, the meaning of the Word might pass through the preacher's words the way that light passes through a clear windowpane. Bonhoeffer does not reflect on the fact that all of these choices are themselves rhetorical and may be as artificial as—and as much a demonstration of one's own accomplishment as—the stylistic moves that he rejects; however, whether or not he views concepts such as restraint, sobriety, and objectivity as rhetorical, the moves he recommends to his students do indeed typically function to distance a speaker from his or her subject matter and conceal the "I" of the speaker from his or her audience—both of which Bonhoeffer hopes to achieve in his sermons.

On the other hand, preachers may adopt the "disposition"—we might say the character or *ēthos*—of the biblical text, provided that they do so in a genuine and humble way.[79] This second approach for allowing "that the *text* come through" helps to prevent one of the pitfalls of the first approach: a stiff or mechanical presentation style. Bonhoeffer notes that "monotony" and a "lack of movement" from the pulpit are untruthful, presumably additional forms of artifice to

---

[76]Bonhoeffer, "Lectures on Homiletics," 506.
[77]Bonhoeffer, "Lectures on Homiletics," 505.
[78]Bonhoeffer, "Lectures on Homiletics," 505-6.
[79]On this point, Bonhoeffer writes, "The subjective side of speaking God's word can consist only in our speaking as those whom the word itself has revealed in our own evil, and that means that we must speak the word as those who we really are, speak it truthfully, in the truthfulness determined by objectivity, in the *humility* due the word of God. This means, however, not that we must use humble intonation, humility as a virtue, humility as a type, but rather that we use them as the genuine disposition of the person speaking. Everything depends on this humility" (Bonhoeffer, "Lectures on Homiletics," 505).

be avoided.[80] Giving rhetorical advice guided by a commitment to biblical truth, Bonhoeffer advocates for "Genuine pathos! Which does not stifle the substance and allow the individual to triumph but rather has genuine enthusiasm for the matter at hand."[81] "*Get in people's face with the text itself!*" he exhorts his students. "The best disposition derives from the text itself."[82] As these passages suggest, the second approach presents the sermon as a face-to-face encounter between the Word and the congregation. Notably absent in this encounter is the face of the preacher.[83] In both this approach and the first one, Bonhoeffer's rhetorical goal seems to be to allow for identification between the Word and the congregation.

In the tradition of past teachers of rhetoric, Bonhoeffer offers advice not only about matters of content and style but also about the composition process of the sermon, from its drafting to its ongoing life after having been delivered to the congregation. First of all, preachers need to prepare in order to ensure the "highest possible objectivity"; a lack of preparation often leads to the kinds of self-referential rhetorical moves that Bonhoeffer rejects elsewhere in the lectures, including "noise, pathos, [and] appeal to teary emotions."[84] And *when* one prepares is

---

[80]Instead, even as one maintains "[a]s much *reticence and reserve* as possible toward the word itself" (in line with the first approach), one should also speak with "[a]s much *enthusiasm* as possible for the subject matter" and "[a]s much *confidence* and cheerfulness in the exclusive power of the word" (Bonhoeffer, "Lectures on Homiletics," 505-6).

[81]Bonhoeffer, "Lectures on Homiletics," 505-6.

[82]Bonhoeffer, "Lectures on Homiletics," 498.

[83]Bonhoeffer warns his students that preachers should not insert themselves into the message: "I am not permitted to accentuate my own natural demeanor; that demeanor is not permitted to become conscious of itself. For the sake of the congregation, one is not permitted simply to let oneself go in the pulpit or simply to give free rein to one's uniqueness" (Bonhoeffer, "Lectures on Homiletics," 505-6). He goes on to contend that preachers should not only avoid showcasing their own external demeanors but also avoid revealing their internal thoughts and feelings to their congregations. Doing so might lead a congregation to confuse the "inner life" of its preacher with "the one who is actually life itself, namely, Christ" (Bonhoeffer, "Lectures on Homiletics," 522). He continues, "Hence no reference to my own distress and deliverance but to the Savior alone. After all, I cannot save anyone with that which was granted me; it is Christ who must save."

[84]Bonhoeffer, "Lectures on Homiletics," 497.

almost as important as *that* one prepares. To prevent excessive excitement that is not befitting of the biblical text, preachers should avoid composing sermons at night or composing them in one sitting.[85] They may also want to avoid rehearsing the sermon beforehand, particularly if such practice is likely to result in an overly impassioned delivery.[86] After delivering the sermon, preachers should continue to hide themselves away by not dwelling on their own words. "Preacher be quiet," the lecture notes record, "Hear what is said about the sermon, never again!"[87] The implication here is that preachers shouldn't solicit any feedback on their sermons because by doing so they risk making themselves, and not the Word, the center of attention.[88]

Though Bonhoeffer seems to want to hold preachers to a higher standard than that of other orators, his aversion to self-centered discourse extends to all speech.[89] Bonhoeffer's widely read *Life Together,* for example, offers congregations what his homiletics lectures offer pastors. Published as the 1930s drew to a close, the book can be read as a kind of rhetorical invitation to relinquish our individuality and claims of self-sufficiency. Again and again in *Life Together*, Bonhoeffer frames the value of particular liturgical practices along these lines. Why do we read the Psalter? Because the psalms "teach us to pray as

---

[85]Bonhoeffer, "Lectures on Homiletics," 496.

[86]Bonhoeffer suggests that one should not practice "rhetorical elements of a sermon" or its "gestures," perhaps because doing so ensures a greater degree of artifice (Bonhoeffer, "Lectures on Homiletics," 506).

[87]Bonhoeffer, "Practical Exercises in Homiletics," 343.

[88]However, according to Bonhoeffer, there are two acceptable means for assessing the quality of one's preaching, both of which are consistent with his insistence on the centrality of biblical text and his related conviction that the preacher must get out of the way. One test involves considering how weary the pastor is after delivering the sermon. Bonhoeffer notes, "Being completely exhausted [after preaching] is a bad sign: it derives from an improper disposition. It is not the pastor who is to deplete himself in the pulpit but rather God" (Bonhoeffer, "Lectures on Homiletics," 530). The second test involves considering the reading habits of the congregation. "*The best sign of a good pastor*," he suggests, "*is that the congregation reads the Bible*" (Bonhoeffer, "Lectures on Homiletics," 497).

[89]As Ronald Arnett rightly observes, "Bonhoeffer rejected the individual as the fulcrum point of communication" (*Dialogic Confession*, 12).

a fellowship."[90] Why do some psalms contain two different voices? It is "a hint that one who prays never prays alone."[91] What is the value of the difficult psalms? They call us beyond what we can individually comprehend to the whole church and, ultimately, to its head, Jesus Christ.[92] Why do we read long passages of Scripture? To know that the text "far surpasses our understanding" and "points to Jesus Christ himself."[93] Why do we read all of Scripture in order? So that by "forgetting and losing ourselves, we, too, [may] pass through the Red Sea, through the desert."[94] How should we read the Bible aloud? In an "artless" and "objective" way, thereby directing the focus away from ourselves.[95] What is the reason for our singing? So that we can "unite in the Word."[96] How should we pray? Together.[97] Whose prayers should we pray? Ours, not mine: "The free prayer in the common devotion should be the prayer of the fellowship."[98] What if one doesn't feel like praying? He or she must do it anyway; it is not about one's own feelings.[99] What is implied in the "table fellowship?" Complete commitment to one another: "we are firmly bound to one another not only in the Spirit but in our whole physical being."[100] What does our work accomplish? It liberates us from the self.[101] The Christian, Bonhoeffer seems to emphasize, ought to hide one's self away amid the body of Christ.

In the first years of the next decade, as the German state exerted more and more control on Bonhoeffer's comings and goings, he

---

[90]Bonhoeffer, *Life Together*, trans. John W. Doberstein (New York: HarperCollins, 1954), 48.
[91]Bonhoeffer, *Life Together*, 49.
[92]Bonhoeffer, *Life Together*, 45-46.
[93]Bonhoeffer, *Life Together*, 52.
[94]Bonhoeffer, *Life Together*, 53.
[95]Bonhoeffer, *Life Together*, 55-56.
[96]Bonhoeffer, *Life Together*, 59.
[97]Bonhoeffer, *Life Together*, 61-62.
[98]Bonhoeffer, *Life Together*, 63.
[99]Bonhoeffer, *Life Together*, 64.
[100]Bonhoeffer, *Life Together*, 68.
[101]Bonhoeffer, *Life Together*, 70.

would come to see such concealment as even more fundamental to Christian witness. Tracing this extension of his thought requires that we turn to two oft-cited letters from the last years of his life.

A "quiet and hidden" cause: Identification with the world and the arcane disciplines. In late December of 1942, Bonhoeffer wrote a letter titled "After Ten Years" to his friends, reflecting on the events of the past decade.[102] When he sent the letter, it had been more than five years since the Finkenwalde seminary had been forced to close by the German state. Bonhoeffer had surely hoped that the illegal seminary would allow Christ-centered theological education to continue in Germany, perhaps even giving rise to new Christian congregations that would undermine the power of the Führer. Such hopes were gone. With an SS presence in every corner of the country, the notion that such a program would reform Germany Christianity was simply impossible. Churches still dotted the country's landscape like so many stars, but their visible "witness" masked diabolical realities and often served as yet another form of political surveillance. In "After Ten Years," Bonhoeffer suggests that he and his companions faced "a great historical turning point" in which "something genuinely new was coming to be that did not fit with the existing alternatives."[103] The moment represented, as Larry Rasmussen puts it, "an epochal break in time" for Bonhoeffer, necessitating a form of faithful action that he and others had not yet realized.[104] However,

---

[102]It is possible that the letter's recipients were reading these reflections on the past decade in the first week of the new year, perhaps even on January 6, the Feast of the Epiphany.

[103]In this kairotic moment, Bonhoeffer stresses the importance of "obedient and responsible action," based not upon one's "reason, his principles, conscience, freedom, or virtue" but rather "founded in a God who calls for the free venture of faith to responsible action and who promises forgiveness and consolation to the one who on account of such action becomes a sinner" (Bonhoeffer, "After Ten Years," in *Dietrich Bonhoeffer Works, Volume 8: Letters and Papers from Prison,* ed. John W. de Gruchy, trans. Barbara and Martin Rumscheidt [Minneapolis: Fortress, 2009], 40-41).

[104]Larry Rasmussen, "The Ethics of Responsible Action," in *The Cambridge Companion to Dietrich Bonhoeffer* (Cambridge: Cambridge University Press, 2006), 206.

despite the significance of the moment, both this letter and the other one that we will consider do not mark a watershed in Bonhoeffer's views about the rhetoric of Christian witness—"none of this is new," he writes in "After Ten Years"—as much as they serve to justify and develop his previous ideas.[105]

As we have already seen, Bonhoeffer had argued that the God-man identified with "the likeness of sinful flesh," simultaneously veiling himself from the world and unveiling himself to people of faith. He had advised preachers to distance themselves from the Word and the congregation, hiding away their own identities and allowing for the revelation of the Word to the congregation. And he had called Christians to identification with one another, concealing the self and revealing the body of Christ. Now Bonhoeffer doubled down on these ideas. He proposed that a small group of courageous disciples must join together through obedient private prayer and responsible public action—distancing themselves from the visible church and all of the trappings of institutionalized religion while identifying themselves with one another, the suffering, and even the secular and the worldly.[106]

In "After Ten Years," Bonhoeffer describes the small band of disciples as a kind of aristocracy of the faithful—an "order" of people of character—who are linked not by their economic status but by their trust, responsibility, bravery, obedience, simplicity, and honesty.[107] This aristocracy must not adopt the misanthropy of their adversaries; rather, like God, who "did not hold human beings in contempt but became human for their sake," they must identify with fellow humans in love: "The only fruitful relation to human beings—particularly to

---

[105]Bonhoeffer, "After Ten Years," 37

[106]Bonhoeffer, "After Ten Years," 47-52; Marsh, *Strange Glory*, 367.

[107]Bonhoeffer, "After Ten Years," 46-48, 52. For a more thorough summary of and reflection on "After Ten Years," see Marsh, *Strange Glory*, 340-42.

the weak among them—is love, that is, the will to enter into and to keep community with them."[108] Bonhoeffer is careful to distinguish between the work of Christ and Christians, noting, "Certainly, we are not Christ, nor are we called to redeem the world through our own deed and our own suffering."[109] However, at least to some degree, Christ's identification with the sinfulness and suffering of humanity— the identification with humanity that gave rise to the christological incognito—is necessary for Christians themselves to practice. "We are not Christ," Bonhoeffer repeats, "but if we want to be Christians it means that we are to take part in Christ's greatness of heart."[110] "It remains an experience of incomparable value," he writes in the letter's final paragraph, "that we have for once learned to see the great events of world history from below, from the perspective of the outcasts, the suspects, the maltreated, the powerless, the oppressed and reviled, in short from the perspective of the suffering."[111] Here, in "After Ten Years," the Bonhoeffer of the christological incognito meets the Bonhoeffer of _Life Together_.

Sixteen months later, and more than a year after his imprisonment, Bonhoeffer ruminated on and extended these ideas in a letter to his friend Eberhard Bethge. In that letter, dated April 30, 1944, Bonhoeffer wondered what it might mean for Christianity that "a completely religionless age" was nearly upon them.[112] The letter raises more questions than it answers, but one important takeaway is that Bonhoeffer believes that the practices, structures, and traditions characterizing Christianity are devoid of power.[113] Framing the problem Bonhoeffer poses in this chapter's terms, rhetorical identification with religious practices,

---

[108]Bonhoeffer, "After Ten Years," 45.
[109]Bonhoeffer, "After Ten Years," 49.
[110]Bonhoeffer, "After Ten Years," 49.
[111]Bonhoeffer, "After Ten Years," 52.
[112]"Letter to Eberhard Bethge," in _Dietrich Bonhoeffer Works, Volume 8_, 362.
[113]"Letter to Eberhard Bethge," in _Dietrich Bonhoeffer Works, Volume 8_, 362-63.

structures, and traditions is no longer an option for people of genuine faith.[114] What, Bonhoeffer wonders, is the way forward for the faithful?[115]

Here again Bonhoeffer extends his previous ideas, looking outwardly to the world (as he did in the Christology lectures) and looking inwardly to the community of the faithful (as he did in both the homiletics lectures and *Life Together*). Christian rhetorical identification must proceed both centrifugally and centripetally, and radically so.[116] Thinking centrifugally, Bonhoeffer asks Bethge, "How do we go about being 'religionless-worldly' Christians, how can we be . . . those who are called out, without understanding ourselves religiously as privileged, but instead seeing ourselves as belonging wholly to the world?"[117] And then, directing his thoughts centripetally, he asks, "In a religionless situation, what do ritual and prayer mean? Is this where the 'arcane discipline[s]' [*Arkandisziplin*] . . . have new significance?"[118] Though Bonhoeffer does not provide direct answers to these questions (at least not in the April 30, 1944 letter), the questions themselves strongly imply that Christians' break with religion ought to be accompanied, on the one hand, by an even more radical alignment with the suffering and sinful world and, on the other hand, by an even more robust commitment to the

---

[114]Arnett writes, "Religionless Christianity . . . stresses the need for religious life to meet the secular world and for persons of faith to avoid equating faith with institutional commitments" (*Dialogic Confession*, 132).

[115]Or as Charles Marsh summarizes one of Bonhoeffer's key questions, "How could one be a disciple, clothed not in the garb of tradition, but having, as Paul tells the Galatians, 'put on Christ'?" (*Strange Glory*, 367). "Bonhoeffer's answers," Marsh continues in a characteristically beautiful passage from *Strange Glory*, "revealed a faith chastened by history, mindful of its failures and misuses—imprisoned by consequence!—yet abidingly and hilariously confident that Christ has broken the chains of death. In the meantime, the Christian witness shall be limited to prayer and righteous action. 'All Christian thinking, talking, and organizing must be born anew, out of that prayer and action.' Until the time that people will once again be able to speak the word of God 'with power,' the 'Christian cause will be a quiet and hidden one'" (367).

[116]James K. A. Smith uses these metaphors when discussing worship and missions in *Imagining the Kingdom: How Worship Works* (Grand Rapids: Baker Academic, 2013), 156. I return to them again at the end of the next chapter when reflecting on the stations of the cross.

[117]"Letter to Eberhard Bethge," in *Dietrich Bonhoeffer Works, Volume 8*, 364.

[118]"Letter to Eberhard Bethge," in *Dietrich Bonhoeffer Works, Volume 8*, 364-65.

private fellowship of the faithful.[119] Note that, in this dual movement toward the world and toward one another, Christians go deeper and deeper into hiding. Not unlike the Christ who conceals himself as "the likeness of sinful flesh," Christians embrace worldliness, hiding themselves from the so-called righteous ones. And even as Christians fully immerse themselves in the world and embrace worldliness, they continue to meet with one another in private, practicing those "secret" disciplines, "whereby the mysteries of the faith are protected from profanation."[120]

Yet despite this twofold concealment, Christ is doubly revealed to the world.[121] In Christians' embrace of worldliness, the sinful and the suffering identify, as Christ does, with the sinful and suffering. And in their practice of the *Arkandisziplin*, the centripetal identification centered in Christ ultimately gives way to centrifugal identification for the world. Worship gives way to witness. Robert J. Dean writes that "the practice of the Arcanum is not an insular or inward-focused activity. As the practice of the presence of Jesus, it can only direct the disciple towards the world which has been reconciled to God in Christ."[122] Bonhoeffer himself offers us an embodied illustration of these points. His practices in prison were deeply devout, but "he refused to pray upon the emotional vulnerability of his fellow prisoners by attempting to thrust the Gospel upon desperate men . . . and instead simply sought to be present to them during times of crises."[123]

---

[119]"Letter to Eberhard Bethge," in *Dietrich Bonhoeffer Works, Volume 8*, 364-65; Marsh, *Strange Glory*, 368.

[120]John de Gruchy, quoted in Dean, *For the Life of the World*, 187.

[121]"This is the power of Christ that is the weakness of Christ," writes Marilynne Robinson in an essay on Bonhoeffer. "He is present even where he is forgotten and efficacious even where he is despised" ("Bonhoeffer," in *The Death of Adam: Essays on Modern Thought* [New York: Picador, 2005], 122).

[122]Dean goes on to quote Bethge, who has noted, "In the *Arcanum* Christ takes everyone who really encounters him by the shoulder, turning them around to face their fellow human beings and the world" (*For the Life of the World*, 187).

[123]Dean, *For the Life of the World*, 187. Some readers may find it strange that I have included a figure who advocated for "religionless" Christianity in a book structured around Christian

His was a worldly piety and a pietistic worldliness, simultaneously concealing and revealing Christ to the world. Here again, then, Bonhoeffer offers us a rhetoric of witness consistent with the witness of Epiphany.

A Witness of Epiphany

As we have already seen, Bonhoeffer's own reflections on Epiphany remind us that the Epiphany of Christ entails not only a manifestation, a "making public," of his glory but also a concealment of that glory from public view. Even the historical beginnings of the Epiphany feast seem to bear witness to this fact for Bonhoeffer. Referring to these beginnings in the opening lines of his reflections, he observes that there is a "strange indeterminacy that lies over the feast of Epiphany," noting, "Its origins are in the dark."[124] He proceeds by highlighting that, historically, the feast has been associated with four events from the life of Christ: his birth, his visitation by the Magi, his baptism, and

---

liturgical practices. As a response to these readers, Larry Rasmussen's work is worth citing at length: "What is striking in those letters and papers from the jail cell is the intense piety: Paul Gerhardt's hymns, a memorized stanza of '*Frolich soll mein Herz springen*' commended to a friend, daily use of the Herrnhuter *Losungen*, prayers, a sermon or two, poetry and so on. Yet even these constitute second-order examples. The telling point is that in prison, while he lamented 'religion' and applauded the world's coming of age, Bonhoeffer practiced regular prayer and meditation . . . surely part of what he meant by 'secret' or 'hidden' discipline (*Arkandisziplin*). He in fact lived by the church year, often dating his mail by the ecclesiastical calendar. His last action in community was to conduct a worship service among fellow prisoners on the way to the last concentration camp, and his last action in solitude was to pray quietly, on his knees and naked, before the steps of the gallows. Cultus counted for Bonhoeffer in his life and thought, in his last days, and for the future he envisioned" (Larry Rasmussen and Renate Bethge, *Dietrich Bonhoeffer: His Significance for North Americans* [Minneapolis: Fortress, 1990], 58). In *The Death of Adam*, Marilynne Robinson makes a similar point ("Bonhoeffer," 111-12).

[124]Bonhoeffer, "*Epiphany*," 534. Philip H. Pfatteicher's account of the origins of the feast in *Journey into The Heart of God: Living the Liturgical Year* (Oxford: Oxford University Press, 2013) suggests that, in the nearly eight decades since Bonhoeffer wrote his reflections, this indeterminacy has not yet been entirely resolved (111-13). Pfatteicher highlights that the feast has been commemorated in different ways in the West and East: the former emphasizes the visitation of the Magi, while the latter emphasizes the baptism of Jesus Christ. In this respect, Bonhoeffer's meditations, which give more space to Christ's baptism, share more with the Eastern celebrations of the feast.

his first miracle.[125] What is noteworthy for my purposes is that the echoes of the christological incognito reverberate throughout Bonhoeffer's reflections on these events. He suggests that "the appearance of the Godhead of Jesus Christ is only a call to believe in the poor child in the manger."[126] The star that guided the Magi to that manger "is *not* a sign that would have visibly announced the birth of the King of Jews to the world"; "Herod did *not* see it" because the star "must be recognized and believed in."[127] Christ's baptism involved "self-humiliation for the sake of sinners."[128] And finally, Christ's revelation in the act of turning water into wine at the wedding feast of Cana involved concealment. "What is decisive," Bonhoeffer writes, "is that this sign of the divine power of Jesus remains hidden from the guests, from the chief steward, and from the bridegroom of the wedding; instead, it serves the faith of the disciples alone."[129]

One can easily add to Bonhoeffer's list of examples. In John 8:6-8, Christ writes an inscrutable message in the dust;[130] in Mark 4:10-12, he tells the disciples that he speaks in parables to prevent some from comprehending his message; and in Matthew 17:9, he exhorts them to refrain from speaking about his transfiguration until after his death and resurrection. This final example brings us back to Bonhoeffer's own reflections on Epiphany, in which he writes the following:

> The glory of Jesus is hidden in his humility and is perceived only in faith. Here, the content of the feast of Epiphany is closely connected again with the Christmas story, so that it becomes understandable that at one time the day of Epiphany was also the appearance of the one who had "no form

---

[125]Bonhoeffer, "*Epiphany*," 534.
[126]Bonhoeffer, "*Epiphany*," 537.
[127]Bonhoeffer, "*Epiphany*," 537.
[128]Bonhoeffer, "*Epiphany*," 535.
[129]Bonhoeffer, "*Epiphany*," 537.
[130]For a rhetorical take on this episode, see Thomas Deans, "The Rhetoric of Jesus Writing in the Story of the Woman Accused of Adultery (John 7.53-8.11)," *College Composition and Communication* 65, no. 3 (2014): 406-29.

or majesty." With this, Epiphany points to the next season in the church year: to the Passion. It makes good sense that the last pericope of the season of Epiphany is the transfiguration of Jesus on his way to Jerusalem.[131]

The meaning of Epiphany is only rightly understood when it is seen in light of the seasonal bookends of Christmas and Lent, which present us with the lowliness of the manger and the shame of the cross. By faith we glimpse the glory of Christ in his humility, or not at all. Bonhoeffer's rhetoric made manifest this truth.

---

[131]Bonhoeffer, "*Epiphany*," 537.

4

CALLING FOR REPENTANCE

Desmond Tutu and Lenten Constitutive Rhetorics

"Yet even now," declares the LORD,
"return to me with all your heart,
with fasting, with weeping, and with mourning;
and rend your hearts and not your garments."
Return to the LORD your God,
for he is gracious and merciful,
slow to anger, and abounding in steadfast love;
and he relents over disaster.

JOEL 2:12-13

Remember that you are dust, and to dust you shall return.

ASH WEDNESDAY LITURGY, *THE BOOK OF COMMON PRAYER*

We are bound up in a delicate network of interdependence because, as we
say in our African idiom, a person is a person through other persons. To
dehumanize another inexorably means that one is dehumanized as well. . . .
Thus to forgive is indeed the best form of self-interest since anger, resentment,
and revenge are corrosive of that summum bonum, *that greatest good,*
communal harmony that enhances the humanity and personhood of all in
the community.

DESMOND TUTU, *NO FUTURE WITHOUT FORGIVENESS*

IN THE MIDDLE OF THE LENTEN SEASON OF 1988, Desmond Tutu
firmly rebuked South African leaders from the pulpit of St. George's
Cathedral in Cape Town. The message was not an uncommon one
for the South African archbishop, who knew that his country's

policy of apartheid was antithetical to the gospel of Jesus Christ and had worked throughout his career to dismantle it. But the atmosphere at St. George's was particularly charged that day. South African President P. W. Botha had recently granted the country's security police additional powers so that they could squelch any anti-apartheid activities, and the police had already broken up or prevented several rallies. In response to these crackdowns, Tutu and others decided to hold the service at St. George's. According to eyewitness Jim Wallis, the security police entered the cathedral while Tutu was preaching. Like an infernal version of the stations of the cross, the police stood along the walls of the nave, armed with guns and "wielding writing pads and tape recorders to record whatever [Tutu] said and thereby threatening him with consequences for any bold prophetic utterances."[1]

But despite the great darkness surrounding him, Tutu did not shrink from his prophetic duty to call the armed members of his audience to account. He declared, "Your cause is unjust. You are defending what is fundamentally indefensible, because it is evil. It is evil without question. It is immoral. It is immoral without question. It is un-Christian. Therefore, you will bite the dust! And you will bite the dust comprehensively."[2] A fiery take on the Lenten words "ashes to ashes, dust to dust," Tutu's words fired up the congregation. Jumping up, they started to dance exuberantly, an act uniting joyful worship with political witness. Wallis recalls, "We danced out of the cathedral to meet the awaiting police and military forces of apartheid who hardly

---

[1] The details of this episode are recounted in a number of places (Desmond Tutu, "Clarifying the Word: A Sermon by Desmond Tutu," in *Crucible of Fire: The Church Confronts Apartheid*, ed. Jim Wallis and Joyce Hollyday (Maryknoll, NY: Orbis, 1989), 32-39; Wallis, "Into the Crucible of Fire: The Church Steps forward in South Africa," in Wallis and Hollyday, eds., *Crucible of Fire*, 1-2; John Allen, *Rabble-rouser for Peace: The Authorized Biography of Desmond Tutu* (New York: Free Press, 2006), 290-91; Jim Wallis, *God's Politics: Why the Right Gets It Wrong and Left Doesn't Get It* (New York: HarperSanFrancisco, 2005), 348.

[2] Tutu, "Clarifying," 34. Also quoted in Allen, *Rabble-rouser for Peace*, 291.

expected a confrontation with dancing worshipers. Not knowing what else to do, they backed up to provide the space for the people of faith to dance for freedom in the streets of South Africa."[3] Events like this one helped to cement St. George's Cathedral as an important site of anti-apartheid activity. It was as if the words of Tutu and other activists had, to borrow a line from Sayers's *The Zeal of Thy House*, "soaked into the stones and sanctified them," constituting the building and those who found a home there as a powerful and prophetic witness against the state.[4]

Tutu's sermon at St. George's was not the first time that he found himself ministering in the midst of a hostile audience, nor would it be his last. In *Rabble-rouser for Peace*, John Allen's excellent and aptly titled biography of Tutu, Allen characterizes Tutu's approach to the pastorate as "interventionist" and chronicles several other events in which Tutu traded his own physical security for an opportunity to minister to others.[5] An early example occurred in the late sixties at the University of Fort Hare, one of only a small number of South African schools that admitted black students at that time. In late August of 1968, several Fort Hare students—who had just participated in a campus week of missions, sponsored by a group of Christian organizations—drafted a petition to the university's administration in the hopes of addressing inequality and discrimination in the community. When the administration did not respond favorably to students' requests, some students decided that graffiti might be a more effective approach than petition. Over the next two weeks, the security police were brought in to investigate the incident, and students staged a sit-in. On September 6, almost three hundred students were

---

[3]Wallis, *God's Politics*, 348.

[4]Dorothy L. Sayers, *The Zeal of Thy House* (Eugene, OR: Wipf & Stock, 2011), 31.

[5]The examples from Allen's book (*Rabble-rouser for Peace*) that I recount in this paragraph appear on pages 102-3, 110-11, 115.

suspended and told to leave the campus that afternoon. Tutu, who was teaching nearby at Federal Theological Seminary and serving as a chaplain at Fort Hare, had been an encouragement to students throughout the whole ordeal. And when the security police showed up on campus that afternoon, Tutu "waded into the fray."[6] Barney Pityana, one of the Fort Hare students who was suspended, recounted Tutu's courageous act as follows:

> We had been surrounded by police, with dogs snarling at us. We were petrified, for nearly two hours. Some people were crying . . . The staff of the university, the white people—some of them armed—these professors were watching and nobody said a word, nobody . . . Desmond [came] almost from nowhere, in a cassock . . . broke the police cordon and came to be among us. I recall moving scenes of young women kneeling to pray with Desmond for blessings. Even today when I recall that I get very emotional. For me that was the greatest example I could think of, of what to be a priest was about.[7]

The parallels with Tutu's experience at St. George's are unmistakable. Tutu's ministry often involved stationing himself with the marginalized and the suffering, and his willingness to preach and comfort in the midst of charged situations, whether at Fort Hare or St. George's, was preparation for the work that he would be called upon to do after apartheid crumbled in the early nineties. When that happened, President Nelson Mandela asked Tutu to serve as the chairperson of the South African Truth and Reconciliation Commission (TRC).

South Africans had elected Mandela through a democratic process, but despite this miraculous event, the evils of apartheid were still very real to a majority of South Africans. Many recognized that if the country's transition from apartheid to democracy was to succeed,

---

[6]Allen, *Rabble-rouser for Peace*, 111.
[7]Quoted in Allen, *Rabble-rouser for Peace*, 111.

decades of violence and discrimination needed to be acknowledged and addressed; however, the approach needed to be one that members of all political parties could agree upon. The difficulty, as Tutu himself often presented it, was to find and adopt a course of action that avoided both the lack of accountability resulting from total amnesty and the retributive justice resulting from Nuremberg-like trials.[8] The TRC was the South African Parliament's solution to this problem. The TRC invited survivors of human rights violations to tell their stories at its public hearings, listened to and attempted to legitimate these stories, and awarded reparations. The commission also invited perpetrators of human rights violations to participate in hearings, and the perpetrators were granted individual amnesty if they confessed their crimes.[9]

For Tutu, serving as chairperson of the TRC did not involve checking his Christianity at the door. During the public hearings, Tutu usually wore his clerical collar and a cross around his neck, as well as his purple cassock—a garment often worn by priests throughout the Lenten season. And much like his attire, Tutu's exchanges with survivors and perpetrators were frequently pastoral in nature. He framed their testimonies in terms of Christian notions of repentance and forgiveness, made an effort to empathize with them, and sang with and prayed for them.[10] Tutu's spiritualization of the commission drew criticism from some South Africans, but he found it impossible to run things any other way. A story from theologian Piet Meiring illustrates

---

[8]Tutu, *No Future Without Forgiveness* (New York: Doubleday, 1999), 30; James Beitler, "Making More of the Middle Ground: Desmond Tutu and the *Ethos* of the South African Truth and Reconciliation Commission," *Relevant Rhetoric: A New Journal of Rhetorical Studies* 3, no. 1 (Spring 2012).

[9]There were certain stipulations for being awarded amnesty. The crimes had to have happened between 1960 and 1994 and had to be "politically motivated" (Tutu, *No Future*, 49-50).

[10]Tutu, *No Future*, 81-82; see also Philpott, "Beyond Politics as Usual: Is Reconciliation Compatible with Liberalism?," in *The Politics of Past Evil: Religion, Reconciliation, and the Dilemmas of Transitional Justice*, ed. Daniel Philpott (Notre Dame: University of Notre Dame Press, 2006), 31-32; Beitler, "Making More of the Middle Ground," 3.

the point.[11] As the commission was commencing its public hearings in Johannesburg, several people working with the TRC approached Tutu and asked him to temper his religious rhetoric. In response, Tutu agreed to start the day's hearing with silence instead of prayer. But according to Meiring, when the moment of silence was over, Tutu thought better of the idea. After a bit of hemming and hawing, he cried out, "No! This is not the way to do it. We cannot start without having prayed. Close your eyes!" Thanks in large part to Tutu's influence and persuasiveness, the hearings frequently felt more like worship than legal proceedings, and Tutu continued to bring this *ēthos* to the TRC throughout its operation.[12]

TRC scholars and commentators have discussed Tutu's Christian rhetoric at length, and many have questioned whether it was appropriate for the chairperson of a state-sponsored institution to talk in such ways.[13] Tutu's critics worried that, in spite of his good intentions, the use of Christian rhetoric may have undermined the very democratic ideals that Tutu sought to strengthen.[14] Others worried that

---

[11]Philpott, "Beyond Politics as Usual," 31.

[12]The criticism that Tutu Christianized the TRC assumes the efficacy of Tutu's rhetoric. Tutu's persuasive abilities are highlighted in John Allen's biography of the former archbishop. According to Allen, Tutu's father often quipped, "Don't raise your voice. Improve your argument"—and Tutu repeated the phrase often during anti-apartheid struggle (*Rabble-rouser for Peace*, 22). About Tutu's early experiences teaching juniors and seniors, Allen writes, "Some teachers used their fists to keep order, but the new teacher used persuasion" (50). And near the end of his book, Allen cites Al Gore, who claimed, "His [Tutu's] power is the power to persuade" (394). Even Tutu's harshest critics would likely agree with Gore's assessment.

[13]Created by an act of Parliament, the South African TRC had been granted the power to subpoena witnesses, grant amnesty to perpetrators of human rights violations, and award reparations to survivors of violence and abuse. The commission was, in these ways, a mechanism and mouthpiece of the state.

[14]Communication scholar John B. Hatch succinctly summarized the problem as follows: "It is one thing to call a church congregation, or even a village or clan with a shared religious tradition, to live into the drama of a divine history and destiny. To expect the same of a pluralistic, secular state is another matter. To some extent, Tutu's presence conflated the two; it appeared to go beyond *informing* transitional politics with a sacred understanding of reconciliation to *pressing* a model of confession, forgiveness, and transcendence to a watching nation. Faith in the power of human agency to transcend (rather than punish) horrific crimes would seem to rest on thin ice unless grounded in some faith that the world is created and sustained by a transcendent Being who ultimately sets the world to right and puts it in good order. Not all citizens share such

encouraging acts of forgiveness by those unable or unwilling to grant them reinscribed apartheid's violence. It silenced those who did not want to understand their past in Christian terms and denied survivors' rights to justice. Such critiques are difficult to dispute, especially when one considers that, more than two decades after the TRC was created, inequalities in South Africa persist.[15]

This chapter does not aim to challenge these critiques. I have been persuaded that, given Tutu's position on a state-sponsored commission, his rhetoric may have been problematic at times. It probably did alienate some people from the TRC process, and in such cases it compromised the freedoms that the commission was attempting to ensure. Furthermore, while the South African TRC did forestall physical violence and probably helped to facilitate the country's democratic transition, I would hesitate to recommend that other countries should embrace the South Africa TRC model wholesale. Despite the similarities among emerging democracies, transitional contexts are too unique for that.[16] All that said, we Christians still have much to learn from Tutu. The rhetoric that fails when proclaimed with the authority of the state may succeed when performed within communities of faith.[17] Among people who share Christian convictions (and

---

a sanguine faith, nor does such faith render all individuals equally ready to forgive those who have irrevocably harmed them" (*Race and Reconciliation: Redressing Wounds of Injustice* [Lanham, MD: Lexington, 2008], 78-79).

[15]Richard C. Marback, *Managing Vulnerability: South Africa's Struggle for a Democratic Rhetoric* (Columbia: University of South Carolina Press, 2012), 2-3.

[16]On this point I have come to agree with rhetorician and truth commission expert Erik Doxtader, who warns that adopting the SATRC as a blueprint elsewhere "may not be risk-free" ("The Potential of Reconciliation's Beginning: A Reply," *Rhetoric & Public Affairs* 7, no. 3 [2004]: 379-80).

[17]John Hatch describes reconciliation's potential when it is sought in and by communities of faith: "The *spirit* of reconciliation displayed by leaders and citizens of faith can reanimate a disenchanted public with fresh visions of human potential for creating a common good; it may also heighten their disillusionment when the *realpolitik* of reconciliation achieves little more than the lessor of two evils (e.g., South Africa's present socioeconomic apartheid and disorderly peace in place of political apartheid and the bloodbath it nearly engendered). Yet disillusionment need not have the final word; this is the promise of reconciliation in the thick of the faith tradition" (*Race and Reconciliation*, 79).

especially among those who have voluntarily joined a church with the expectation that the community will help guide and chasten them as they attempt to live out their convictions), Tutu's rhetoric is not simply appropriate; it is the gospel. Christians are commanded in Scripture to forgive and be reconciled to one another (Mt 18:21-35).

In this chapter, then, I set aside questions about the appropriateness of state-sponsored Christian rhetoric in South Africa or elsewhere, considering instead what Tutu's rhetoric might teach Christians about witnessing. I begin by giving an overview of what communication theorists refer to as constitutive rhetoric and discussing Tutu's constitutive "rhetoric of interdependence."[18] Then I explore Antjie Krog's response to Tutu and the TRC in her magnificent and haunting book *Country of My Skull: Guilt, Sorrow, and the Limits of Forgiveness in the New South Africa.* An Afrikaner journalist who covered the TRC, Krog embraces and extends Tutu's rhetoric of interdependence, and her book serves as a powerful public act of repentance. My exploration of Tutu's rhetoric and Krog's response to it resonates with the postures of worship that Christians are called to adopt throughout the Lenten season.

---

[18]My dissertation was titled "Rhetorics of Interdependence: Composing the *Ethos* of the Greensboro Truth and Reconciliation Commission." In this chapter, I draw on some of the research from that project and from the resulting book, *Remaking Transitional Justice in the United States: The Rhetorical Authorization of the Greensboro Truth and Reconciliation Commission* (New York: Springer, 2013). For those interested in exploring Desmond Tutu's rhetoric or the rhetoric of the South African transition in more detail, Philippe-Joseph Salazar's *An African Athens: Rhetoric and the Shaping of Democracy in South Africa* (Mahwah, NJ: L. Erlbaum, 2002) and Erik Doxtader's scholarly corpus are excellent starting points. Salazar's book describes Tutu's role in helping to rhetorically reconstitute and unify the South African nation-state (*African Athens*, 2-16, 77-78), and Doxtader's work focuses on the rhetoric of reconciliation, highlighting its connections to *ubuntu* ("Making Rhetorical History in a Time of Transition: The Occasion, Constitution, and Representation of South African Reconciliation," *Rhetoric & Public Affairs* 4, no. 2 [2001]: 228); the way it functioned to summon adversaries to engage in rhetorical relationship with one another (*With Faith in the Works of Words: The Beginnings of Reconciliation in South Africa, 1985–1995* [East Lansing: Michigan State University Press, 2009], 90-91, 159; "Reconciliation—a Rhetorical Concept/ion," *Quarterly Journal of Speech* 89, no. 4 [2003]: 268-69); and its power to prompt redefinition, as opposed to renewed violence, in South Africa ("Reconciliation," 268-69; "The Potential of Reconciliation's Beginning: A Reply," *Rhetoric & Public Affairs* 7, no. 3 [2004]: 379).

Constitutive Rhetorics of Interdependence

In the previous chapter, I discussed Kenneth Burke's innovative distinction between the "old" rhetoric of persuasion and the "new" rhetoric of identification.[19] Burke's distinction, communication scholar Maurice Charland observes, contributed much to the understanding of how rhetoric works. The old model of rhetorical activity assumed that rhetors design discourse strategically, hoping to persuade audience members whose identities are relatively stable and outside the discourse at hand.[20] Burke's new model, Charland notes, enabled "a rethinking of judgment and the working of the rhetorical effect, for he does not posit a transcendent subject as audience member, who would exist prior to and apart from the speech to be judged, but considers audience members to participate in the very discourse by which they would be 'persuaded.'"[21] In other words, without completely dismissing the deliberate design of persuasion or the ability to make rhetorical judgments, Burke highlighted that the identities of both rhetor and audience are fashioned in and through the language we use. The language we use not only *references* but also *shapes* reality.[22] As Burke famously writes in *Language as Symbolic Action,* "Even if any given terminology is a *reflection* of reality, by its very nature as a terminology it must be a *selection* of reality; and to

---

[19]Kenneth Burke, "Rhetoric—Old and New," *Journal of General Education* 5, no. 3 (1951): 203.

[20]Maurice Charland, "Constitutive Rhetoric: The Case of the Peuple Québécois," *Quarterly Journal of Speech* 73, no. 2 (1987): 133. I summarize Charland's argument in more detail elsewhere (Beitler, *Remaking Transitional Justice,* 64).

[21]Charland, "Constitutive Rhetoric," 133.

[22]Language's constitutive function is one of the central topics—or, at the very least, a key theoretical assumption—of much recent rhetorical theory and criticism. James Jasinski's entry on "constitutive rhetoric" from his excellent, encyclopedic *Sourcebook on Rhetoric* (Thousand Oaks, CA: Sage, 2001) mentions several scholars who contributed to the concept's development, including Edwin Black, Maurice Charland, James Farr, Michael Calvin McGee, John Lyne, Steven Mailloux, and James Boyd White (106-8). But Jasinski's exploration of the constitutive function of discourse in his *Sourcebook* is by no means limited to a single entry. One of the implicit arguments that is developed across many of his entries is that rhetoric's constitutive function is one of the field's most important notions and that it needs to receive even greater attention from scholars.

this extent it must function also as a *deflection* of reality . . . any no-
menclature necessarily directs the attention into some channels rather
than others."[23]

Founding political documents such as the Declaration of Independence or the Constitution demonstrate this function of our language
use most clearly. Their composition calls into being new communities
and gives individuals new identities in relation to those communities.[24] But the constitutive function of our language use is not restricted
to these documents alone. Legal-literary scholar James Boyd White
explains, "Whenever you speak [or write], you define a character for
yourself and for at least one other—your audience—and make a community at least between the two of you."[25] From great literature to
grocery lists, church liturgies to corporate logos, biblical criticism to
birthday cards—all language functions constitutively. What is more,
the constitutive functions of language are wide-ranging in their effects.
Sociolinguist James Paul Gee, for example, describes "seven building

---

[23]Kenneth Burke, *Language as Symbolic Action: Essays on Life, Literature, and Method* (Berkeley:
University of California Press, 1966), 45.

[24]Jacques Derrida's "Declarations of Independence" (*New Political Science: A Journal of Politics and
Culture* 15 [1986]: 7-15) remains one of the best pieces on this point.

[25]James Boyd White, *When Words Lose Their Meaning: Constitutions and Reconstitutions of Language, Character, and Community* (Chicago: University of Chicago Press, 1984), xi. My approach
in what follows draws primarily on James Boyd White's conception of constitutive rhetoric—in
part because White explores language's constitutive functions without suggesting that humans
do not have rhetorical agency (as some proponents of constitutive rhetoric suggest). Quoting
White's book *Hercules' Bow,* James Jasinski describes White's conception of constitutive rhetoric
as "the activity and art 'of constituting character, community, and culture in language'" (*Sourcebook on Rhetoric,* 107). As even this brief description shows, White's theory of language acknowledges that it is both instrumental (it involves an "activity and art" that we can practice consciously and judge) and constitutive (it creates, whether we are aware of it or not, our "character,
community and culture"). For White, we make—and thus act through—language, even as it
makes us and shapes our experience of reality. People, he writes, "at once form and are formed
by their language and the events of their world" (White, *When Words Lose Their Meaning,* 4).
"When language changes meaning, the world changes meaning, and we are part of the world"
(4). White's analytical method involves exploring how a given text "[works] upon a world it
defines and [leads] its reader to a position within it" (x). For extended illustrations of White's
approach to reading texts, see *Justice as Translation: An Essay in Cultural and Legal Criticism*
(Chicago: University of Chicago Press, 1990); and *Living Speech: Resisting the Empire of Force*
(Princeton: Princeton University Press, 2006).

tasks of language."[26] According to Gee, language constructs significance, activities, identities, relationships, politics, connections, sign systems, and knowledge.[27] While a specific utterance may be more or less effective in building reality in these ways, the fact remains that our language and the language that surrounds us influences all aspects of our lives.

This idea is congruent with the biblical and apostolic witness.[28] God creates through his Word, and the Genesis account suggests that, as image bearers of the creating God, humans have been granted the ability to use language to create from what he has made. That said, the *ways* we use language to constitute ourselves, others, and our communities may be more or less consistent with Scripture and church doctrine. Therefore, our goal as Christian witnesses should involve, to borrow ideas from Andy Crouch's *Culture Making, critiquing* constitutive rhetorics that are inconsistent with Scripture and church doctrine and *creating* and *cultivating* constitutive rhetorics that advance the gospel of Jesus Christ.[29]

During the operation of the Truth and Reconciliation Commission, Desmond Tutu resolutely advanced a constitutive rhetoric that defined personhood in terms of human interdependence and,

---

[26]James Paul Gee, *An Introduction to Discourse Analysis: Theory and Method*, 2nd ed. (New York: Routledge, 2005), 11-13.

[27]Gee writes, "Whenever we speak or write, we always and simultaneously construct or build . . . seven areas of 'reality'" (*Introduction to Discourse Analysis*, 11). Gee's "seven building tasks of language" include using language to "make things significant"; "engag[e] in a certain sort of activity"; "tak[e] on a certain identity or role"; "signal what sort of relationship we have, want to have, or are trying to have with our listener(s), reader(s), or other people, groups, or institutions about whom we are communicating"; "convey a perspective on the nature of the distribution of social goods"; "render certain things connected or relevant (or not) to other things"; and "build privilege or prestige for one sign system or knowledge claim over another" (11-13).

[28]Acknowledging that rhetoric functions constitutively does not require one to assert that *all* truth is socially and rhetorically constructed. One may admit that our language use shapes individual and community identities while maintaining belief in truth that transcends our own rhetorical constructions.

[29]Andy Crouch, *Culture Making: Recovering Our Creative Calling* (Downers Grove, IL: InterVarsity Press, 2008), 10, 68, 73-77.

in so doing, exemplified Gee's three building tasks of identity, connection, and relationship simultaneously. Time and time again, Tutu positioned South Africans of all backgrounds as dependent upon and responsible for one another's flourishing as humans. His most overt expression of this notion came through his discussion of the South African concept of *ubuntu*—the idea that, as he puts it in *No Future Without Forgiveness*, humans "are bound up in a delicate network of interdependence" and "a person is a person through other persons."[30] The language of *ubuntu*, it should be noted, was not unique to Tutu. The concept had been part of the democratic South Africa from its inception. The famous postamble to South Africa's Interim Constitution affirmed "a need for ubuntu" in the country, and this exigency was used to justify the TRC's creation in Parliament's subsequent Promotion of National Unity and Reconciliation Act.[31] But Tutu was arguably *ubuntu*'s most prominent spokesperson, championing the concept throughout the TRC's operation.

Tutu used *ubuntu* to highlight that one's identity—even one's very being—cannot be understood apart from others. Personhood is, in part, a socially constructed reality. In a speech on the concept that he delivered in the United States, Tutu put it this way: "I am human ultimately only because I belong. I would never know . . . to be able to speak as a human being. I wouldn't know how to think as a human being. I wouldn't be able to walk as a human being. Yes, I wouldn't know how to be human. I need other human beings to help me to

---

[30]Tutu, *No Future*, 35. I have discussed *ubuntu* at length elsewhere (*Remaking Transitional Justice*, 38, 51-74). As I have noted, the concept of *ubuntu* is multifaceted and has been described in a variety of ways (52-54). For my purposes here, however, I will focus primarily on Tutu's use and description of the term. For a robust theological account of Tutu's use of the concept of *ubuntu*, see Michael Battle's *Reconciliation: The Ubuntu Theology of Desmond Tutu* (Cleveland, OH: Pilgrim, 1997), and "Ubuntu: Learning from the African Worldview," *Sewanee Theological Review* 53, no. 4 (2010): 404-16.

[31]Beitler, *Remaking Transitional Justice*, 37-38, 54; Doxtader, "Making Rhetorical History"; Tutu, *No Future*, 45.

become human."[32] But Tutu's *ubuntu* does not simply suggest that reality is socially constructed; it also points toward the fact that reality is divinely constructed. God in his wisdom designed humans to complement one another, compensating for one another's shortcomings. By describing *ubuntu* in this way, Tutu calls his audience members to embrace a vision of humanity not unlike Paul's description of the church as a unified body comprised of many diverse parts (1 Cor 12).[33] He offers a constitutive rhetoric of interdependence that beckons his audiences to embrace a view of themselves more aligned with the constitutive rhetorics of the body of Christ.

Moreover, because we are interdependent creatures, our actions toward others have consequences for ourselves and vice versa. Tutu contends that when we harm or belittle others, we ourselves are diminished. Immediately after defining *ubuntu* in *No Future Without Forgiveness,* he writes, "To dehumanize another inexorably means that one is dehumanized as well. It is not too surprising that, having been involved in a policy as evil and dehumanizing as apartheid, Cabinet minister Jimmy Kruger could heartlessly declare that the death in detention of a Steve Biko 'left him cold.'"[34] In other words, apartheid and the horrible human rights violations that were employed to uphold it did not just have an effect on the victimized. Such acts injured *both* victim *and* perpetrator. And for Tutu, the converse is also true. When we treat others with dignity and respect, we enhance our own dignity as humans. Here again we are presented with a vision of humanity that resonates with Paul's ecclesiology. Shortly after Paul

---

[32]Desmond Tutu, "Reconciling Love: A Millennium Mandate," 2005–2006 Bryan Series Lectures on Spirit and Spirituality, Hege Library, Guilford College, Greensboro, NC, 2005.

[33]In an interview with Jim Wallis, Tutu describes "interrelatedness" in an overtly Christian way. He says, "I think one has to say God is pretty smart, because we have an interrelatedness in the body of Christ. So we are not alone. . . . It isn't my struggle, it isn't even the struggle of the people of South Africa. It's the struggle of all the people of God" ("Clarifying the Word: A Sermon by Desmond Tutu," in Wallis and Hollyday, eds., *Crucible of Fire*, 68).

[34]Tutu, *No Future*, 35.

describes the church as a body made of many parts, he adds, "If one member suffers, all suffer together; if one member is honored, all rejoice together" (1 Cor 12:26).[35]

In line with Gee's claim that building reality with language always involves engaging in particular activities, Tutu tried to make his constitutive rhetoric take hold by encouraging South Africans to participate in the formal mechanisms of the TRC: public confession, truth-telling, repentance, and forgiveness. He suggested that, through confession, perpetrators could acknowledge the ways that they had dehumanized others and themselves; through truth-telling, survivors might begin to reclaim the voice, agency, and human dignity diminished by violence; through repentance, perpetrators could recognize the humanity of those they had harmed; and through forgiveness, survivors might help restore the humanity of those who had done them harm. Taken together, the hope (which was not always realized, of course) was that these practices might create opportunities for individuals and groups to recognize their interdependence upon one another and move forward together as a united but wonderfully diverse nation.

Tutu's claims about *ubuntu* and the mechanisms of the TRC were not the only means by which he advanced his rhetoric of interdependence. He also portrayed Nelson Mandela and the TRC as its individual and communal embodiments—models for South Africans to emulate.[36] In *No Future Without Forgiveness*, Tutu describes Mandela as the "heroic embodiment of reconciliation and forgiveness," and later, amplifying the point, he presents him as "the most

---

[35]On a related note, Michael Battle has observed that Tutu's conceptualization of *ubuntu* was influenced by his "Anglican heritage with its eucharistic understanding of community" ("Ubuntu," 416).

[36]For a related example, in which Mandela was associated with the truth and reconciliation commission model to justify the TRC approach, see my analysis of Rev. Bongani Finca's address at the Swearing in and Seating Ceremony of the Greensboro Truth and Reconciliation Commission (*Remaking Transitional Justice*, 60-61).

spectacular embodiment of the ANC's commitment to peace and reconciliation."[37] According to Tutu, this posture was forged through the suffering Mandela endured in prison, which, in keeping with Tutu's emphasis on interdependence, Tutu describes as a "suffering on behalf of others."[38] Later in the book, Tutu praises those who have modeled their own actions on Mandela and expresses his strong desire for more people to do so.[39] In Mandela we see the person that Tutu's rhetoric of interdependence invites South Africans to become.

In a similar fashion, in the TRC we see the community that Tutu's rhetoric invites South Africa to become. The TRC was, Tutu suggested in the foreword to the commission's final report, a miniature South Africa, modeling for the country as a whole what relationships and interactions ought to look like.[40] Commissioners were "a microcosm of our society," and the fact that a diverse group of commissioners had been able to overcome "alienation, suspicions, and lack of trust in one another" served as "a sign of hope" for Tutu that South Africans could achieve unity.[41] Such language presented the TRC as both a realization of the Interim Constitution's (and Tutu's own) call for *ubuntu* and a corporeal reiteration of that call, transmitted through the commissioners' interactions with one another to the people of South Africa. In other words, the commission itself was a key facet of Tutu's constitutive rhetoric.[42]

---

[37]Tutu, *No Future*, 39, 42.

[38]Tutu, *No Future*, 39.

[39]Tutu, *No Future*, 164.

[40]Tutu, "Foreword by Chairperson," in *Truth and Reconciliation Commission of South Africa Report*, vol. 1 (New York: Grove's Dictionaries, 1999), 22. I have discussed this point in much greater detail elsewhere (see Beitler, "Making More of the Middle Ground," 15; *Remaking Transitional Justice*, 76). Tutu also writes more on this point in *No Future Without Forgiveness* (79-80).

[41]Tutu, "Foreword by Chairperson," 22.

[42]Tutu claimed as much in a subsequent paragraph of the foreword. Comparing the TRC to and quoting from the Interim Constitution, he wrote, "Like our Constitution, the Commission has

Tutu's own *ēthos* was an additional aspect of his rhetoric of interdependence. I have already discussed Tutu's willingness to enter into the midst of dangerous situations, risking his own safety and authority to care for those who had neither. But during the operation of the TRC, the archbishop upended unjust social structures and demonstrated human interdependence in yet another way. At various points throughout the TRC process, Tutu, arguably one of South Africa's most prominent and powerful orators, reconfigured the rhetorical situation by repositioning himself as an audience member. This reconfiguration of the rhetorical situation was most evident at the commission's public hearings. During the hearings, survivors and perpetrators of human rights violations gave testimonies or confessed their wrongdoing before members of the TRC and the public, and—though Tutu would certainly sermonize at the hearings from time to time—he seems to have made a conscious effort to listen, ask questions, and acknowledge the value of participants' stories.[43] Tutu was often deeply moved by what he heard and saw, but he claims that he tried to avoid shedding tears whenever possible, not because he sought to be a perfectly neutral observer but because when he cried, "the media then concentrated on [him] and took their attention away from those who should have had it, the witnesses."[44] Such acts of "rhetorical listening" upended

helped in laying *the secure foundation for the people of South Africa to transcend the divisions and strife of the past*" ("Foreword by Chairperson," 23).

[43] As he notes in *No Future Without Forgiveness,* Tutu offered commentary after each day of hearings "to capture the mood of the day and to sum up what had been its chief features," "to affirm those who had testified as well as the communities from which they came," "to draw lessons" from the testimonies, and "to appeal to . . . white compatriots not to shun the commission but to embrace it" (118).

[44] Tutu, *No Future,* 144. But Tutu did weep—a fact that many critics have commented on when discussing Tutu's role as chair of the TRC (Beitler, "Making More of the Middle Ground," 3). Personally, I have come to see Tutu's tears in light of the apostle Peter's lament after denying Jesus. Quoting from a sermon of Dietrich Bonhoeffer's, theologian Jennifer M. McBride writes, "Peter is the one who 'denied his Lord,' indeed on 'the same night Judas betrayed him.' But Peter is also the one who 'went out and wept bitterly.' Thus, Bonhoeffer concludes, 'Peter's church is not only the church which confesses its faith, nor only the church which denies its Lord; it is the

the power dynamic between the archbishop and the people. The archbishop's control of his voice and emotions gave voice to the people and reinforced Tutu's claims about the interdependency of human persons.[45]

Tutu's attempts to reinforce his claims about interdependence through rhetorical listening did not require that he efface himself completely or attempt to mask his views about apartheid; rather, his stated position was, as Richard C. Marback has elaborated upon in his excellent book *Managing Vulnerability: South Africa's Struggle for a Democratic Rhetoric*, one of "even-handedness."[46] Marback writes, "In the foreword to the final report of the TRC, Tutu characterizes his gesture of conciliation not as open-handed, not as an unconditional invitation to cooperation, but as even-handed, a gesture balancing his condemnation of apartheid with his willingness to consider the motives of apartheid's administrators."[47] For Marback, such a stance

---

church which still can weep'" (*Radical Discipleship* [Minneapolis: Fortress, 2017], 122). A few sentences later, McBride instructively adds, "The church of Peter is the church that laments the specific ways it denies and ostracizes those who, like Jesus in his final days, are most despised" (122). During the TRC hearings, Tutu served as an instrument of the "church of Peter," expressing lament about the ways that South Africans—and, indeed, many South African Christians—had wounded others.

[45]Listening as a rhetorical practice has attracted interest from scholars of communication in recent decades. Krista Ratcliffe's book *Rhetorical Listening: Identification, Gender, and Whiteness* (Carbondale: Southern Illinois University Press, 2005) is an excellent theoretical account of the topic, and the book is also worth highlighting because it includes a brief discussion of Tutu and his notion of interdependence (73-74). Drawing on both Kenneth Burke's and T. Minh-ha Trinh's writings, Ratcliffe holds Tutu's work up as a model of "non-identification," which may allow people to avoid identification's elision of difference (58) and disidentification's rejection of it (62). TRC testimonies, Ratcliffe writes, "were 'simply' allowed to lie alongside one another as a cultural quilt whose purpose was to provide an understanding of the past in hopes of reinventing the future" (74).

[46]Richard C. Marback, *Managing Vulnerability: South Africa's Struggle for a Democratic Rhetoric* (Columbia: University of South Carolina Press, 2012), 85-104. For a more thorough summary of Marback's *Managing Vulnerability*, see my review of the book (James E. Beitler, Review of *Managing Vulnerability: South Africa's Struggle for a Democratic Rhetoric*, by Richard C. Marback, *Rhetoric Review* 32, no. 4 [2013]: 490-93). Michael Battle links vulnerability to Tutu's conceptualization of *ubuntu*, noting, "Ubuntu is the environment of vulnerability" ("Ubuntu," 416). And Jennifer M. McBride discusses vulnerability in the context of Lent in her book *Radical Discipleship* (128-30).

[47]Marback, *Managing Vulnerability*, 86.

is consistent with Tutu's notion of *ubuntu*. Both even-handedness and *ubuntu* demand that people "become vulnerable [yet] have integrity," seeking accountability for past wrongs "without allowing [their] pain to embitter the present."[48]

To summarize the preceding points, Tutu established a constitutive rhetoric of interdependence through his claims about *ubuntu*, his depictions of Mandela and the TRC, and his own appeals to *ēthos*—which involved a willingness to position himself in the midst of volatile situations on behalf of others as well as a willingness to listen to others even-handedly. While a significant number of South Africans embraced Tutu's constitutive rhetoric, many white Afrikaners simply chose not to participate in the TRC process. And yet some were deeply moved by Tutu's words. South African journalist Antjie Krog was one such Afrikaner, and her response to Tutu and the TRC offers a powerful illustration of the rhetoric of interdependence taking hold in another person's life and work.

"I Was Scorched / A New Skin": Repentance in Antjie Krog's *Country of My Skull*

In *Country of My Skull: Guilt, Sorrow, and the Limits of Forgiveness in the New South Africa*, Krog presents readers with a collage-like account of the TRC's operation. The book is composed of stories, poems, and testimonies, pages and pages of which do not contain any commentary from Krog. It's also part memoir. Krog weaves her own testimony into her account of the TRC, and consequently, a good deal of scholarship has looked at the way in which she positions herself in the text. For example, Gillian Whitlock argues that

---

[48]Marback, *Managing Vulnerability*, 96-97, 103. "Tutu's even-handedness," Marback writes, "refuses to dehumanize the victims of apartheid by refusing to compromise on what is just and unjust, while also refusing to constrain the humanity of post-apartheid South Africans of all colors by holding out hope for forgiveness. . . . For Tutu, *ubuntu* is the strongest expression of this sense of integrating past, present, and future" (96). For more on Tutu's rhetoric of *ubuntu*, see Marback, *Managing Vulnerability*, 20-21, 102-103.

Krog's memoir "becomes a way of reinventing the self as an ethical subject."[49] This move, Whitlock claims, functions as "a gesture of reconciliation," and it also allows Krog to explore the difficulties of representing trauma.[50] Laura Moss contends that Krog establishes not one but four different subject positions for herself in the text, and that her creation of multiple first-person narrators "illustrates the . . . fragmented subject who emerges from the forced separation of people and communities."[51] According to Moss, the creation of several narrators "convincingly expresses the ambiguity of Afrikaner responses to the process of reconciliation."[52] For Carli Coetzee, what is important about Krog's positioning work is that it allows her to "publicly distance" herself from the "language . . . of the men of her race" and to identify herself with "what she calls the country of her skull, a country into which she wishes to be invited by black South Africans."[53] (It is a move that, according to Coetzee, Krog can never quite manage, since her Afrikaner identity is part and parcel of who she is.) According to Kay Schaffer and Sidonie Smith, Krog's identification with her Afrikaner identity is actually crucially important to the rhetorical work that the text is doing. They note how the truth commission constructed "victim" and "perpetrator" as "binary identities" and failed to account for the position of the "beneficiary"—"those who benefited from the everyday policies and practices of the apartheid regime."[54] Beneficiaries "were neither identified [by the TRC] as complicit in

---

[49]Gillian Whitlock, "Consuming Passions: Reconciliation in Women's Intellectual Memoir," *Tulsa Studies in Women's Literature* 23, no. 1 (2004): 14.

[50]Whitlock, "Consuming Passions," 14, 25-26.

[51]Laura Moss, "'Nice Audible Crying': Editions, Testimonies, and *Country of My Skull*," *Research in African Literatures* 37, no. 4 (2006): 91.

[52]Moss, "Nice Audible Crying," 99.

[53]Carli Coetzee, "'They Never Wept, the Men of My Race': Antjie Krog's *Country of My Skull* and the White South African Signature," *Journal of Southern African Studies* 27, no. 4 (2001): 685.

[54]Kay Schaffer and Sidonie Smith, "Human Rights, Storytelling, and the Position of the Beneficiary: Antjie Krog's *Country of My Skull*," *PMLA* 121, no. 5 (2006): 1577.

perpetuating systemic violence nor called to account."[55] Shaffer and Smith consider how Krog's book helps to establish this important subject position.[56]

A gesture of reconciliation, a testament to the fragmentation of identity, a representation of reconciliation's ambiguities, an act of distancing and identification, a deconstruction of binaries: Krog's *Country of My Skull* probably functions in many or all of these ways simultaneously. In what follows, however, I synthesize several ideas from this past scholarship to show that Krog also uses the book to affirm Tutu's rhetoric and, ultimately, to repent.[57]

Krog's portrait of Tutu in *Country of My Skull* is a tender, even loving, one.[58] She gives us multiple scenes of Tutu at prayer—describing him as both a "man interceding" and a "man praying"—and highlights his insight and wisdom throughout the text. She does not hide the fact that the TRC process took a great toll on Tutu, yet she balances her descriptions of Tutu's weariness with frequent illustrations of his good humor. He is "humanity at its fullest—humanity as it was meant to be." He is also presented as absolutely crucial to the TRC process and the country's transition from apartheid to democracy. When Tutu is hospitalized to undergo cancer testing, Krog notes, "The process is unthinkable without Tutu. Impossible." A few pages later, she adds, "We cannot finish what we have started without this man." "Don't look so concerned," Tutu tells her when she visits him

---

[55]Schaffer and Smith, "Human Rights," 1577.

[56]Schaffer and Smith, "Human Rights," 1579.

[57]Note that I am not arguing that the text functions as a conversion narrative. As Carli Coetzee notes, "Narratives of conversion can too easily be self-referential in the sense that they perform the author's self-absolution," and I think Coetzee is right when she claims that Krog avoids "self-consolation" ("They Never Wept," 691). It is also worth noting that, while Coetzee and I cite some of the same passages in what follows, my argument differs from hers in that I focus on *Country of My Skull* as a response to Tutu and an act of repentance.

[58]The examples and quotations in this paragraph appear on the following pages of *Country of My Skull: Guilt, Sorrow, and the Limits of Forgiveness in the New South Africa* (New York: Three Rivers, 2000): 63, 201, 203-4, 206-7.

in the hospital. "I will be okay . . . besides, we are fighting . . . on the side of the angels."

In addition to praising his leadership of the TRC process, Krog stresses how crucial Tutu's language is for South Africans, herself included. Early in the book, Krog records a conversation that she had with friend and colleague Mondli as the hearings were getting underway. After Mondli celebrates the fact that South Africans "are finally breaking through to one another" and Krog refers to their "common humanity," Mondli laughs and says, "We're all starting to talk like Tutu."[59] Later in the book, Krog amplifies Mondli's point: "Whatever role others might play, it is Tutu who is the compass. He guides us in several ways, the most important of which is language. It is he who finds language for what is happening."[60] Tutu's language, Krog adds, "shoots up like fire" and "drags people along with the process." Though only the views of one person, Krog's comments here provide at least some confirmation that the archbishop's constitutive rhetoric has been successful.

Additionally, Tutu's language of *ubuntu* permeates the book. In one chapter, Krog provides her readers with an extended definition of the concept, and she also offers us several illustrations that highlight what Tutu's *ubuntu* looks like in practice.[61] While visiting Tutu in the hospital, for example, Krog recalls the story of Chris Hani's funeral, one of the most famous times that Tutu "waded into the fray." The situation was indeed explosive. People were absolutely incensed about Hani's assassination, and the funeral orations for the anti-apartheid activist were "furiously bitter."[62] "But Tutu got up," Krog writes, "spoke into that crowd of thousands, and got them—all of

---

[59]Krog, *Country of My Skull*, 61.
[60]Krog, *Country of My Skull*, 201.
[61]Krog, *Country of My Skull*, 143.
[62]Krog, *Country of My Skull*, 203.

them—to wave their hands in the air, saying, 'We are all God's children—black and white.'" To give a second example, Krog's book records that when members of the National Party threatened to sue the TRC, Tutu stressed just how much everyone in the country needed each other if reconciliation was to become a reality.[63] Krog includes Tutu's remarks about F. W. de Klerk, the last South African president to serve during apartheid: "You see, we can't go to heaven alone. If I arrive there, God will ask me: 'Where is De Klerk? His path crossed yours.' And he also—God will ask him: 'Where is Tutu?' So I cried for him, I cried for De Klerk—because he spurned the opportunity to become human."

Krog's most powerful affirmation of Tutu's rhetoric, however, is her own gesture of repentance and desire for belonging in the new South Africa. The notion of repentance as presented in Scripture requires that an individual *turn around* by acknowledging one's past sins and changing one's course, and as we will see in what follows, Krog certainly uses *Country of My Skull* to turn from past wrongdoing. That said, she does not repent solely (or even primarily) of her own individual acts; instead, she grapples with her identity as an Afrikaner who, though not personally responsible for human rights abuses, nonetheless benefited from the evils of apartheid.[64] While Krog cannot completely jettison her Afrikaner identity, she does, as Coetzee notes, distance herself from it at various points throughout the book, and these episodes can be read as the means by which she turns and ultimately comes to a place where she is able to ask for forgiveness in the book's closing pages.[65]

---

[63]Krog, *Country of My Skull*, 209-10.

[64]Shaffer and Smith, "Human Rights," 1577.

[65]By simultaneously distancing herself from other Afrikaners (as Coetzee suggests) and establishing her own beneficiary position (as Shaffer and Smith demonstrate), Krog is able to speak against injustice in South Africa without succumbing to self-justification, to condemn evil while acknowledging her own role in it.

For one thing, she stridently condemns the actions of many National Party leaders and cuts herself off from many other Afrikaners as well.[66] When she confronts P. W. Botha about his crimes, for example, Botha snaps back at her, and she realizes that she cannot identify with the man: "I try to find a pathway in my thoughts to him. A link. An Afrikaner connection. No. I can still find common ground with those who are battling to deal with a dramatically changed order, with our part in the past—but with this swaggering fool, there is nothing."[67] Rejecting P. W. Botha and what he stands for may not seem like a particularly impressive act of turning from one's past, but Krog does not stop there. Other instances in which she turns from her Afrikaner identity throughout the book are much more costly to her personally.

In one episode, which Krog recounts in an early chapter of the book, she finds herself questioning the actions of her own brother.[68] The scene takes place on her family's farm. Krog recounts being woken up in the night by the sound of her brothers, Andries and Hendrick, talking urgently on the family shortwave radio. She hears Andries say that someone is trying to take the family's cattle and that Hendrick should come with his gun. After that, Krog and her parents remain by the radio, listening anxiously and waiting. When they hear what sounds like gunfire, Krog finds herself wondering, "Who did the shooting? Who has been shot? And which is worse? What fierce scenes are being played out in the veld?" The next morning Antjie's brothers tell her what happened over breakfast: they had confronted the thieves, hoping that they did not have guns—and the thieves had fled. When Andries suggests that *he* is the victim by claiming that he has "become brutalized" and is "learning to fight, to kill, to hate,"

---

[66]Coetzee, "They Never Wept," 689-90.
[67]Krog, *Country of My Skull*, 354.
[68]Krog, *Country of My Skull*, 7-8.

Krog challenges him: "Ja, but it was always like that for millions of black people."[69]

Krog ends the chapter by recounting a conversation with Mondli about theft. Mondli says he was raised to believe that "stealing from whites is actually not stealing," adding, "Way back, Africans had no concept of stealing other than taking cattle as a means of contesting power. But you whiteys came and accused us of stealing—while at that very same minute you were stealing everything from us!"[70] Ending the chapter with these comments allows Krog to call into question Andries's contention that he has been wronged. The truth is more complex. Apartheid created an unjust set of laws, some of which forced many people from their land. In such a society, some actions deemed illegal may not be immoral. To move beyond apartheid, so-called illegal acts like trespassing and stealing need to be understood in light of the contexts and histories that gave rise to those acts. Thus, through the juxtaposition of the cattle-stealing episode on her family farm and Mondli's comments about stealing, Krog acknowledges that she and her family members are implicated in the policies of apartheid and begins to turn her back on such policies. In the process, of course, she distances herself from her brothers and their views.[71]

Later in the book, Krog distances herself from her mother's views as well. She does so by indirectly challenging the views that her mother expressed in a highly nationalistic essay written in Afrikaans.[72] In Carli Coetzee's article, she persuasively shows how Krog, by translating her mother's piece from Afrikaans into English, uses

---

[69]Krog, *Country of My Skull*, 17.

[70]Krog, *Country of My Skull*, 18.

[71]Schaffer and Smith, "Human Rights," 1580.

[72]Krog, *Country of My Skull*, 124-25. In the piece, her mother wrote, "I prayed that my hand should fall off if I ever write something for my personal honor at the cost of my people and what has been negotiated for them through years of tears and blood; that I will always remember that to write in Afrikaans is not a right, but a privilege bought and paid for at a price—and that it brings with it heavy responsibilities" (125).

the episode to reject the language of Afrikaners. Krog's book constructs an "argument for the necessity of betraying the language of
the ancestors."[73] During apartheid, Afrikaans was a means of shor-
ing up inequalities, and the language has become so intertwined
with injustice that Krog feels she must turn her back on her mother
tongue and thus, to some degree, her mother. She completes this
turn in her poem at the end of the book when she suggests that the
language of the new South Africa will be one of "soft intimate clicks
and gutturals."[74]

As Krog turns her back on aspects of her identity, she finds that she
is also distanced from her own children. Reporting on the TRC, she
writes about "becoming a family" with her fellow journalists, but such
bonds come at a price.[75] In the very next paragraph, she describes
what it is like to come back to her house and family after covering the
hearings: "I walk into my home one evening. My family are excitedly
watching cricket on television. They seem like a happy, close-knit
group. I stand in the dark kitchen for a long time. Everything has
become unconnected and unfamiliar. I realize that I don't even know
where the light switch is."[76] The contrasts that Krog sets up in this
passage—the brightness of the television versus the darkness of the
kitchen, the play of a cricket match (with all of its English associations) versus the difficult work of the South African TRC, the family's
excitement and happiness versus Krog's motionlessness and disorien-
tation, the connection among her family members versus her own
feelings of disconnectedness—all reinforce the turn that Krog is
making from her biological family to her fellow journalists and,

---

[73]Coetzee, "They Never Wept," 690. Schaffer and Smith also point to this episode as one that
"locate[s] the narrator in and also distance[s] her from a conservative Afrikaner family"
("Human Rights," 1580).
[74]Krog, *Country of My Skull*, 364. Coetzee, "They Never Wept," 687, 692-93.
[75]Krog, *Country of My Skull*, 63.
[76]Krog, *Country of My Skull*, 63.

ultimately, to the TRC. Krog's defamiliarization continues a few pages later. She writes, "I enter my house like a stranger. And barren. I sit around for days. Staring. My youngest walks into the room and starts. 'Sorry, I'm not used to you being home.'"[77] Then, anticipating the inclusion of her mother's essay later in the book, Krog echoes a phrase of her mother's: "No poetry should come forth from this. May my hand fall off if I write this."[78] No longer comfortable in her own home, Krog is, to cite Exodus, "a stranger in a strange land" (Ex 2:22).

Through the stories she tells in *Country of My Skull,* Krog turns from her leaders, her language, and her family. Ultimately, and most personally, she turns away from her*self*. This turn begins during the TRC hearings. As Krog listens to the testimony of the victims of human rights abuses, she loses hair and teeth and, most notably, develops rashes.[79] Krog's report of her physical reaction to the testimony is a significant (and often-discussed) moment in the narrative: Shaffer and Smith note that the rash is a means by which she identifies with the victims.[80] The testimonies of the TRC witnesses, they write, "infect the narrator with a horror she internationalizes, takes on in her body." Coeztee suggests that the rash also speaks to Krog's self-rejection.[81] As a result of what she learns from the TRC, her own body turns from itself.

But Krog's self-rejection is not the final word. In her poem at the end of the book, Krog suggests that the TRC hearings have also been transformative. She writes, "The retina learns to expand / daily because by a thousand stories / I was scorched / A new skin / I am changed forever."[82] The imagery here is overflowing with meaning. Once again, it serves to identify Krog with the victims: many bodies were incinerated during

---

[77]Krog, *Country of My Skull*, 65.
[78]Krog, *Country of My Skull*, 66.
[79]Krog, *Country of My Skull*, 65.
[80]Schaffer and Smith, "Human Rights," 1581.
[81]Coetzee, "They Never Wept," 693.
[82]Krog, *Country of My Skull*, 364-65.

the apartheid years.[83] And it also attests to Krog's rejection of herself and her heritage: Coetzee notes that the "image of the scorched skin . . . speaks of the desire to shed the white skin that connects the author to her ancestral shame."[84] But the imagery also bears witness to another aspect of Krog's transformation. The TRC testimonies were, to borrow language from Malachi 2, a fire that has refined Krog. Her skin has been figuratively blackened and her point of view—her "retina"—expanded. She concludes the poem with a litany of forgiveness and an appeal for reconciliation, pleading, "Forgive me / forgive me / forgive me / You whom I have wronged, please / take me / with you."[85]

In one of the final scenes before the book's epilogue, Krog recalls covering a TRC event on Robben Island—the site off of the coast of Cape Town where Mandela and many others were once held prisoner. Gazing back at the mainland, Krog is overcome with emotion and offers us a final vision of *ubuntu*: "There is a rawness in my chest. It is mine. I belong to that continent. My gaze, my eyes, are one with the thousands of others that have looked back over the centuries toward Africa. Ours. Mine. Yes, I would die for this. It slips out, like a smooth holy sound. And I realize that it is the commission alone that has brought me to these moments of fierce belonging."[86] Journeying back from the island by boat, Krog watches Tutu, who is, fittingly, riding in the prow of the vessel.[87] "Because of him," she concludes.

---

[83]Tutu, *No Future*, 129-30.

[84]Coetzee, "They Never Wept," 693. Coetzee suggests that Krog's writing does not convey the desire to "to be black" (which, Coetzee notes, would be "problematic in many ways") but rather the longing "to be heard and acknowledged by a black audience" (695-96). She adds that *Country of My Skull* is "aware of the limitations and contradictions in such a move" (696).

[85]Krog, *Country of My Skull*, 365. As further support for my argument, Laura Moss suggests that Krog's poem draws on the language of a sermon of Tutu's from 1990 entitled "We Forgive You" (Moss, "Nice Audible Crying," 92). Coetzee and Schaffer and Smith reference the poem as well. Coetzee calls attention to Krog's rejection of her skin ("They Never Wept," 692-93). Schaffer and Smith argue that, in her plea to be forgiven, "Krog invokes an abstract universality as the foundation of a common humanity and of reconciliation" ("Human Rights," 1582). This call for forgiveness reverses racialized divisions that marked the apartheid era.

[86]Krog, *Country of My Skull*, 363. See also Coetzee, "They Never Wept," 695.

[87]Krog, *Country of My Skull*, 363.

Lenten Witnesses

Whether or not Tutu's rhetoric was appropriate given the TRC's state-sponsored authority, his call to interdependence and Krog's response to it serve as a powerful reminder to the church about what Christian witness to the world must look like: the shape of our witness must never be far from postures and practices we embrace during Lent.[88] Developing as a liturgical response to Christ's period of prayer and fasting in the desert in preparation for his public ministry, Lent is a forty-day season that begins with an image akin to scorched skin. On the first day of Lent, Christians throughout the world gather at their churches to celebrate the Ash Wednesday liturgy, during which the priest dips a finger into a bowl of ashes and uses them to draw the sign of the cross on parishioners' foreheads. While doing so, the priest often echoes words that God declared to Adam after he sinned in the Garden of Eden (Gen 3:19). _Remember that "you are dust, and to dust you shall return."_ This temporary scarring is meant to remind Christians of our sin, our resultant mortality, and our need for Christ's grace and forgiveness. During the remainder of the Lenten season, Christians prepare to celebrate Easter through acts of prayer, self-examination, penitence, and charity toward others. Like the season of Advent, Lent places a strong emphasis on our need for repentance, and the color most often associated with it is purple—which, as I have noted, Tutu wore throughout the TRC's public hearings. Since that time, the garb has become a fixed aspect of his public persona. Tutu is the priest in purple, a living embodiment of the call to "celebrate a holy Lent."

---

[88]In addition to Tutu's calls for repentance, his careful listening and expressions of lament during the TRC hearings were also deeply Lenten practices. Jennifer M. McBride writes, "The social and political significance of Lent and Holy Week is . . . _lament_—the ability to open oneself up to the pains and needs of the world. This may only happen when we _listen_ to the depth of suffering experienced by people victimized by structural sin and grieve the ways we have overlooked or ignored the pain" (_Radical Discipleship_, 122-23, emphases added).

The wisdom of the Lenten season—which is, in many ways, exemplified in Tutu's rhetoric and Krog's response—includes a reminder to Christians that, as fallen humans who live in interdependence with other humans, we ourselves sin and are often the beneficiaries of systemic injustice. In light of our fallenness and the fallenness of the world, our witness must involve acts of private and public repentance—our own turnings—alongside our call to others to repentance. In fact, the power of our witness may ultimately rest not in our ability to convince others of their need for repentance but in our willingness to make ourselves vulnerable to others by confessing to—and actively seeking to redress—the injustices we have perpetuated.

As I alluded to in the previous chapter, theologian Jennifer McBride develops an argument along similar lines in her important book, *The Church for the World: A Theology of Public Witness*. McBride notes that, all too often, Protestant churches in the United States practice a "theology of glory" in place of a "theology of the cross," resulting in a warped view of "a dominating God" and a distorted understanding of the church's place in the world.[89] Such views about God have significant consequences for Christian witness. McBride writes, "A privileged and affluent community trying to reflect this [dominating] God will be formed by that domineering image, becoming—perhaps without even noticing—a self-assured and/or defensive people."[90] When that happens, the form that our presentation of the gospel takes can undermine the content of the message, hindering our ability to serve as ambassadors of the One who chose the form of the cross as his primary bearing in relation to the world. To respond to this problem, McBride draws on the writings of Dietrich Bonhoeffer and others, arguing that an important and neglected posture of public witness for

---

[89]McBride, *Radical Discipleship*, 5.
[90]McBride, *Radical Discipleship*, 5.

Christians to take on is "confession of sin unto repentance."[91] "Protestant churches in the United States," she writes, "may witness to Christ in a nontriumphal manner through an overlapping confession of their own sin and the sin of broader society, which finds public expression in repentant activity."[92] To be effective witnesses, churches must admit and take responsibility for their own wrongdoing as well as their complicity in social and institutional sins, which inevitably occur when we participate in public life.

Lent concludes with Holy Week, during which we contemplate Christ's triumphal entry into Jerusalem on Palm Sunday, his establishment of the Lord's Supper (as well as his acts of foot-washing and prayer) on Maundy Thursday, his crucifixion on Good Friday, the deep silence of the tomb on Holy Saturday, and his resurrection on Easter Sunday. Like Tutu's speeches and writings, the worship practices of Holy Week are part of a constitutive rhetoric, calling us to an interdependence that is, in this case, grounded in the person and work of Jesus Christ.[93] By confessing and repenting of our sins, reconciling with one another, sharing in the Eucharist, washing one another's feet, and praying together through the night, we allow ourselves to be constituted as the people of God—a people who bear witness to God's reconciling love for the whole world.[94]

---

[91]McBride, *Radical Discipleship*, 16.

[92]McBride, *Radical Discipleship*, 6.

[93]Though Tutu was often criticized for Christianizing the TRC process, his descriptions of *ubuntu* read in the context of the church may not ultimately go far enough for Christians, since they are not always clearly grounded upon the person and work of Jesus Christ. Even as the Holy Week liturgies affirm that our personhood is bound up with others, they go further than Tutu's *ubuntu*, highlighting the Person upon whom all our lives depend.

[94]The notion that liturgy is constitutive of character and community is not new, as even a brief survey of definitions of the term illustrates. Theologian Maggi Dawn defines liturgy, etymologically, as "work that is first for God, that also transforms our world and benefits people" ("Liturgy—It's *Not* the Work of the People," *Maggidawn.net*, September 21, 2009). Theologian Simon Chan defines liturgy as "the people's common response to [God's Word], their acceptance of the Word, which constitutes them as the covenant people"—and later Chan notes, "Worship . . . makes or realizes the church" (*Liturgical Theology* [Downers Grove, IL: InterVarsity Press, 2006], 40, 46). And philosopher James K. A. Smith defines liturgies as "rituals of ultimate

Viewing our worship practices as a Christ-centered constitutive rhetoric productively blurs the distinction that many Christians make between worship and witness. Consider, by way of conclusion, how the Holy Week liturgy known as the stations of the cross positions worshipers as witnesses.

The stations of the cross grew out of Christian pilgrimages to the Holy Land, a centuries-old practice. When early pilgrims journeyed to Jerusalem, many "wanted to follow literally in the footsteps of Jesus, tracing the path from Pilate's house to Calvary."[95] As generation after generation walked along Christ's path to Golgotha, it became customary to stop at fixed points along the way—often designated as holy places—to worship, pray, or meditate on particular aspects of the Passion narrative. When the Franciscans were charged with maintaining these sites of pilgrimage toward the end of the fourteenth century, they "erected tableaux [at these stops] to aid the devotion of the visitors."[96] In the middle of the fifteenth century, Englishman William Wey went on two of these pilgrimages to Jerusalem, and his account of the experiences contains the earliest known instance in which the pilgrims' stops are described as "stations."[97] As the devotional practice grew in popularity—promoted in large part by the work of the Franciscans—it began to be practiced elsewhere. In the seventeenth and eighteenth centuries, it became increasingly common for stations

---

concern: rituals that are formative for identity, that inculcate particular visions of the good life, and do so in a way that means to trump other ritual formations. . . . They are a certain species of ritual practice that aim to do nothing less than shape our identity by shaping our desire for what we envision as the kingdom—the ideal of human flourishing" (*Desiring the Kingdom* [Grand Rapids: Baker Academic, 2009], 86-87). Taken together, these definitions suggest that liturgy is constitutive on several levels. It constitutes the character of individual Christians, the community of the people of God, and the world itself (or so we hope).

[95]*Common Worship: Services and Prayers for the Church of England: Times and Seasons* (London: Church House Publishing, 2006), 236.

[96]*Common Worship*, 236.

[97]Colin Morris, "Pilgrimage to Jerusalem in the Late Middle Ages," in *Pilgrimage: The English Experience from Becket to Bunyan*, ed. Colin Morris and Peter Roberts (New York: Cambridge University Press, 2002), 141.

to be erected *inside* Franciscan churches, and in 1741 Pope Benedict XIV urged *all* priests to put up stations in their churches.[98]

Contemporary congregations that practice the stations of the cross typically arrange images depicting the story of Christ's Passion on the walls of the nave. For much of the year, the images remain on the periphery of (but are never incidental to) the church's worship practices. However, on Good Friday, the periphery becomes the center. During the worship service, the clergy (and, in some churches, all of the worshipers) travel from station to station, meditating on events from Christ's final hours and his death. The placement of the stations on the walls of the nave is significant. As the clergy process from station to station over the course of the service, they travel the liminal space between the church and the world. Because members of the congregation face or join this processional, they find themselves turning in a complete circle through the course of the liturgy, directing their gaze at the suffering Christ on the walls of the church and, beyond the images of the suffering Christ, to the suffering world beyond—north, south, east, and west. Unlike the militaristic version of the stations with which I opened the chapter, this one encourages Christians to witness in and through our own vulnerability and brokenness.[99] The movements that the service asks of individual worshipers serve as a call to embody the character of Christ and to go forth, processing through the world, bearing his cruciform likeness.

---

[98]Darius Liutikas and Alfonsas Motuzas, "The Pilgrimage to the Hill of Crosses: Devotional Practices and Identities," in *Redefining Pilgrimage: New Perspectives on Historical and Contemporary Pilgrimages*, ed. Antón M. Pazos (Burlington: Ashgate, 2014), 120.

[99]Jennifer M. McBride captures the dynamic of looking at the world in and through the suffering Messiah when she writes, "The crucified Christ commands that we turn to his cross for salvation and see in him all of society's victims; for when we turn towards our victims in repentance and reconciliation, we transcend the victim-oppressor cycle and are liberated into beloved community" (*Radical Discipleship*, 151-52).

But the movement of the service also encircles all those who happen to make their way into the building. As such, the rhetorical force of the stations of the cross has, to borrow a phrase from James K. A. Smith, "centripetal and centrifugal dynamics."[100] Even as the liturgy prepares worshipers for witness outside the church, it calls them, as well as any visitors present, inward. In this respect, the rhetorical activity that takes place during the stations of the cross serves as an apt metaphor for the rhetoric of all orthodox worship. By participating in worship, individuals are called to adopt particular appeals to character out in the world and, at the same time, constituted as a people—the people of God!—who together create a rhetorical dwelling place for wanderers and wayfarers. Christian witness in this context does not simply involve a discussion between a single Christian and his or her non-Christian audience member but immersion (to draw on baptismal language), in which the audience is surrounded by the worshiping body of the crucified Christ. And in the worshiping congregation, the message of the cross, which is pure foolishness in the world, functions as common sense. It is, therefore, in and among worshiping Christians that the kind of rhetoric practiced by Tutu may be at its most persuasive.

---

[100]James K. A. Smith, *Imagining the Kingdom* (Grand Rapids: Baker Academic, 2013), 156. This section of my argument draws heavily on Smith's views about worship and mission (153-57).

5

HOSTING THE GUEST

Marilynne Robinson and the *Ēthos* of Eastertide

How lovely is your dwelling place,
O LORD of hosts!

PSALM 84:1

Whoever feeds on my flesh and drinks my blood has eternal life, and I will
raise him up on the last day. For my flesh is true food, and my blood is
true drink. Whoever feeds on my flesh and drinks by blood abides in me,
and I in him.

JOHN 6:54-56

We do not presume to come to this thy Table, O merciful Lord, trusting
in our own righteousness, but in thy manifold and great mercies. We
are not worthy so much as to gather up the crumbs under thy Table. But
thou art the same Lord whose property is always to have mercy. Grant us
therefore, gracious Lord, so to eat the flesh of thy dear Son Jesus Christ,
and to drink his blood, that we may evermore dwell in him, and he in
us. Amen.

THE PRAYER OF HUMBLE ACCESS, THE BOOK OF COMMON PRAYER

Today was Lord's Supper, and I preached on Mark 14:22, "And as they were
eating, he took bread, and when he had blessed, he brake it, and gave to
them, and said, Take ye: this is my body." Normally I would not preach
on the Words of Institution themselves when the Sacrament is the most
beautiful illumination of them there could be. But I have been thinking
a great deal about the body these last weeks. Blessed and broken. I used
Genesis 32:23-32 as the Old Testament text, Jacob wrestling with the Angel.
I wanted to talk about the gift of physical particularity and how blessing and

sacrament are mediated through it. I have been thinking lately how I have loved my physical life.

MARILYNNE ROBINSON, GILEAD

IN HER GILEAD TRILOGY, Marilynne Robinson invites readers to dwell with characters for whom the Christian faith matters deeply. The characters' stances in relation to faith differ considerably—we are presented with individuals who find Christianity to be truthful and familiar (John Ames and Robert Boughton), familiar yet alienating (Jack and, to some extent, Glory), alienating and strange (Doll and Doane), and strange yet truthful (Lila)—but few in Robinson's world are spared confrontation with Christian truths, and many must wrestle with its most vexing problems, predestination central among them. On this side of Robinson's Pulitzer Prize for *Gilead,* it is easy to overlook what a risk that first book in the trilogy must have been. The publication of an unhurried epistolary novel written from the point of view of a frail pastor living in what some would consider to be the middle of nowhere and exploring what Robinson elsewhere refers to as a "thorny doctrine" of Calvinism is itself a marvel.[1] However, the magnitude of Robinson's accomplishment comes into full view when we turn to reviews of *Gilead* and the two subsequent novels in her trilogy, *Home* and *Lila.* Reviews indicate that Robinson's books have found acclaim among Christians and non-Christians alike, revitalizing stale religious concepts in the process.[2] Some reviewers even claim that the books have made faith's unseen realities more believable

---

[1]Marilynne Robinson, "Marguerite de Navarre," in *The Death of Adam: Essays on Modern Thought* (New York: Picador, 2005), 187.

[2]Regarding the last point, A. O. Scott's review of *Home* for *The New York Times* states that Robinson "is somehow able to infuse what can sound like dowdy, common words—words like courtesy and kindness, shame and forgiveness, transgression and grace—with a startling measure of their old luster and gravity" ("Return of the Prodigal Son," *The New York Times,* September 19, 2008).

and faith's central questions more significant for unbelievers—a fact worth further exploration by those interested in the intersections of Christianity and rhetoric.[3] The present chapter asks, therefore, What does the Gilead trilogy, along with the favorable reception it has received, have to teach us about the rhetoric of Christian witness?

The persuasiveness of Robinson's trilogy, I suggest in what follows, results in part from the rhetorical character of the world that she invites us to inhabit. In the Gilead trilogy, Robinson doesn't recite the creeds or preach at us; rather, she acts more like a faithful church usher, who is always at her post, Sunday after Sunday. She makes the place more habitable, welcomes us in, and then turns our attention forward, to the sacraments of baptism and the Eucharist. In doing so, she points us to the new life. Borrowing a line from Robinson's book *Housekeeping,* Jennifer L. Holberg has remarked that Robinson's writing involves the "resurrection of the ordinary."[4] The description seems particularly apt to me because it signals her narrative world's sacramental character as well as the way that her landscapes (and the stories of their inhabitants) seem to bend and strain toward rebirth and final homecoming. In and through the elements of Robinson's dwelling places, we are presented with an earthly glimpse of the resurrection life. Her rhetoric beckons us toward the realities of the Easter season.

Thomas F. Haddox's insightful book *Hard Sayings: The Rhetoric of Christian Orthodoxy in Late Modern Fiction* is a useful place to begin

---

[3]In a review of *Gilead* in *Slate,* Ann Hulbert remarks, "What elicits tears at the book's close . . . is a highly unusual literary experience: Robinson (in her role as author of this creation) allows even a faithless reader to feel the possibility of a transcendent order, thanks to which mercy can reign among people on Earth" (quoted in Lisa M. Siefker Bailey, "Fraught with Fire: Race and Theology in Marilynne Robinson's *Gilead,*" *Christianity and Literature* 59, no. 2 [2010]: 276). And Cathleen Schine, in her review of *Lila* for *The New York Review of Books,* writes, "Robinson poses doctrinal questions about predestination and grace, about the afterlife and who will be there and who will not, serious questions only for the sincerest of believers, yet they become serious in Robinson's telling for the rest of us as well" ("A Triumph of Love," *The New York Review of Books* 61, no. 16 [2014]).

[4]Jennifer L. Holberg, "'The Courage to See It': Toward an Understanding of Glory," *Christianity and Literature* 59, no. 2 (2010): 283.

a discussion of Robinson's rhetoric. Haddox explores the persuasive power of Christian doctrine in the works of Robinson and five other late-modern writers, not just for Christian readers but also "among educated audiences most committed to secular principles."[5] Christianity's force and continued relevance comes through clearly in Haddox's account; however, while his overarching argument is both persuasive and encouraging, I am not convinced by all of his claims about Robinson. What is rhetorically notable about Robinson's works, Haddox argues, is not so much her own affirmation of orthodoxy but rather her employment of orthodoxy for other "political and aesthetic" ends.[6] On Haddox's reading, Robinson's works privilege believers' experiences over their doctrinal commitments and make use of Christian belief to promote humanistic values, especially equality.[7] But while "Robinson succeeds in making Christian orthodoxy attractive to her readers," there is a cost: she "does so in a way that emphasizes cultural critique instead of truth—and in doing so empties it of much of its specificity."[8] Later Haddox suggests that Robinson casts off those aspects of Calvinism that do not line up with her views as a liberal humanist.[9] Robinson leaves us, he seems to imply, with the husk of truth, not its fruit.

I agree that Robinson cares deeply about religious experience and uses orthodoxy in the ways Haddox describes, but I have reservations with his suggestion that Robinson gives less importance to the "question of whether Christian orthodoxy is true" and does not emphasize a "commitment to it" in her Gilead novels.[10] At issue here is what counts as a commitment to Christian orthodoxy within the genre of the novel, and I think that the view presented in *Hard*

---

[5]Thomas F. Haddox, *Hard Sayings: The Rhetoric of Christian Orthodoxy in Late Modern Fiction* (Columbus: Ohio State University Press, 2013), 20.

[6]Haddox, *Hard Sayings*, 19-20, 166, 188, 202.

[7]Haddox, *Hard Sayings*, 20, 188, 202.

[8]Haddox, *Hard Sayings*, 20.

[9]Haddox, *Hard Sayings*, 192.

[10]Haddox, *Hard Sayings*, 188, 202.

Sayings may be too narrow. When Haddox states, for example, that Robinson's "treatment of Christian orthodoxy is more accurately described as a use of Christian orthodoxy than an argument in favor of it," he seems to restrict support for orthodoxy to argumentative and expositional modes of discourse, the consequence being that he neglects to fully consider how Robinson might use narration—and, in particular, the relationship between character and setting—in her books to bear witness to truth.[11] In relation to this point, we would do well to remember that many of the words we use to express our opinions and beliefs (stance, position, standpoint, perspective, attitude, outlook, viewpoint) have spatial connotations, calling attention not only to our discursive assertions but also to our places and postures in the world. Keeping that in mind, I want to suggest in the pages that follow that Robinson's commitment and witness to Christian orthodoxy, and to Christian orthodoxy as true, may be less akin to the zealous defense of a claim and more like the loyal and hospitable occupation of a post.[12] Her narratives' affirmation of Christian hospitality—a form of obedience to Scripture's commands to care for outsiders and strangers—may itself represent a deep commitment to orthodoxy.[13]

---

[11]Haddox, *Hard Sayings*, 19-20. Likewise, in response to Haddox's assertion that Robinson "does not *press the claims* of whether the Calvinist Christianity that she advocates is true," I would respond that pressing a truth claim in narrative discourse might look very different than it does in argumentative and expository discourse (Haddox, *Hard Sayings*, 188, emphasis added).

[12]Rebecca M. Painter also reflects on the theme of loyalty in Robinson's prose ("Loyalty Meets Prodigality: The Reality of Grace in Marilynne Robinson's Fiction," *Christianity and Literature* 59, no. 2 [2010]: 321-40). Painter highlights the importance of loyalty to Robinson's thought, noting, "The essay 'Family' from Robinson's *The Death of Adam: Essays or Modern Thought* (1998) equates love with loyalty, declaring loyalty to be not only 'the antidote to fear, distrust, [and] self-interest' but also '[t]he balm for failure or weakness' (89). In the absence of loyalty, 'all attempts to prop the family economically or morally or through education or otherwise will fail. The real issue is, will people shelter and nourish and humanize one another? This is creative work, requiring discipline and imagination' (89). Robinson's novelistic endeavors take up this challenge" (321).

[13]In her book *Prophets of the Posthuman: American Fiction, Biotechnology, and the Ethics of Personhood* (Notre Dame: University of Notre Dame Press, 2013), Christina Bieber Lake rightly notes that *Gilead* presents us with "a powerful picture of an ethic of hospitality" (180). On a similar

Gilead itself would seem to make a similar point. One of the relevant scenes takes place, not insignificantly for my purposes, in John Ames's church. Alienated from his home, his family, and his family's faith, Jack Boughton visits Ames in his church, hoping, it would seem, to overcome his estrangement and find a place for himself—and, more important, for his African American wife and their child—in the racially and religiously homogeneous town of Gilead. Jack is not ready to tell Ames about his interracial family, so the conversation centers on a feeling of alienation that he can talk about and that Ames can, perhaps, help him rectify: his unbelief. As the discussion unfolds, Jack wants Ames to play the apologist's role, convincing him to believe in the truth of Christianity through argumentation. Here Robinson presents us with the apologist's dream scenario: imagine that a biblically literate unbeliever comes to you at your church desperately desiring to be convinced of Christianity's veracity.[14] But Ames resists, knowing from long experience that he can't give his namesake what he wants. Reflecting on the conversation later, he explains why he refuses "to defend religion" to people.[15] Doing so only serves to shore up their doubts, since "nothing true can be said about God from a posture of defense." Ames later elaborates on the point, giving the following advice in his long letter to his son, Robby: "Don't look for proofs. Don't bother with them at all. They are never sufficient to the question, and they're always a little impertinent, I think, because they claim for God a place within our conceptual grasp."[16] What is more, trying to prove one's beliefs has a disconcerting effect on the arguer. Even if the arguments persuade one's listeners, they tend to ring hollow to the

---

note, Alex Engebretson writes, "The drama of hospitality, whether to accept or reject the stranger, is Robinson's most persistent theme" ("Marilynne Robinson's Singular Vision," *The Millions*, November 24, 2014). Building off of such a claim, one of my aims in this chapter is to demonstrate how Robinson's novels rhetorically enact the hospitality that they illustrate.

[14] Marilynne Robinson, *Gilead: A Novel* (New York: Farrar, Straus, and Giroux, 2004), 171.

[15] Robinson, *Gilead*, 177.

[16] Robinson, *Gilead*, 179.

speaker. Ames then offers Robby the following counsel, based on Matthew 5:16: "'Let your works so shine before men,' etc. It was Coleridge who said Christianity is a life, not a doctrine, words to that effect."

Haddox suggests that these responses to Jack (as well as Ames's reflections on the scene later in the book) provide additional support for the claim that Robinson's "treatment of Christian orthodoxy is more accurately described as a use of Christian orthodoxy than an argument in favor of it."[17] For Haddox, Ames's refusal to answer Jack's questions about predestination seems to serve as further evidence that Robinson views "belief as experience" (as opposed to "belief as meaning") and that she wants to avoid taking up "inquiries into the truth of predestination—or, indeed, of any religious matters."[18] While Ames and Robinson do indeed care about belief as experience, I think that the primary purpose of these scenes is to acknowledge that, when trying to convince someone of the truth of Christianity, some modes of discourse should be used sparingly, if at all. Here it is important to note that, in refusing to answer Jack, Ames is not rejecting all truth claims or dismissing theological discussion entirely. Much of his life has, in fact, been spent reading theological arguments and engaging in debate with his best friend and fellow pastor, Robert Boughton. What Ames is questioning here (and what Robinson seems to be questioning through the character) is the profit of using argumentation to compel belief.[19]

---

[17]Robinson, *Gilead*, 19-20, 198-200.

[18]Robinson, *Gilead*, 199-200.

[19]Amy Hungerford (who is cited fairly extensively by Haddox) offers a related and extremely insightful reading of the discussions about predestination that take place in *Gilead* and *Home*, which hinges on two different views about what theological discourse is *for*. Hungerford writes, "Jack, a professed unbeliever, wants to be convinced through the conceptual content of religious discourse; his difference from his father and from Ames is only underscored by his lack of what Ames calls 'sympathy' with theology—his mistaking it for a discourse of answers rather than a discourse of relationship. He mistakes it, that is, for a discourse that could *produce* individual belief rather than a discourse that *enacts* shared belief" (*Postmodern Belief: American Literature and Religion since 1960* [Princeton: Princeton University Press, 2010], 118).

In the Coleridge quotation above, Ames offers his son an alternative to argumentative forms of witness: embodied faithfulness. And the very church building where Ames and Jack sit to discuss questions of belief provides an example of such embodied faithfulness in action: when doing that for which it was properly made (that is, enabling Christian worship), the church offers a more persuasive presentation of the truth of Christianity than Ames could ever hope to offer Jack with skillful argument.[20] Ames tells Jack, "When this old sanctuary is full of silence and prayer, every book Karl Barth ever will write would not be a feather in the scales against it from the point of view of profundity."[21]

By the end of Ames's long letter to his son, it would seem that he has come to see himself as exactly this sort of witness: one who has, despite his father's and brother's desertions of Gilead and dismissal of it as "a backwater," stood his ground and remained loyal to the Lord *and* loyal to his place in the world (which are two different things, as Ames notes).[22] "I love this town," he writes. "I think sometimes of going into the ground here as a last wild gesture of love—I too will smolder away the time until the great and general incandescence."[23] Likewise, at the end of *Home,* Glory decides to stay put in Gilead, awaiting the return of Jack's son and serving as a kind of steward of her family's memories of the place.[24] Robinson's world may, indeed, present us with a husk of truth, but this husk (a word that comes from

---

[20]Significantly for my purposes, Robinson's presentation of embodied faithfulness in her Gilead trilogy is congruent with what Jennifer M. McBride writes about Easter. McBride notes, "The significance of Easter is so much more than *mere belief* in the resurrection. Plenty of believers readily affirm that Jesus rose from the dead even as they maintain the status quo and deny the possibility of substantial this-worldly change. The significance of Easter is *embodied hope*—the revolutionary vision and energy by which the risen Jesus intends his disciples *to live*" (*Radical Discipleship,* 197, emphases added).

[21]Robinson, *Gilead,* 173.

[22]Robinson, *Gilead,* 26, 235, 247.

[23]Robinson, *Gilead,* 247.

[24]Robinson, *Gilead,* 299-300, 308, 324-25.

the German *hüske,* meaning "little house") is not empty but inhabited.[25] Such a claim brings us back to the concept with which we began our study of the rhetoric of Christian witness—*ēthos.*

Ēthos as Dwelling Place

In previous chapters I have introduced several concepts from the Western rhetorical tradition that, I believe, can refresh our discussions about Christian witness, including *ēthos, eunoia, enargeia,* identification, and constitutive rhetoric. The first of these, *ēthos,* has served as the book's conceptual common thread: each of the chapters can be read as an attempt to bring different facets of that key term into focus. In this final chapter before the epilogue, we turn our attention directly to *ēthos* once again—not by summarizing Aristotle but by reflecting on recent scholarly conversations about his concept. More specifically, I consider Aristotelian *ēthos* from the standpoint of postmodern (or, if you prefer, late-modern) rhetorical theory. Sketching the postmodern recovery of a premodern notion, my focus here is a description of *ēthos* at once old and new.

As noted earlier in the book, the term *ēthos* has often been translated into English as "character." (This one-word definition still routinely shows up in high school and college English courses, mine included.) However, though this shorthand may be useful in some situations, simply swapping the English word *character* for *ēthos*

---

[25]Christianity's truths are embodied ones, affirmed not only through our beliefs but also through our practices. At one point in his chapter on Robinson, Haddox notes that Ames's views about faith "resonate with an entire tradition that holds Christianity to be not merely a set of beliefs, but a whole way of life, which cannot be 'questioned' in the same way that one might question the logic of an argument" (*Hard Sayings*, 198). On this point, I find myself in agreement with Haddox—and Ames. In an essay on Dietrich Bonhoeffer, Marilynne Robinson makes a comment that suggests that Bonhoeffer might also agree with Ames's view. Robinson writes, "In 1932 [Bonhoeffer] wrote, 'The primary confession of the Christian before the world is the deed that interprets itself.' An obedient act owes nothing to the logic or the expectations of the world as it is, but is affirmed in the fact of revealing the redeemed world. Action is revelation" ("Bonhoeffer," in *Death of Adam*, 110-11).

limits our understanding of Aristotle's concept.[26] In his 1974 article "Aristotle on Habit (ἔθος) and Character (ἦθος): Implications for Rhetoric," Arthur B. Miller implies that the "character" signified by the Greek word *ēthos* is, for Aristotle, both a *temporal* and *spatial* phenomenon. *Ēthos's* temporal connotations stem from the fact that its Greek spelling, ἦθος, differs by only one letter from the word ἔθος, meaning "habit," "custom," or "use; usage—rite; institution."[27] He makes a compelling case that—although Aristotle did not write explicitly about the connections between the two terms—when he used ἦθος "to designate the character of a speaker as revealed in a speech, he was thinking of the speaker's habits, customs, traditions, or manners of life."[28] Character is, in other words, formed over time, through repeated practices—an observation that recent work by James K. A. Smith has brought back into focus for those interested in Christian higher education. In addition to discussing *ēthos's* temporal connotations, Miller also highlights that *ēthos* has spatial connotations, stemming directly from the word ἦθος itself. Miller writes, "Significantly, the basic denotation [of ἦθος] is *not* character, but '*an accustomed place*' and in the plural may refer to the '*haunts* or *abodes* of animals'; it also may refer to '*the abodes of men*.'"[29] The polis, Miller contends, is one example of such an accustomed place or abode.[30]

---

[26]Nedra Reynolds, "*Ethos* as Location: New Sites for Understanding Discursive Authority," *Rhetoric Review* 11, no. 2 (1993): 327.

[27]Arthur B. Miller, "Aristotle on Habit (ἔθος) and Character (ἦθος): Implications for Rhetoric," *Speech Monographs* 41, no. 4 (1974): 309-10.

[28]Miller, "Aristotle on Habit," 310, 314. According to Miller, one of the places where Aristotle comes closest to making the connection between character and habit explicit occurs in book 2 of the *Nichomachean Ethics*; Miller notes that, for Aristotle, "moral or ethical virtue is the product of habit [ἔθος], and has indeed derived its name with a slight variation of form, from that word" ("Aristotle on Habit," 309). Invoking one of the Burkean metaphors that I introduced in chapter three, Miller continues, "There is basic consubstantiality between the two words. Not only does etymology bear out this statement, but so does the good sense observation that a man's habits are indicative of his character" (309).

[29]Miller, "Aristotle on Habit," 309.

[30]Miller, "Aristotle on Habit," 311. Hints of this spatial, more communal aspect of *ēthos* are present, though not fully developed, in Aristotle's *On Rhetoric*. Though Aristotle focuses on establishing

The second of Miller's etymological observations here—that the term *ēthos* was used to refer to an accustomed place, haunt, or abode—has had staying power in rhetorical studies for the last forty years.[31] S. Michael Halloran, for example, presents *ēthos* as follows:

> *Ethos* emphasizes the conventional rather than the idiosyncratic, the public rather than the private. The most concrete meaning for the term in the Greek lexicon is "a habitual gathering place," and I suspect that it is upon this image of people gathering together in a public place, sharing experiences and ideas, that its meaning as character rests. To have *ethos* is to manifest the virtues most valued by the culture to and for which one speaks.[32]

More recently, communication scholars have devoted an entire volume, *The* Ethos *of Rhetoric,* to this "originative meaning of *ethos.*"[33] One reason for the continued interest in this particular etymology is its consistency with what Reynolds refers to as "postmodern subjectivity," particularly with respect to its "spatial and social emphases."[34]

ēthos within the rhetorical situation, he contends that *ēthos* can also come about from outside of the rhetorical situation, i.e., from the "prior reputation" that a speaker brings to the rhetorical situation (Craig R. Smith, "*Ethos* Dwells Pervasively: A Hermeneutic Reading of Aristotle on Credibility," in *The Ethos of Rhetoric*, ed. Michael J. Hyde [Columbia: University of South Carolina Press, 2004], 16). Based on this evidence and more, Smith makes a persuasive case that "Aristotle *assumes* the knowledge of the Athenian fore-structure of *ethos* as a dwelling place and then reformulates the notion of dwelling place to present a rhetorical understanding of *ethos*" (2).

[31]Reynolds, "*Ethos* as Location," 326-28; S. Michael Halloran, "Aristotle's Concept of *Ethos*, or If Not His Somebody Else's," *Rhetoric Review* 1, no. 1 (1982): 60; Judy Holiday, "In[ter]vention: Locating Rhetoric's *Ethos*," *Rhetoric Review* 28, no. 4 (2009): 389; Michael J. Hyde, ed., *The* Ethos *of Rhetoric* (Columbia: University of South Carolina Press, 2004), xiii; Calvin O. Schrag, foreword to Hyde, ed., *The* Ethos *of Rhetoric*, vii; Smith, "*Ethos* Dwells Pervasively," 2. Judy Holiday offers a thorough (and particularly helpful) summary of this scholarship ("In[ter]vention," 389). I draw on many of the same sources as Holiday does, and I have also summarized this literature elsewhere (James E. Beitler, "Making More of the Middle Ground: Desmond Tutu and the *Ethos* of the South African Truth and Reconciliation Commission," *Relevant Rhetoric: A New Journal of Rhetorical Studies* 3, no. 1 (Spring 2012).

[32]Halloran, "Aristotle's Concept of *Ethos*," 60; quoted in Reynolds, "*Ethos* as Location," 328, and Holiday, "In[ter]vention," 389.

[33]Schrag, foreword to *The* Ethos *of Rhetoric*, vii.

[34]Reynolds, "*Ethos* as Location," 326, 327. Judy Holiday speaks to both of these points: "Incorporation of the social nature of *ethos* moves beyond simplistic or modernist definitions of *ethos* as individual 'character'—where character might denote a rhetor's reputation, a rhetor's intrinsic character, or a textual performance enacted and controlled by a rhetor (oratorical competence).

Unlike "modern notions of the person or self," which suggest that one's identity is self-governing and fixed, postmodern descriptions stress that it is impossible to understand identity apart from one's environment: the so-called self is shaped by one's material, discursive, and social surroundings, especially the local places that we inhabit.[35] The importance of place and location to postmodern thought is further evidenced by the language sometimes used to refer to identity. Identity, which is said to involve *occupying* one or more subject *positions,* is a *constructed* and *embodied* phenomenon.

When Christian engagement with the questions raised by postmodernity was still in its heyday, most Christian scholars did not reject the fruits of postmodernity wholesale, and rightly so: though the postmodern critique of metanarratives and universal truth claims necessitated thoughtful replies from disciples of Jesus Christ, postmodernity productively exposed Christianity's problematic entanglements with modernity. "We have learned from the postmoderns that knowledge is not disembodied," writes theologian Kevin J. Vanhoozer. "On this point, postmodernity and incarnational Christian faith are agreed."[36] Building upon this consensus, Vanhoozer offers a suggestion about how Christians might witness to the good news of Jesus Christ in a postmodern context. "What is needed," he asserts, "is a translation of the Gospel that goes beyond conveying propositions— a translation that would *concretize* the Gospel in individual and communal shapes of living."[37] Along similar lines, theologian Stanley Hauerwas argues that to witness effectively, Christians must not only

---

Such [modernist] characterizations are insufficient because, among other reasons, they do not incorporate a postmodern critique of the individual in which, James Baumlin explains, 'the rhetorical situation renders the speaker an element of the discourse itself, no longer simply its origin (and the consciousness standing outside of the text) but rather a signifier standing *inside* an expanded text'" ("In[ter]vention," 389).

[35]Halloran, "Aristotle's Concept of *Ethos*," 60.

[36]Kevin Vanhoozer, "Theology and the Condition of Postmodernity," in *The Cambridge Companion to Postmodern Theology* (Cambridge: Cambridge University Press, 2003), 24.

[37]Vanhoozer, "Theology and the Condition of Postmodernity," 24

tell others about the truth but also show the communal embodiment of that truth. He writes, "The needed incentive not just to entertain but to live Christian convictions requires the display of *a habitable world* exemplified in the life of the Christian community."[38] What these theologians call for, to reframe Vanhoozer's and Hauerwas's claims in terms of the etymology of *ēthos*, is for Christians to build, inhabit, and invite others into "dwelling places" of faith.[39] Marilynne Robinson's narrative rhetoric offers an answer to this call.

The remainder of this chapter considers the Gilead trilogy in light of the scholarly recovery of "*ethos* as location," reflecting on the "communal shapes" or "dwelling places" that Robinson establishes in her novels and invites us, as readers, to inhabit for a time.[40] The trilogy presents us with a variety of dwelling places to consider, such as Ames's and Boughton's homes (and their gardens, porches, kitchens, and bedrooms); Jack's hideaway in Boughton's barn; the town of Gilead and its different churches; the gravesites of Ames's grandfather and first wife and child; Gilead's rural surroundings, including the home of Jack's first child and Lila's shack; the revival where members of Doane's group find temporary respite; a St. Louis brothel; and—more expansively—mid-century middle America. By identifying common characteristics of these dwelling places, we can begin to see why Christians and non-Christians alike have found Robinson's faith-infused world habitable. In what follows, I highlight four interrelated characteristics of Robinson's dwelling places. First, they are charged

---

[38]Stanley Hauerwas, *With the Grain of the Universe: The Church's Witness and Natural Theology* (Grand Rapids: Brazos, 2013), 214, emphasis added.

[39]Hyde, Ethos *of Rhetoric*, xiii. In *The Gospel in a Pluralist Society* (Grand Rapids: Eerdmans, 1989), Lesslie Newbigin uses the same metaphor as Hyde does to explain what Christian belief entails: "The Christian believer has to learn to *indwell* the tradition. Its models and concepts are things which he does not simply examine from the perspective of another set of models, but have to become the models through which he understands the world. *He has to internalize them and to dwell in them*" (49, emphasis added).

[40]Reynolds, "*Ethos* as Location," 325, 330; Vanhoozer, "Theology and the Conditions of Postmodernity," 24; Hyde, Ethos *of Rhetoric*, xiii.

with both theological and aesthetic significance; second, they are inhabited by faith's insiders and outsiders, both of whom are presented sympathetically; third, despite such significance and sympathy, they portray belonging realistically (in part because her "haunts" are haunted); and fourth and comprehensively, they include room for mystery.[41] My primary aim in describing these characteristics is to show how Robinson's narrative rhetoric "grants such *living room* to" the Christian faith, helping her readers to "feel more *at home*" with belief and some of its most difficult questions.[42] And in the process, Robinson's rhetoric, seasoned with the realities of Easter, points us toward a more permanent dwelling place.

Characteristics of Robinson's Dwelling Places

Robinson's dwelling places are imbued with aesthetic and theological significance. It is not uncommon for Robinson's reviewers to comment

---

[41]Rowan Williams's talk "Native Speakers: Identity, Grace and Homecoming" (*Christianity and Literature* 61, no. 1 [2011]: 7-18) jump-started my thinking about several features of Robinson's dwelling places. The piece is a must-read for those exploring Robinson's work from a theological perspective, and it is particularly helpful in explaining what Robinson is saying to us about identity and hospitality.

[42]Hyde, Ethos *of Rhetoric*, xiii. Reflecting on *faith's* dwelling places—i.e., on the connections between belief and *ēthos*'s spatial dimensions—has precedent from rhetoricians and theologians alike. In his introduction to *The* Ethos *of Rhetoric,* for example, Michael Hyde draws a connection between *ēthos* and the Jewish word *shechinah* ("the dwelling place of God") (xx). Hyde limits his remarks about the dwelling place of God to the *shechinah,* but for Christians there is, of course, much more to say. In the coming of the God-man Jesus Christ, God dwells in the midst of his people as one of them. Foretold by the prophet Isaiah, he is the one called Immanuel or "God is with us" (7:14). While the truth of God-as-Immanuel has many implications for the rhetoric of Christian witness, what is important for our present purposes is that such witness involves inviting others into the places where God promises to dwell with his people—most notably, the church—and supporting them as they themselves learn how to inhabit those places, too.

Drawing on Hyde's work, communication theorist Robert Stephen Reid has attempted "to provide a critical means to clarify the identifying features of a Christian *ēthos* that dwells rhetorically in the presentation of the self linguistically configured in oral or written texts" ("A Rhetoric of Contemporary Christian Discourse," in *Journal of Communication and Religion* 31, no. 2 [2008], 113). Reid's project is more general and theoretical than mine: he aims to develop a framework to help the critic identify and analyze any argument to determine whether its *ēthos* is "predominantly Christian" or not (113-14). I, on the other hand, simply aim to reflect on the particular features of Robinson's narratively constructed dwelling places.

on the beauty of her prose.[43] Her writing has been celebrated for its "precision and lyrical power," its "measured and absorbing elegance," and its freedom from cliché.[44] Robinson's verbal artistry—and her clear desire to describe rural Iowa in beautiful and even majestic ways—explains in part why so many readers want to spend time in her world. But there is another, related reason. Robinson's own deep concern for the beauty of her world is an attitude she grants to almost all of her characters, reinforcing her readers' affection for the world and its various dwelling places.

Examples are myriad. In a poignant moment in Ames's grandfather's graveyard, after father and son have spent time "putting things to rights," young Ames kisses his father's hand, alerting him to the unexpected and heartening beauty of their celestial surroundings.[45] "I would never have thought this place could be beautiful," his father remarks. "I'm glad to know that."[46] As the first novel of the trilogy unfolds, readers learn that Ames's attention to beauty—to light and darkness, water and land, laughter and quiet—has developed into a habitual posture as he has grown older. His exclamations of awe at the splendors of his surroundings repeat with such frequency throughout his letter that at times his epistle reads like a liturgy in praise of creation; and viewing the world through Ames's eyes, we too learn how to appreciate an empty church building or the Iowan prairie.

---

[43]Ron Charles, "Their Father's House," _The Washington Post_, September 7, 2008; Scott, "Return of the Prodigal Son"; Wood, "The Homecoming," _The New Yorker_, September 8, 2008.

[44]Wood, "Homecoming"; Diana Johnson, "Moral of the Story," _The New York Times_, October 3, 2014; James Kidd, Review of _Lila_ by Marilynne Robinson, _The Independent_, October 11, 2014; Sameer Rahim, "Quiet Epiphanies," _The Telegraph_, July 29, 2015; John Wilson, Review of _Lila_ by Marilynne Robinson, _The Chicago Tribune_, October 10, 2014. Reviewers have also praised Robinson for the simplicity _and_ grandeur of her prose, as James Wood does, in a single sentence, in his review of _Home_. The novel, Wood writes, "begins simply, eschewing obvious verbal fineness, and slowly grows in luxury—its last fifty pages are magnificently moving, and richly pondered in the way of 'Gilead'" ("Homecoming").

[45]Robinson, _Gilead_, 13, 15.

[46]Robinson, _Gilead_, 15.

But Ames is not alone in his perspective. It is one that is shared by many of the trilogy's central characters, including Lila, Glory, and even Jack. Robinson occasionally reveals these characters' appreciation for beauty as explicitly as she does with Ames. We learn, for example, that Lila is drawn not only to the lighting and music of Ames's church but also to these same elements of the camp meeting.[47] However, these characters' appreciation of beauty is more often manifested through the ways that they take care of their surroundings. For Lila, this involves tending to Ames's garden and his family's gravesite, while Glory and Jack improve the Boughton homestead by gardening, repairing steps on the porch, cooking an aromatic meal, and fixing the car. As with Ames's delight in the world's beauty, these characters' care for Gilead enlarges our own appreciation of the dwelling places of Robinson's world.

Robinson's narrative rhetoric does not merely function aesthetically, however; it moves us theologically as well.[48] As Michael Vander Weele indicates in an article that touches on Robinson's rhetoric, books like *Gilead* can persuade us to embrace specific ethical positions in addition to cultivating our aesthetic sensibilities.[49] He writes that *Gilead* invites "us to be part of a community that loves the elements of this world, that recognizes them as gifts, and that refuses to lose sight of their gift-character even amidst the keenly registered sorrows and flaws of our world."[50] Vander Weele's comments about the "gift-character" of the things of the world begin to point us toward the theological significance of Robinson's dwelling places, but we must go further about the nature of the gift. Through Ames's

---

[47] Robinson, *Lila*, 28, 66.

[48] Christina Bieber Lake highlights that Robinson's vision of the end, or "telos," of human life "is aesthetic—and distinctly theological" (*Prophets of the Posthuman*, 176-77).

[49] Michael Vander Weele, "Marilynne Robinson's *Gilead* and the Difficult Gift of Human Exchange," *Christianity and Literature* 59, no. 2 (2010): 237.

[50] Vander Weele, "Marilynne Robinson's *Gilead*," 237.

theological reflections and his expressions of awe at the beauty of the world, Robinson presents readers with a sacramental view of *ēthos* as dwelling place, suggesting that the "elements of this world" are not just gifts in themselves but also means of grace. At the same time, through the other characters' acts of caretaking in these dwelling places, Robinson gestures toward a Christian understanding of stewardship, the notion that God has called humans to work as creation's custodians.

As sites of both sacrament and stewardship, Robinson's dwelling places offer gifts of grace and work to their inhabitants—and they suggest to readers that, at least in Robinson's world, the boundary between spiritual and mundane, divine and human is very thin indeed. This spirit of the place, coupled with Ames's and Boughton's religious language and Jack's and Lila's struggle with belief, imbues nearly all of the places of Robinson's world (and most of their "elements," as Vander Weele aptly puts it) with theological significance. Whether or not they believe in God, most of Robinson's characters are conscious of this aspect of their world. Lila, for one, is troubled by it, wondering to herself why preachers assign meaning to natural objects (like Communion bread) and events (like Christ's death).[51] While wrestling with these ideas, she decides to get baptized, not because of what the water represents theologically or does spiritually but because "there might be something about that water on her forehead that would cool her mind."[52] Sometime after her baptism (the episode actually comes earlier in the book), Lila returns to the river to undo it. Robinson writes, "The river smelled like any river, fishy and mossy and shadowy, and the smell seemed stronger in the dark, with the chink and plosh of all the small life. . . . The river was like the

---

[51]Robinson, *Lila*, 34.
[52]Robinson, *Lila*, 34.

old life, just itself. Nothing more to it."[53] The naturalistic perspective that Robinson lends to Lila's voice here and elsewhere in the book only underscores for the reader how theologically charged this world is otherwise. And later, speaking to her son Robby before he's born, Lila warns him about Gilead, "The world has been here so long, seems like everything means something. You'll want to be careful. You practically never know what you're taking in your hand."[54]

In spite of Lila's wariness about such matters, if book reviews are any indication, Robinson's readers seem to find the theological richness of her world as appealing as its beauty. One explanation for this appeal has to do with the fact that, for Robinson, the two are actually inextricably connected to each other.[55] Put another way, the persuasiveness of Robinson's theologically infused landscape stems from the fact that, in the words of reviewer Cathleen Schine, her "spirituality is indistinguishable from her lyricism."[56] Comments made by reviewers such as A. O. Scott would suggest that another explanation may have to do with the continuing appeal of the aesthetics of romanticism and, more precisely, the rhetorical potency of the sublime. Praising *Home,* Scott writes that the "quotidian facts of what Glory thinks of as 'difficult, ordinary life' feel, in Robinson's hand, like vessels of the terrible, the sublime, the miraculous."[57] A third explanation for the

---

[53]Robinson, *Lila*, 22.

[54]Robinson, *Lila*, 135.

[55]To borrow a line from rhetorician Kenneth R. Chase's article "Christian Rhetorical Theory," "truth is not separable from eloquence and it certainly does not deny eloquence" ("Christian Rhetorical Theory: A New (Re)Turn," *Journal of Communication and Religion* 36, no. 1 [2013]: 36).

[56]In a piece appearing in *The New Yorker,* Mark O'Connell writes, "Even though I'm more or less a fully paid-up atheist, I'm more drawn to Robinson's Christian humanism than I am to the Dawkins-Dennett-Hitchens-Harris school of anti-theist fighting talk. Perhaps that's because *Robinson's moral wisdom seems inseparable from her gifts as a prose writer*" ("The First Church of Marilynne Robinson," *The New Yorker,* May 30, 2012, emphasis added). Of Ames's language, he later notes, "This is not the kind of voice I normally associate with religious people, and it makes me wonder whether we might not be listening to the wrong voices."

[57]On a related note, Kidd writes about *Lila,* "The nomadic sections have something of Cormac McCarthy's *The Road* about them—the sacred tinges to the language, the pared-down wonder and sudden burst of violent 'ferociousness' (to use Lila's word)" (Kidd, Review of *Lila*).

persuasiveness of the trilogy's theological richness may be that it is not only conveyed to us by the book's pastors but also filtered to us through other voices and viewpoints, including, for example, Lila's aforementioned naturalism. To explain why this enhances the persuasiveness of the trilogy, we must turn to the second characteristic of Robinson's dwelling places.

Both insiders and outsiders of Robinson's dwelling places are sympathetically presented. Nearly all of Robinson's dwelling places are occupied by both insiders (those accustomed to the place) and outsiders (those unaccustomed to or alienated from the place), and often the distinction between insider and outsider hinges on matters of faith. Robinson repeatedly brings Christian characters into contact with characters who do not believe, pairing Ames and Edward, Ames and Jack, Ames and Lila, Boughton and Jack, Glory and Jack, the women of Ames's church and Lila, churchgoers and Doane, Christians at the revival meeting and Doane's band of interlopers, and eventually Lila and the boy at her shack.[58] Even Ames's recollection of baptizing cats as a young boy brings this dynamic into relief, since it left Ames and his friends pondering the cats' spiritual status.[59]

Significantly, Robinson is persistent in presenting her Christian characters and their beliefs sympathetically; in the trilogy's dwelling places, faith remains a virtue. Ames, one of the most lovingly portrayed pastors in late-modern literature, is the primary example. His grief surrounding the loss of his first wife and child; his tender affection toward Lila and Robby; his deep reverence for the physical

---

[58]Robinson sometimes turns the insider-outsider distinction inside out. When it comes to baseball, for instance, Jack is the insider and Ames is the outsider (_Home_, 92). For a more thorough discussion of baseball's place in _Gilead_, see June Hadden Hobbs, "Burial, Baptism, and Baseball: Typology and Memorialization in Marilynne Robinson's _Gilead_," _Christianity and Literature_ 59, no. 2 (2010): 252-57.

[59]Robinson, _Lila_, 23.

world; his capacity for self-reflection and growth; his love for Boughton; his charity toward theological perspectives different from his own (including those of Feuerbach); his willingness to dwell in faith's ambiguities and mysteries; his wisdom in frailty; and even (perhaps especially) the intimacy of the epistolary form of *Gilead* all arouse our sympathies for the character. And Robinson's loving portrayal of religious characters does not stop with Ames. In the storylines devoted to the Boughton household, she gives us a devout father's agony for his wayward son and a sister's deep sorrow, often to the point of tears, for her brother. Jack's return to Gilead is a *via dolorosa* not only for him—the "man of sorrows," as Glory describes him—but also for the faithful around him, and we are made to empathize with them in their grief.[60] Likewise, the supporting cast of Christians in Lila's narrative are good and decent people. While each may have faults, they are not reduced to them. After Doane leaves young Lila on the church's doorstep, the preacher of the church becomes a fierce advocate for her;[61] the Nazarene woman who allows Lila to ride with her in her car from St. Louis to Iowa, though legalistic, seems tenderhearted and may ultimately be the reason that Lila steps into Ames's church;[62] and the women of Gilead who welcome Lila into the life of the church respect her space and allow her to contribute to the community's labors.[63] Doane may have very good reasons to distrust Christians, but Lila's interactions with them throughout this trilogy undermine his warnings.[64]

Furthermore, Robinson treats the characters who struggle to believe (or have difficulty believing in conventional ways)

---

[60]Robinson, *Home*, 318.
[61]Robinson, *Lila*, 53-54.
[62]Robinson, *Lila*, 215.
[63]Robinson, *Lila*, 32.
[64]Robinson, *Lila*, 11, 33.

sympathetically as well. She presents Lila and Jack—who, as the former Archbishop of Canterbury (and Robinson fan) Rowan Williams instructively observes, respectively stand for "unimaginable otherness" and "inaccessible strangeness" in these books—as lovingly as she does Ames.[65] One way that she does so is by keeping the line between character and setting (between *ēthos*-as-character and *ēthos*-as-dwelling place) taut. Lila distrusts others and often experiences a sense of shame that makes intimacy with others difficult for her. But as the trilogy unfolds, Robinson reveals that Lila's bent toward isolation has come about as a result of forces beyond her control: it is a product of injustices toward the impoverished that have forced Lila into dwelling places characterized by psychological and physical abuse, such as the brothel in St. Louis. Lila thinks (in a line that captures so many of her struggles in Gilead), "When you're scalded, touch hurts, it makes no difference if it's kindly meant."[66] Jack's "oldest habit"—his "estrangement" from family, hometown, and faith—may be the result of his own choices to a greater degree than Lila's.[67] He played mean-spirited tricks on Ames when he was boy, impregnated a young girl and then abandoned her and the child, and responds to conflict by drinking excessively.[68] But Robinson ties Jack's personal plight to society's systemic injustices as well. His inability to belong in Gilead is not simply his own doing but also the result of prejudices, both in the town and nationally, toward African Americans, including his wife and child.[69] The people of Gilead once protected African Americans but over time grew less and less welcoming toward them, effectively exiling Jack from his hometown.

---

[65]Robinson, *Lila*, 10.
[66]Robinson, *Lila*, 253.
[67]Robinson, *Home*, 230.
[68]Robinson, *Gilead*, 180-83; Robinson, *Home*, 158.
[69]Robinson, *Gilead*, 36-37, 231; Robinson, *Home*, 97, 155-56, 204, 217.

By sympathizing with both sets of characters, Robinson creates a habitable world for a variety of readers. Through Ames's and (to a lesser extent) Boughton's stories, Robinson affirms the values of readers whose towns, homes, and lives are built upon orthodox Christian beliefs and practices. At the same time, through Lila's and Jack's stories, she reminds us that many of these acts of communal, familial, and individual homemaking in the United States have excluded others on the basis of class and race. As such, Robinson makes a space for those readers who are painfully aware of systemic injustice in our country and its communities. And these are not the only viewpoints that Robinson gives voice to in her trilogy's dwelling places: she presents us with Lila's naturalism and universalism, Glory's conflicted views about domesticity, and Jack's religious skepticism and irony.[70] This plurality of voices, a notion we will return to in chapter six, enhances the rhetorical appeal of Robinson's world insofar as it takes the perspectives of many different readers seriously and speaks to different audiences. Spending time in Gilead, Robinson's readers learn to trust that, even if their views differ from hers, she handles them with the respect they deserve. She is willing to wrestle with her own convictions and represent others' viewpoints in fair and thought-provoking ways.

Robinson's dwelling places offer a realistic portrayal of belonging. Although Robinson charges her dwelling places with aesthetic and theological significance and presents the majority of her characters sympathetically, her scenes are seldom saccharine. In his review in *The Washington Post,* Ron Charles rightly observes that "her books are toxic to sentimentality."[71] One reason for this is that Gilead's

---

[70]Williams, "Native Speakers," 7.
[71]Ron Charles, "Marilynne Robinson's 'Lila': An Exquisite Novel of Spiritual Redemption and Love," *The Washington Post*, September 30, 2014. This point is echoed by many of Robinson's

haunts are haunted.[72] More precisely, in the warp and woof of Robinson's world, insiders and outsiders do not simply coexist in the same spaces; rather, in these dwelling places, insiders are haunted by the presence and perspectives of outsiders and vice versa, leading all of the major characters to wrestle with complex questions about identity and belonging—often in relation to matters of faith. For Gilead's outsiders, this means grappling with the theological doctrines and practices concerned with membership in the body of Christ, the doctrine of predestination and the sacraments of Communion and baptism central among them. So Jack condemns himself as a reprobate and rejects Ames and Boughton's offer of the Communion bread, while Lila attempts to undo her baptism and is confounded by Doll's supposed status among the lost—"[Heathens] sure don't deserve no hellfire," she says.[73] For Gilead's insiders, this involves the difficult task of making room for the others in one's midst and, more to the point, grappling with what it means to be a neighbor to those whom one has alienated. In the words of Rebecca M. Painter, Jack may indeed be "haunted by and unable to understand his own waywardness," but "he is [also] a kind, exquisitely compassionate individual, deeply offended by what has been called our country's original sin, racism."[74] Because of this, Jack forces Boughton and Ames to come face to face with what they and their town have, in their sinfulness,

---

reviewers (Sarah Churchwell, "Marilynn Robinson's *Lila*—A Great Achievement in US Fiction," *The Guardian*, November 7, 2014; Kidd, Review of *Lila*; Scott, "Return of the Prodigal Son"; Wilson, Review of *Lila*).

[72]Many reviews of Robinson's books use similar language. For example, Scott describes the Boughton household as "hold[ing] on to the *ghost* of its former vitality" and refers to the Bible as a book that "still has the power to *haunt and surprise*" Glory ("Return of the Prodigal Son," emphases added); Churchwell notes that Robinson's books "[resurrect] powerful *ghosts* to remind America of a forgotten moral lineage" ("Marilynne Robinson's *Lila*," emphasis added); and Charles refers to the "despair and trauma that *haunt* Lila" ("Marilynne Robinson's 'Lila,'" emphasis added).

[73]Robinson, *Lila*, 225.

[74]Rebecca M. Painter, "Further Thoughts on a Prodigal Son Who Cannot Come Home, on Loneliness and Grace: An Interview with Marilynne Robinson," *Christianity and Literature* 58, no. 3 (2009): 490-91.

excluded.[75] Much of this dynamic between Gilead's insiders and outsiders is encapsulated during a scene in the Boughton household, which takes place in front of the television.[76] Watching news footage of violent actions toward African Americans in the South, Jack cries out, "Jesus Christ!" Upon hearing these words, Boughton immediately takes offense, not because of the racial injustice on the screen but because Jack has taken the Lord's name in vain. In this moment, the distinction between insider and outsider remains tragically fixed: the nature of each figure's cry—one, a response to injustice; the next, to impiousness—pushes the other away.[77]

There is honesty here about the very human longing to be understood and accepted by others and, related to that, to feel at home in the world. There's also a truthfulness about the fact that these types of belonging are seldom fully realized, or at least not often realized in the ways that we expect or hope for. Jack and Robert Boughton are not, of course, exceptional in this regard. The protagonists of all three novels are motivated by different kinds of homesickness—deep longings for belonging—and they are all forced to confront ironies of being at home. Ames doesn't "feel very much at home in the world" until he is physically unable to fully participate in it, and he later admits to being "homesick for a place

---

[75]While Jack does not always manage to treat his godfather respectfully, Ames is also at fault. When he lived alone, he coveted Boughton's family. And while watching Jack with his own child, he covets that which he has not yet lost. It is little wonder, therefore, that Robinson weaves so much about the fifth and tenth commandments into *Gilead*. Ames honors the faith of his fathers but struggles with covetousness toward his neighbors, whereas Jack is concerned with the justice for his neighbors but finds it difficult to honor his fathers and their faith. Masterfully, in this strained relationship between Ames and Jack, Robinson reveals that the final statements in each of Moses' tablets function as a kind of holy diptych, signaling together what it ought to mean to be "at home in the world" (Robinson, *Gilead* 30).

[76]Robinson, *Lila*, 97-98.

[77]This scene between Jack and Robert Boughton reads as a cry from the heart about racial injustice in the US. In an interview with Rebecca M. Painter, Robinson remarked that "for Jack's wife and son Gilead might well be a foreign and perhaps a hostile country. I fervently wish that America will some time be a good, welcoming home to her whole family" ("Further Thoughts on a Prodigal Son," 490).

[he] never left."[78] Glory has to abandon her own vision of home in order to find her place, a place that she is all but "horrified" to inherit.[79] And Lila's understanding of home is, and seemingly always will be, defined by her homelessness. Robinson writes, "She had never been at home in all the years of her life. She wouldn't know how to begin."[80] Such examples ring true to many of us. There are probably few readers among us who cannot find something to identify with in the midst of Jack's discomfort with and alienation from his childhood home; Boughton's despair at his son's estrangement; Glory's humiliation at having to return to Gilead after her idealized vision of home collapsed; Lila's shame about the townspeople's gestures of charity and her impulse that "she'd best try to act like she belonged there"; and Ames's growing detachment from the active life of his son, Robby.[81]

Robinson's realistic portrayal of the difficulties of belonging is amplified by an awareness of the immense challenges that often accompany attempts to practice hospitality, not just for hosts but also for guests. The strained exchanges that Jack has with Ames, Boughton, and Glory are clear examples, but Ames and Lila's interactions offer equally potent illustrations, particularly with respect to the knife that Doll gives Lila. We learn a great deal about the knife's history in the same section of the book where Lila notes that "everything means something," and through these paragraphs and others, we come to understand that the knife does indeed mean much to Lila. The knife was a gift from Doll and, therefore, Lila's only physical connection to the only person who had ever cared for her.[82] But as with much of the rest of the trilogy, there's little room for viewing this

---

[78]Robinson, *Gilead*, 5, 235.
[79]Robinson, *Home*, 298.
[80]Robinson, *Lila*, 107.
[81]Robinson, *Lila*, 23.
[82]Robinson, *Lila*, 133.

"family heirloom" sentimentally, since Doll used it as a murder weapon and Lila concealed it from the sheriff shortly before Doll died.[83] When Lila ends up at the brothel in St. Louis, the madam makes her surrender the knife; but later, when Lila comes to live in Ames's home as his wife, he lets her keep it. We as readers come to realize that, for Lila, the knife represents freedom, the possibility of returning to the old life—and Ames is willing to protect that freedom, even though it comes with uncertainty and the risk of danger or disappointment. And despite the fact that Ames adds yet another layer of meaning to the object by using it to pare apples, the knife's more mundane domestic significance cannot erase its associations with Doll's blood and death.[84] To my mind, the place of the knife in the Ames household is a near perfect illustration of the perils of radical hospitality: for the host, it can come with risk and even danger, and for the guest, it can involve shame, fear of exposure, and ultimately rejection. But it also speaks to the promises of welcoming the stranger into one's midst. If one can avoid the temptation "of capturing and devouring, of absorbing the guest into the host's world" (a temptation Ames avoids by allowing Lila to keep the knife), there is the possibility of joy and even transformation in the direction of holiness—for the one we encounter is none other than Christ himself.[85]

In brief, then, Robinson's dwelling places are realistic about the limitations of belonging and the challenges of hospitality. Perhaps somewhat counterintuitively, this realism makes them credible and, thus, more habitable to Robinson's readers.

Robinson's dwelling places make room for mystery. The three characteristics of Robinson's dwelling places that I have just discussed all point to, and to some degree are all summed up by, the fourth.

---

[83]Robinson, *Lila*, 136-7.

[84]Robinson, *Lila*, 241.

[85]Janis Haswell, Richard Haswell, and Glenn Blalock, "Hospitality in College Composition Courses," *College Composition and Communication* 60, no. 4 (2009): 711.

Robinson's dwelling places embrace mystery and, consequently, make room for many more readers than they otherwise might.[86] To understand this last characteristic, we must turn to an address delivered at the 2011 Conference on Christianity and Literature by Rowan Williams. In his address, Williams spoke to the conference theme, "The Hospitable Text"—a fitting topic for our present purposes.

Williams suggests that Ames and Lila are able to make space for each other (and, ultimately, are able to come to a common understanding and language, and even share a home) because "otherness" or "strangeness" is a central aspect of their identities.[87] The strangeness at the heart of Ames's being stems from his faith, while the otherness at the heart of Lila's being is a result of her wanderings and homelessness, a background very different from Gilead's other inhabitants.[88] Ames is aware, Williams writes, "that he stands under an alien judgement."[89] He continues: "[Ames] may be broadly 'comfortable,' as Lila suggests, but it is not a comfort that defends itself by refusing what is strange. His settled faith is based on awareness of a strangeness at the very center of his identity: Christ in him, in Barth's terms, is a given, a presence not dependent on his own self-correspondence. There is in his identity something that is not mere sameness."[90] These reflections on identity and otherness in Robinson's work bring Williams back to the conference theme:

> If the text of a native language is to be in some sense hospitable, Robinson implies, it must be a text with a shadow or margin, conscious of a strangeness that surrounds it and is not captured by it, a strangeness that

---

[86] Alex Engebretson notes, "The words *mystery* and *complexity*, and their underlying ideas, are two of the most common in Robinson's essays, and they also name two of the fiction's aesthetic effects" (*Understanding Marilynne Robinson* [Columbia: University of South Carolina Press, 2017], 10).

[87] Williams, "Native Speakers," 9, 12.

[88] Williams, "Native Speakers," 10-11.

[89] Williams, "Native Speakers," 11-12.

[90] Williams, "Native Speakers," 12.

interprets it or at least offers the possibility of a meaning to be uncovered, on the far side of questioning. And the paradoxical conclusion is that the person who "inhabits" with integrity the place where they find themselves, in such a way as to make it possible for others to inhabit it in peaceable company with them is always the person who is aware of the possibility of an alien yet recognizable judgement being passed, aware of the stranger already sensed in the self's territory.[91]

Williams's claims here about the strangeness at the heart of hospitable texts tie together many of the other characteristics of Robinson's dwelling places discussed in this chapter. As we have seen, these places are spaces of sublimity and grace, zones where insiders and outsiders both reside and are valued, and haunted haunts that involve difficult encounters and speak to the ironies of home. Williams's arguments are, moreover, reinforced by the third book in the trilogy despite the fact that Williams wrote and delivered his talk before *Lila* was published. In the story, Lila becomes a scribe of sorts, copying down long passages from the Bible.[92] The passages she chooses are some of the most peculiar and difficult to interpret, including passages from Ezekiel. Perhaps worried that such passages will turn off Lila to Christianity, Ames recommends she reads Matthew alongside Ezekiel.[93] But Ames's pastoral instincts may be mistaken in this case, for it is precisely Scripture's unusual and unsettling passages that speak to her and her past experience, an experience very alien from the conventions of Gilead.[94] "It could be," Lila tells us, "that the wildest, strangest things in the Bible were the places where it touched earth"; and then, in one of the book's most enduring images, she compares this potency of the Bible with a whirlwind, filled first with bright river water and then with whatever

---

[91]Williams, "Native Speakers," 12-13.

[92]Robinson, *Lila*, 43.

[93]Robinson, *Lila*, 124-25, 135.

[94]Robinson, *Lila*, 68, 74, 106, 132. Charles puts it well: "The images of desolation and abandonment in Ezekiel don't sound to [Lila] like history or metaphor—they sound like yesterday" ("Marilynne Robinson's 'Lila,'" 3).

else might come in its path: plants, animals, and even people.[95] Lila's presentation of Scripture further supports Williams's point. For her, it is such strangeness that makes the text hospitable—a dangerous hospitality, to be sure, but ultimately a transformative one. "It would," as she says of the whirlwind's power over people and their surroundings, "change everything they thought they knew."

Remarkably, Robinson's trilogy does not simply *represent* the textual hospitality described by Williams; it also *performs* that hospitality for its readers by avoiding a didactic stance and, instead, by dwelling with questions of the Christian faith. A significant number of the trilogy's reviewers imply this is so. Schine speculates, for example, that "Robinson is able to write so powerfully and engagingly about religion, even for the nonreligious . . . because she writes about questions rather than answers."[96] Along similar lines, other reviewers suggest that readers find Robinson's willingness to embrace faith's contradictions especially persuasive. For instance, Scott calls *Home* "a book full of doubleness and paradox, at once serene and volcanic, ruthless and forgiving," adding later that the book "is at once hard and forgiving, bitter and joyful, fanatical and serene." Echoing Glory's comments about the Bible, he concludes of *Home,* "What a strange old book it is."[97]

An Easter Witness

"Reading a Marilynne Robinson novel is like going to church," poet-professor Angela Alaimo O'Donnell perceptively observes. Let me

---

[95]Robinson, *Lila,* 226-27.

[96]Schine, "Triumph of Love," 2. See also Rahim, "Quiet Epiphanies," and Churchwell, "Marilynne Robinson's *Lila.*"

[97]For more on Robinson's embrace of contradiction and paradox, see Wood, "Homecoming," and Leslie Jamison, "The Power of Grace," *The Atlantic,* October 2014. Wood highlights the "tender pain"; Jamison, the "bleed between joy and sorrow." Robinson's willingness to dwell with mysteries and paradoxes is a feature of her prose that Robinson herself likely considers to be characteristically Christian. As she notes in her essay on Bonhoeffer, "Christian thinkers since Jesus have valued paradox as if it were resolution" ("Bonhoeffer," 117).

begin this chapter's conclusion by suggesting one way that this is so. In his book *Liturgical Theology: The Church as Worshiping Community*, Simon Chan reminds us that authentic Christian worship includes two liturgical practices: the proclamation of the Word and the celebration of the table.[98] Chan cites the work of theologian Jean-Jacques von Allmen, who observes that these two components of Christian worship mirror Christ's two central ministerial activities: he preached in Galilee, and he instituted the Eucharist and was crucified in Jerusalem.[99] Like Christ's own acts of self-revelation, the practices of Word and table accomplish different ends. Chan notes, for example, that the proclamation of the Word is an occasion for *reflection*, whereas the celebration of the table is an opportunity for *participation*.[100]

What I want to suggest here is that the rhetoric of Marilynne Robinson's witness in the Gilead trilogy is less like the proclamation of the Word and more like an invitation to the table, and it includes the eschatological orientation that accompanies the latter. Such claims help us move beyond the notion that her books are simply about *using* orthodoxy.[101] For though Robinson does not explicitly advance creedal formulas or make sermonic proclamations to her readers ("Even her preachers do not preach," Schine rightly observes), she does present readers with places where faithful men

---

[98]Simon Chan, *Liturgical Theology: The Church as Worshiping Community* (Downers Grove, IL: InterVarsity Press, 2006), 63.

[99]Jean-Jacques von Allmen writes, "[Divine worship] is an echo of the incarnation in that it includes, like the ministry of Jesus, what one could call a 'Galilean' moment—centered on the sermon—and a 'Jerusalemite' moment—centered on the Eucharist. These two elements, indispensable in the ordinary worship of the Church, are conditioned by one another. The preaching of the Kingdom could not have been properly understood if Jesus had not sealed it with His blood; but neither could the crucifixion have been understood if Jesus had not prepared it by His prophetic ministry. The same is true of the relation between sermon and communion" (quoted in Chan, *Liturgical Theology*, 69).

[100]For more on the ways that Word and table relate to one another, see Chan, *Liturgical Theology*, 63-70. For example, in addition to reflection and participation, Word and table respectively involve "revelation and response" (67-68) and "preparation and fulfillment" (68-70).

[101]Haddox, *Hard Sayings*, 20.

and women are striving toward holy Communion and the new life of Easter.[102]

Robinson's world is one that recognizes and participates in the sacraments. As we have seen, we find among Gilead's haunts an appreciation of things as both beautiful and sublime; a concern for salvation for the wayward individual and healing for the marginalized community; a sympathetic recognition (and even loving portrayal) of others different from ourselves; a longing for belonging and hospitality; an emphasis on the importance of "the alien action of grace"; and a proper respect for mystery (which, of course, comes from the Greek word *mystērion*—a word that was translated into Latin as *sacrament*). Such features of the trilogy's dwelling places are reinforced by the sacramental imagery that Robinson weaves into the novels. In *Gilead,* Ames watches a couple get showered by a rain-soaked tree and sees blessing; in *Home,* after Jack's attempted suicide, Glory prepares rich comfort food, the fragrance of which suffuses "the atmosphere of the house" to remind its inhabitants that they are loved unconditionally; and in *Lila,* we are invited to ponder, with Lila, the idea that "everything means something."[103] But Robinson does not stop at allusion and comparison. Many of the books' most pivotal scenes present us with sacraments. Ames preaches on the Eucharist; Robby receives Communion from Ames at Lila's insistence; Ames

---

[102]Haddox ends his chapter on Robinson by admitting that, despite the fact that she does not proclaim Christianity as much as she uses it for her own ends, her books may serve as an important prelude to Christian witness. In a statement that parallels aspects of my argument about C. S. Lewis's witness from chapter one, Haddox writes, "It may be that until more people are willing to embrace truth as truth, the work of . . . writers [like Robinson] will be useful as a rhetorical model akin to what Pascal described long ago—to make people see that Christianity is desirable, good, and not contrary to reason before they can come to be persuaded of its truth" (*Hard Sayings,* 203). According to this statement, Robinson does not offer the truth to her readers; rather, she merely shows us that "Christianity is desirable, good, and not contrary to reason." Without denying that Robinson's trilogy does present Christianity in these important ways, I have suggested in this chapter that Robinson also offers us something akin to embodied truth. We as readers may not be given explicit truth claims in Robinson's trilogy; however, we are presented with characters trying to live faithful lives in relation to God and one another.

[103]Robinson, *Gilead,* 27-28; Robinson, *Home,* 252; Robinson, *Lila,* 135.

shares the Lord's Supper with Robert and Glory; and Lila is baptized by Ames.[104]

What is more, like the Eucharistic feast that prefigures the marriage supper of the Lamb and the baptismal journey that heralds Christians' passage from death to life at the end of time, Robinson's dwelling places are oriented eschatologically, drawing many of her characters (and, perhaps, even her readers) toward the hope of homecoming and resurrection, the hope of the Easter season. "Behind all of Robinson's work," James Wood correctly observes, "lies an abiding interest in the question of heavenly restoration."[105] Certainly all three books in the Gilead trilogy orient us in this direction. As we have already seen, in an early scene from *Gilead,* the young John Ames and his father put his grandfather's grave "to rights."[106] It is an act that could be read as a sign of their hope for a life beyond the grave. Much later, nearing the end of his life, Ames is preoccupied with the idea of resurrection. He writes to Robby that he will soon "put on imperishability" and reflects on the loveliness of the phrase "the twinkling of an eye"; he ruminates on Boughton's view of heaven; and he concludes his letter to Robby by writing of his burial and, in a beautiful description of the final resurrection of the dead, "the great and general incandescence."[107] When, in the book's final sentence, Ames writes, "I'll pray, and then I'll sleep," we are reminded of the poetry recommendation that he

---

[104]Robinson, *Gilead*, 69-70; Robinson, *Home*, 314; Robinson, *Lila*, 86-88. Some might argue that Robinson's depiction of the sacraments is itself unorthodox, perhaps noting that Ames gives Robby Communion before he is of age and that Lila tries to wash off her baptism. I would respond by suggesting that Robinson may simply be intent on presenting the sacraments to us in their most grace-filled form: they work on us despite the limitations of our understanding or our intention.

[105]I am indebted to literary scholar Alex Engebretson for reminding me of this wonderful line from Wood's review of *Home*. In his book *Understanding Marilynne Robinson,* Engebretson includes the quotation when discussing "the centrality of resurrection" in Robinson's first and fourth novels (*Understanding Marilynne Robinson*, 80; see also Engebretson, "Marilynne Robinson's Singular Vision").

[106]Robinson, *Gilead*, 13.

[107]Robinson, *Gilead*, 53, 166, 247.

gave to Lila many pages earlier, particularly the excerpt of John Donne's "Death, be not proud," which he included in his letter to Robby: "One short sleepe past, wee wake eternally, / And death shall be no more; death, thou shalt die."[108]

Unlike *Gilead*'s closing pages, the ending of *Home* does not invite us to ponder "the great and general incandescence" at the end of time, but it is very much about homecoming and a kind of resurrection life for the Boughton homestead. The book is, of course, a retelling of the story of the prodigal son. Robert had long held out hope that Jack would one day feel "at home" in Gilead and perhaps even embrace the Christian faith. When Jack was a boy, Robert had taken great delight in even the smallest gestures of faith—Jack's presence at an Easter service, for example. After Jack left Gilead, Robert had kept things on the farm unaltered in the hopes that, should Jack return to the town, his childhood home would be familiar and inviting to him.[109] However, in Robinson's version of the prodigal son story, the father's fervent prayer for the son's return and the son's attempt to come home end not in restoration but in misunderstanding, rejection, and failure. And yet, though Jack is unable to stay in Gilead and Robert dies disappointed, the story does not end there. Glory commits to continue her father's preservation project, holding the memory of the home alive for her siblings and, perhaps most important, for Jack's son.[110] Amy Hungerford writes, "The book seems to suggest that someday, through Glory's efforts in the old, odd house with its cumbersome furniture (a metaphor for all we inherit), both young Robert Boughtons, Robert Boughton Miles and Robert Boughton Ames, black and

---

[108]Robinson, *Gilead*, 77.

[109]Robinson, *Home*, 179. Glory muses, "It seemed sometimes as if her father must have meant to preserve all this memory, this sheer power of sameness, so that when they came home, or when Jack came home, there would be no need to say anything. In the terms of the place, they would all always have known everything" (88).

[110]Robinson, *Home*, 299-300, 323-25.

white, may return together *to take up habituation* in this land of their fathers."[111] The book, in other words, holds out the hope that the prayers of Jack and Robert for homecoming and new life will be answered by God—if only in the coming generations. How fitting it is, then, that in the novel's last sentence, Glory echoes the expression that her father uses when he perceives God's providence in life's circumstances: "The Lord is Wonderful."[112]

Robinson's third book beckons readers toward the idea of resurrection as well. When Lila first steps into Ames's church, she does not do so looking for new life; in fact, she is troubled by the notion of resurrection because she finds it to be nonsensical.[113] But after spending time in Gilead, she begins to come around to the idea of resurrection since, she supposes, it would involve a reunion with Doll.[114] Later, when Robert Boughton teaches her about the Last Judgment that accompanies the resurrection of the dead, she does another about-face. Robinson writes, "Lila hated the thought of resurrection as much as she had ever hated anything."[115] How, Lila wonders, could someone who has a life as difficult as Doll's be condemned to perdition? "Who could want to cause her more sorrow?"[116] Lila's final response to such questions is not to jettison the notion of resurrection but to become something of a universalist.[117] She also does her part to work toward resurrection. In a deed that reminds readers of the scene from *Gilead* in which young Ames and his father put his grandfather's gravesite "to rights" (and perhaps even evokes for some readers the moments in *Home* when Jack and Glory tend to the Boughton farm, sustaining the

---

[111]Hungerford, *Postmodern Belief*, 297.

[112]Robinson, *Home*, 167, 215, 325; Williams, "Native Speakers," 13-14.

[113]Robinson, *Lila*, 27-28.

[114]Robinson, *Lila*, 100.

[115]Robinson, *Lila*, 101.

[116]Robinson, *Lila*, 101.

[117]Robinson, *Lila*, 260-61. Though Robinson ends her trilogy on this note, she seems more intent to present us with a number of different views on resurrection: Ames focuses on grace; Boughton, on judgment; Jack, on predestination and perdition; and Lila, on universalism.

memories of the place for future generations), Lila plants and cares for flowers at the gravesites of Ames's first wife and child. As she does so, she sometimes thinks about her husband's own death and resurrection.[118]

What makes Lila's vision of Ames's resurrection so poignant is that, in spite of her work at the gravesite, she is not there. Lila does not envision being buried with the Ames family, and she does not believe that she will rise alongside them at the resurrection. (Here again, even in her understanding of the afterlife, we see that Lila's notion of home is defined, at least in part, by her homelessness.) Nevertheless, Lila seems to believe that she *will* rise and that she won't be alone: "The old man might have his wife and his child. She would have Doll, so that would be all right. There would be such crowds of people, but she would look for her until she found her if it took a hundred years."[119] In the meantime, after Ames's death but before hers, Lila won't be alone. She will "wander a while" with their son, Robby.[120] And because of remarks that Ames made to Lila before their son was born, we are led to believe that Robby, too, may prompt Lila to think of the resurrection from time to time. While decorating their home for Christmas, Ames commented on the timing of the celebration of Jesus's birth, telling Lila (who was pregnant with Robby at the time), "Spring would seem like a better time to celebrate a birth."[121] He then added, "But it's even better for resurrection. Everything coming back to life."[122] Robby was born that spring.

---

[118]The passage is worth quoting in full here: "One day she and the child [Robby] would watch them lower John Ames into his grave, Mrs. Ames on one side and his father, John Ames, on the other, and his mother and that boy John Ames and his sisters, a little garden of Ameses, all planted there waiting for the Resurrection. She knew it was ridiculous, but she always imagined them coming up some June day, right through the roses, not breaking a stem or bruising a petal. Shaking hands, patting backs, too taken up with it all to notice her flowers. Except Mrs. Ames, who might stoop down and pick one to show that baby, This is a rose. See how cool it is, how nice it smells. Holding it away from the baby's hand because in the world as they left it there'd have been thorns" (Robinson, *Lila*, 251).

[119]Robinson, *Lila*, 100.

[120]Robinson, *Lila*, 251.

[121]Robinson, *Lila*, 230.

[122]Robinson, *Lila*, 230.

6

SPEAKING IN TONGUES

The Church and the Heteroglossia of Pentecost

And they were all filled with the Holy Spirit and began to speak in other tongues as the Spirit gave them utterance.

ACTS 2:4

There are many different ways of bringing people into His Kingdom.

C. S. LEWIS, "CROSS-EXAMINATION"

The Power—the Spirit—is thus a social power, working to bring all minds into its unity, sometimes by similarity and at other times by contrast. There is a diversity of gifts, but the same Spirit.

DOROTHY L. SAYERS, "PENTECOST"

Now, after all, still separated, we celebrate Pentecost, the church festival that is in a special way a celebration of community. When the church bells rang this morning, I felt a great longing to be in a worship service. . . . I have also thought a lot again about the peculiar story of the "miracle of tongues." That the Babylonian confusion of languages, through which people are no longer able to understand one another because each speaks his own language, is to end and be overcome by the language of God, which each human being understands and through which alone people are also able to understand one another again, and that the church is where this is to take place—all these are indeed very deep and important thoughts.

DIETRICH BONHOEFFER, PENTECOST 1943

We are bound up in a delicate network of interdependence because, as we say in our African idiom, a person is a person through other persons.

DESMOND TUTU, *NO FUTURE WITHOUT FORGIVENESS*

*It has seemed to me sometimes as though the Lord breathes on this poor
gray ember of Creation and it turns to radiance—for a moment or a year
or the span of a life. And then it sinks back into itself again, and to look
at it no one would know it had anything to do with fire, or light. That
is what I said in the Pentecost sermon. I have reflected on that sermon,
and there is some truth in it. But the Lord is more constant and far more
extravagant than it seems to imply. Wherever you turn your eyes the world
can shine like transfiguration. You don't have to bring a thing to it except a
little willingness to see.*

MARILYNNE ROBINSON, *GILEAD*

THE CHRISTIANS GATHERED TOGETHER in this book each witness
in myriad ways. Though I selected each of the figures with particular
liturgical and rhetorical practices in mind and am of the opinion that
each figure's place in the book is fitting, I am certainly not making the
case that my designations are the definitive ones. I would argue, in fact,
that each figure discussed here could be used to illustrate all of the
seasons of the church year and worship practices that I have touched
on in the preceding pages. For example, while Lewis's rhetoric clearly
resonates with the call to worship and Advent, a case could surely be
made that other aspects of his life and work witness in ways that are
consistent with the creeds and Christmas, sermonic language and
Epiphany, confessional discourse and Lent, and the sacraments and
Easter.[1] What is more, particular worship practices and specific church
seasons offer us rhetorical postures other than those embodied by the
figures in this book: in our own contexts, bearing witness with an eye

---

[1]One reason for this is that we are all able to witness in multiple ways. Another reason is that the
emphases of the liturgical seasons overlap with one another. As Jennifer M. McBride rightly
notes, "No liturgical season is whole in and of itself. The boundary lines are fluid indeed as each
points forward and backward, often in surprising ways, to central themes emphasized in the
other, to themes like hope and repentance" (*Radical Discipleship* [Minneapolis: Fortress,
2017], 26).

to Advent may look very different than Lewis's appeals to goodwill. Furthermore, there are many important moments of the liturgical year, such as Ascension Day, that I simply did not have space to discuss in these pages.

Such admissions speak to the limitations of each of my chapters; however, they also reinforce my book's larger claim that our liturgical practices offer us a variety of rhetorical resources for Christian witness. And if this is so, I believe that one of our tasks as Christians ought to involve more reflection about how we can make use of these liturgical-rhetorical resources. Through the case studies in this book, I hope to have brought a few of the connections between rhetorics of worship and witness into relief, not as models to slavishly reproduce but as inspirations to enliven our attempts to bear witness in our own challenging times.

In what follows, I begin by acknowledging some additional limitations of this project, not simply because that is what academic arguments do to establish credibility but because such admissions support my views about the *ēthos* of the body of Christ, the church. Then I turn to a configuration of *ēthos* that builds upon the work of twentieth-century literary theorist Mikhail Bakhtin. More specifically, I consider ways that Bakhtin's concept of heteroglossia might relate to the rhetorical manifestation of the body of Christ. Our collective rhetoric of Christian witness, I suggest, resonates with postures that we are invited to embrace on Pentecost. After exploring what Lewis, Sayers, Bonhoeffer, Tutu, and Robinson have to say to us about the witness of Pentecost, I conclude by offering a few final reflections on worship and witness.

This book's limitations and shortcomings are many, and they are my own. I am very aware that the arguments here have been shaped by my own place in the church and in the world. It has focused on the traditions and practices of Western Christianity and the Western rhetorical tradition, and—while there is much more to say about the liturgical-rhetorical resources of these traditions—the traditions and practices of the East and the global South offer many other liturgical-rhetorical resources for Christian worship and witness. Likewise, looking across the chapters of this project, I recognize the need to spend more time learning from scholars and practitioners who are writing about Christian witness in ways that better recognize and celebrate differences of race, ethnicity, class, and gender. More could also be learned by considering the liturgical-rhetorical practices of Christianity's other branches. This project would have offered valuable insights had it been written from a Roman Catholic or Eastern Orthodox perspective. And then there is the matter of my disciplinary affiliations. As an English professor who studied rhetoric and composition in graduate school, it is not surprising that the genres I focus on in this book include the essay, the radio play, the sermon, the memoir, and the novel. But there are other disciplinary approaches to take with respect to this topic, with a focus on other genres, sites of inquiry, and forms of evidence.[2] In short, there are a multitude of voices in the church worth celebrating and learning from, which brings us to the final theoretical concept that we will consider here: heteroglossia.

Mikhail Bakhtin on Heteroglossia

Mikhail Bakhtin's heteroglossia is the conceptual linchpin of his brilliant and wide-ranging essay "Discourse in the Novel," the primary goals of which are to highlight the inability of late-nineteenth- and

---

[2]Jennifer M. McBride's _Radical Discipleship_, which I mentioned in the introduction and have cited repeatedly, is an excellent example. McBride's "constructive theology" focuses more on contemporary social issues than my book does, calling us to different but absolutely vital forms of Christian witness (5). She encourages Christians to "reduce distance between ourselves and those who are oppressed, be they the incarcerated or the homeless, immigrants or refugees, or people enduring Islamophobia and other forms of racism" (237; see also 246-48). The rhetorics of witness that I have explored in this book are probably at their most persuasive when practiced by Christians who identify with the oppressed, as McBride recommends.

early-twentieth-century stylistics to make sense of the genre of the novel and to offer a theory of novelistic prose (and of prose discourse and language-in-use more generally) that does justice to it.[3] *Heteroglossia*, which is literally translated from Greek as "other tongues," describes the "multi-languageness" of any given language.[4] The concept speaks to the fact that a cultural or national language is not a monolithic and unified phenomenon; rather, every language is actually composed of diverse and multitudinous layers of "sub-languages or idioms," each with their own characteristic meanings and linguistic features.[5] Thus, for Bakhtin, *writing a novel* involves an "orchestration of meaning by means of heteroglossia."[6] Authors arrange their own speech in relation to "the speeches of narrators, inserted genres, and the speech of characters," allowing "a multiplicity of social voices" to converse with one another in their works.[7] *Analyzing a novel's stylistics,* in turn, requires understanding how it embraces the heteroglossia of a language.[8]

To help his readers understand the concept of heteroglossia, Bakhtin relies heavily on metaphor. Taken together, Bakhtin's figures of speech are remarkably interdisciplinary, drawn from fields such as geology (language is "stratified"), geometry ("'languages' of

---

[3]M. M. Bakhtin, "Discourse in the Novel," in *The Dialogic Imagination: Four Essays*, ed. Michael Holquist, trans. Caryl Emerson and Michael Holquist (Austin: University of Texas Press, 1981), 260-67, 415.

[4]Bakhtin, "Discourse in the Novel," 274.

[5]James Jasinski, "Heteroglossia," in *Sourcebook on Rhetoric: Key Concepts in Contemporary Rhetorical Studies*, ed. James Jasinki (Thousand Oaks, CA: Sage, 2002), 295.

[6]Bakhtin, "Discourse in the Novel," 371.

[7]Bakhtin, "Discourse in the Novel," 263; Jasinski, "Heteroglossia," 296.

[8]Bakhtin, "Discourse in the Novel," 416-18. Bakhtin presents such analysis as an absolutely Herculean (if not impossible) task, given the complexities of both heteroglossia and its instantiation in the novel. He writes, for example, that "the real task of stylistic analysis consists in uncovering all the available orchestrating languages in the composition of the novel, grasping the precise degree of distancing that separates each language from its most immediate semantic instantiation in the work as a whole, and the varying angles of refraction of intentions within it, understanding their dialogic interrelationships and—finally—if there *is* direct authorial discourse, determining the heteroglot background outside the work that dialogizes it" (416). And for Bakhtin, that is only the beginning of what is required methodologically (416-18).

heteroglossia intersect each other"), astronomy (language can be understood in "Galilean" and "Ptolemaic" ways), music (words have "timbre" and may be in or out of harmony with their surroundings), and optics (intention in language interacts with heteroglossia the way that a "ray of light" passing through the "atmosphere" undergoes "spectral dispersion" and "makes the facets of the image sparkle"). Words also have the "taste" of their contexts, and languages "cohabit with one another." The piece is truly a metaphorical marvel, and this metaphorical richness helps Bakhtin convey a sense of the complexity of heteroglossia and, in turn, the stylistic complexity of the novel.[9]

Perhaps because of the metaphorical richness of Bakhtin's prose, the concept of heteroglossia has been a generative concept for scholars working in a variety of fields. Rhetoricians are no exception. James Jasinski observes that "rhetorical critics are now devoting considerable effort to unpacking the play of languages within specific texts and trying to describe the process of 'orchestration' that Bakhtin saw as basic to prose composition and rhetorical invention."[10] Following in the footsteps of these critics, I would suggest that Bakhtin's notion of heteroglossia helps us make sense of the rhetoric of Christian witness writ large. In order to understand how this is so, it will be useful to begin with a brief summary of this book's central concept: *ēthos*.

In the introduction and chapter one, I presented *ēthos* in Aristotelian terms, describing it in terms of the character or credibility of the rhetor and noting that, for Aristotle, one can appeal to *ēthos* by establishing

---

[9]The metaphors mentioned in this paragraph are scattered throughout Bakhtin's piece ("Discourse in the Novel," 228, 277, 291, 293, 327, 415). Bakhtin also uses metaphors when discussing specific literary texts, describing Charles Dickens's *Little Dorrit*, for example, as "everywhere dotted with quotation marks that serve to separate out little islands of scattered direct speech and purely authorial speech, washed by heteroglot waves from all sides" (307).

[10]Jasinski, "Heteroglossia," 297. I count myself among these critics, having drawn on John Murphy's appropriation of Bakhtin to develop my methodology for the study of the rhetorical activity of truth commissions (James E. Beitler, *Remaking Transitional Justice in the United States: The Rhetorical Authorization of the Greensboro Truth and Reconciliation Commission* [New York: Springer, 2013], 16-17).

eunoia, or goodwill, with one's audience. This association between *ēthos* and audience was reinforced in each of the subsequent chapters, offering a sketch of several important conceptual innovations from the Western rhetorical tradition that might be considered offspring, or at least distant relatives, of the appeal to *ēthos.* Chapter two's focus on *enargeia* considered how acts of vivid description—of bringing an event before one's eyes and allowing oneself and, by extension, one's *ēthos* to be overtaken by it—might carry off one's audience members and persuade them. Chapter three's reflections on identification explored rhetorical activity that aligns rhetors and their audiences, effectively uniting *ēthos* and *pathos.*[11] Chapter four's emphasis on constitutive rhetoric, which explored how rhetors call audience members to adopt particular identities, might be understood as mapping a corporate character or *ēthos* onto an entire audience. And chapter five's return to premodern uses of *ēthos* considered the persuasive characteristics of one's dwelling places. This journey has taken us from a consideration of the rhetor and audience's shared attitude (goodwill) to their shared experience (*enargeia*), to their shared identity (identification), to their shared community (constitutive rhetoric), to their shared environment (*ēthos* as dwelling place). Now our consideration of the rhetoric of Christian witness turns to language itself—and difference (heteroglossia).

Heteroglossia not only proves to be a useful concept for understanding national or cultural languages; it also helps us make sense of the languages and sub-languages of the body of Christ, the church as it has existed in all times and places. Through the authoritative revelation of Scripture, the guiding of the Spirit, and the doctrines and practices of Christian orthodoxy, the heteroglossia of the church may be pruned, but it is not destroyed. Unlike monologic utterances that, to borrow a line from Bakhtin, "[destroy] all traces of social

---

[11]Jeanne Fahnestock and Marie Secor, *A Rhetoric of Argument,* 3rd ed. (New York: McGraw-Hill, 2004), 55.

heteroglossia and diversity of language," the church's heteroglossia survives and even flourishes in response to the limits imposed by the illimitable Word.[12] Scripture itself speaks to these realities, describing both the origin of "multi-languageness" and its Spirit-directed manifestation in the church. The origin is, of course, the account of the tower of Babel, in which God responds to human pride by complicating the people's speech and scattering them one from another (Gen 11:1-9). Often referred to as both a punishment and a blessing, God's response causes disarray and drives people apart, but—more important for our purposes—it also results in a linguistic diversity that is rich and beautiful. Through the "Tower-of-Babel mixing of languages," God continues the work recorded in the first two chapters of Genesis, bringing about new opportunities for acts of human creativity— novel-writing among them.[13] In creating these opportunities, God amplifies the ways he can be glorified and witnessed to, as we see in Scripture's remarkable account of the day of Pentecost:

> When the day of Pentecost arrived, they were all together in one place. And suddenly there came from heaven a sound like a mighty rushing wind, and it filled the entire house where they were sitting. And divided *tongues as of fire* [γλῶσσαι ὡσεὶ πυρός, transliterated as *glōssai hōsei pyros*] appeared to them and rested on each one of them. And they were all filled with the Holy Spirit and began to speak *in other tongues* [ἑτέραις γλώσσαις, transliterated as *heterais glōssais*] as the Spirit gave them utterance. Now there were dwelling in Jerusalem Jews, devout men from every nation under heaven. And at this sound the multitude came together, and they were bewildered, because each one was hearing them speak in his own language. (Acts 2:1-6, emphases added)

Here we are presented with an absolutely astonishing depiction of the church's heteroglossia, which draws people from all over the world to

---

[12]Bakhtin, "Discourse in the Novel," 296.
[13]Bakhtin, "Discourse in the Novel," 278.

one another and reverses the course that God had put humanity on at the tower. And ultimately, as Bonhoeffer wrote in a letter to his parents on Pentecost of 1943, the "confusion of languages . . . is to end and be overcome by the language of God."[14] In the account of the language of God that we are given in the book of Acts, linguistic diversity still flourishes, but it is now understood by the people and sanctified by the Spirit: the disciples' "other tongues" are joined by "tongues as of fire." Such an image of diverse and holy Christian witness grants us a glimpse of the *ēthos* of the body of Christ for the world.

Pentecostal Witnesses

To begin to understand what it means to be a witness of Pentecost, we need look no further than our five exemplars: Lewis, Sayers, Bonhoeffer, Tutu, and Robinson. As we will see in what follows, each of these figures have significant things to say to us about the season, and their individual rhetorical approaches, when considered together, also have much to teach us about the witness of Pentecost. Let me briefly highlight their individual insights about the season before turning to what I think they say to us collectively.

Though I focused on his appeals to *ēthos* in chapter one, C. S. Lewis is often praised for his appeals to *logos*. Lewis himself knew he was skilled at crafting clear and logical arguments, but he also described this strength as a potential liability. "My own work," he admitted, "has suffered very much from the incurable intellectualism of my approach."[15] On occasion, his audience agreed. For instance, when Lewis addressed members of the Royal Air Force, people in the audience were—according to Lewis biographer George Sayer—"put off by

---

[14]Dietrich Bonhoeffer, "Letter to Karl and Paula Bonhoeffer, Pentecost 1943, June 14," in *Dietrich Bonhoeffer Works, Volume 8: Letters and Papers from Prison*, ed. John W. de Gruchy, trans. Barbara and Martin Rumscheidt (Minneapolis: Fortress, 2009), 105.

[15]C. S. Lewis, "God in the Dock," in *God in the Dock: Essays on Theology and Ethics*, ed. Walter Hooper (Grand Rapids: Eerdmans, 1970), 244.

his cool, rational approach, by the lack of emotional and obvious devotional content."[16] One's witness, Lewis realized as he practiced his craft and watched other evangelists work, was more powerful when logical appeals were combined with passionate appeals.[17] However, Lewis did not believe he had the skills to pull off direct emotional appeals of the "come to Jesus" sort.[18] It is not surprising, therefore, that he advocated for two-person missionary teams. The first speaker could appeal to logic to expose bias and faulty thinking about matters of faith, while the second speaker could appeal to the emotions to bring about a change of heart.[19] Keenly aware of his own weaknesses, Lewis did not feel compelled to witness as evangelists like Billy Graham did.[20] Let Jack be Jack and Billy be Billy. "There are many different ways," Lewis wrote, "of bringing people into His Kingdom."[21]

Desmond Tutu presents us with a view of human beings that is consistent with, and provides the grounds for, Lewis's argument about the importance of two-person missionary teams. As we saw in chapter four, Tutu challenges conceptions of humanity that give pride of place to the autonomous individual and instead champions the South African concept of *ubuntu*. *Ubuntu* announces that "I am who I am because of who you are," which suggests that human personhood and identity are social realities. For Tutu, *ubuntu* also presents personhood and identity as theological realities. In a characteristically playful excerpt from one of his speeches, Tutu remarked,

---

[16]Quoted in Philip G. Ryken, "Winsome Evangelist: The Influence of C. S. Lewis," in *C. S. Lewis: Lightbearer in the Shadowlands: The Evangelistic Vision of C. S. Lewis*, ed. Angus J. L. Menuge (Wheaton: Crossway, 1997), 59.

[17]Lewis, "God in the Dock," 244; Michael Ward, "Escape to Wallaby Wood: Lewis's Depictions of Conversion," in Menuge, ed., *C. S. Lewis: Lightbearer in the Shadowlands*, 146.

[18]Lewis, "God in the Dock," 244; Christopher W. Mitchell, "Bearing the Weight of Glory," in *The Pilgrim's Guide: C. S. Lewis and the Art of Witness*, ed. David Mills (Grand Rapids: Eerdmans, 1998), 6; Ward, "Escape to Wallaby Wood," 143.

[19]Lewis, "Christian Apologetics," in *God in the Dock*, 99.

[20]Ward, "Escape to Wallaby Wood," 143.

[21]Lewis, "Cross-Examination," in *God in the Dock*, 262.

"God is smart. God has created us so that we could never really be self-sufficient. I need you to make up for what I lack, as I make up for what you lack. And you can almost see God rubbing God's hands in glee and saying, 'Ah, even if I have to say so, that really is smart.'"[22] For Tutu, spiritual gifts and human finitude are actually two sides of the same coin, and Tutu locates the source of both in a grand and brilliant act of divine creation. This description of God's orchestration of human gifts and shortcomings offers us the theological and anthropological warrants for the claim that the character of Christian witness ought to be marked by rich diversity. In light of the gifts and shortcomings granted to us and our audiences, Christians should not strive to witness in identical ways. Or, to borrow another metaphor from Tutu, if we truly are part of "the rainbow people of God," we need not try to spread light on the same wavelength.[23] "*Non omnia possumus omnes,*" Lewis noted in "Christian Apologetics."[24] "Not all things can we all do."

Even as Pentecost reminds us to speak to others in the ways appointed to us, it also trains our ear to hear what Dietrich Bonhoeffer referred to as the "polyphony of life" in a letter to Eberhard Bethge from May 20, 1944.[25] Bonhoeffer had been thinking a lot about Pentecost from his cell in Tegel prison during the last weeks of May of 1944, and his comments on polyphony seem to be inspired, at least in part, by the season.[26] His May 29 letter to Eberhard Bethge begins,

---

[22]Desmond Tutu, "Reconciling Love: A Millennium Mandate," 2005–2006 Bryan Series Lectures on Spirit and Spirituality, Hege Library, Guilford College, Greensboro, NC, 2005.

[23]Tutu used the rainbow metaphor repeatedly before, during, and after the operation of the South African TRC. To give just one example (which is particularly noteworthy, given one of my book's key figures), Tutu referred to the "rainbow nation" when he and Alex Boraine accepted the Evangelical Church in Germany's "Dietrich Bonhoeffer-Prize" on behalf of the TRC.

[24]Lewis, "Christian Apologetics," 99.

[25]Bonhoeffer, "Letter to Eberhard Bethge, May 20, 1944," in *Dietrich Bonhoeffer Works, Volume 8: Letters and Papers from Prison*, ed. John W. de Gruchy, trans. Barbara and Martin Rumscheidt (Minneapolis: Fortress, 2009), 393-94.

[26]Pentecost fell on May 28 in 1944. A few days before the feast, Bonhoeffer had sent three meditations on passages from the Moravian daily lectionary to Renate and Eberhard Bethge,

"I hope that despite the air raids you both [Eberhard and Renate] are enjoying to the full the peace and beauty of these warm, summery days of Pentecost."[27] Such opening remarks are not simply small talk for Bonhoeffer. One's capacity for enjoyment in the midst of danger is part and parcel of his reflections in the letter. Bonhoeffer goes on to observe that, in prison during wartime, many of the people around him can only focus on one thing at a time. He writes, "When bombers come, they are nothing but fear itself; when there's something good to eat, nothing but greed itself; when they fail to get what they want, they become desperate; if something succeeds, that's all they see. They are missing out on the fullness of life and on the wholeness of their own existence."[28] The Christian faith, however, frees us from such tunnel vision, placing "us into many different dimensions of life at the same time; in a way we accommodate God and the whole world within us."[29] Shortly after citing Paul's comments in Romans 12:15,

---

and each of his reflections focused on the workings of the Spirit in the life of the Christian ("*Daily Text* Meditation for Pentecost 1944," in *Dietrich Bonhoeffer Works, Volume 16: Conspiracy and Imprisonment: 1940-1945*, ed. Mark S. Brocher, trans. Lisa E. Dahill [Minneapolis: Fortress, 2009], 626-29). The reflection most relevant to Bonhoeffer's concept of polyphony focused on the fruits of the Spirit: "There is a danger for us today that patience appears as the sole and most important Christian stance, and that we thereby severely curtail the riches of God. In the midst of times of discipline, the entire fullness of the Holy Spirit wants to unfold and to ripen, and we should give it full space within us for the sake of God, for the sake of others, and for our own sake. The entire world of God, the dear Father, wants to be born in us, to grow and ripen" (628). Here Bonhoeffer warns that the Christian's posture when facing challenging times should not become too fixed, because we may close ourselves off to the other fruits of the Spirit (which Bonhoeffer goes on to list). All of the fruits, not just patience, have a place in the midst of difficulty. Bonhoeffer's counsel that Christians should open themselves up to "the entire fullness of the Holy Spirit" does not seem too far afield from (and may provide the underpinnings for) the idea that the Christian faith better allows one to hear and embrace the "polyphony of life." After May 28 came and went without a letter, Bonhoeffer wrote to Bethge that he had been "a bit disconcerted and perhaps even saddened not to have a letter from anyone for Pentecost this year" ("Letter to Eberhard Bethge, May 29, 1944," in *Dietrich Bonhoeffer Works, Volume 8*, 405).

[27]Bonhoeffer, "Letter to Eberhard Bethge, May 29, 1944," in *Dietrich Bonhoeffer Works, Volume 8*, 404.

[28]Bonhoeffer, "Letter to Eberhard Bethge, May 29, 1944," in *Dietrich Bonhoeffer Works, Volume 8*, 405.

[29]Bonhoeffer, "Letter to Eberhard Bethge, May 29, 1944," in *Dietrich Bonhoeffer Works, Volume 8*, 405.

Bonhoeffer adds, "Life isn't pushed back into a single dimension [for people of faith], but is kept multidimensional, polyphonic."[30]

For Bonhoeffer, then, Pentecost is not simply a time to commemorate the church's proclamation of the gospel with many voices; it also serves as a fitting occasion to remind ourselves to embrace all of the richness of human existence. This embrace of the "polyphony of life" is connected, as Robert J. Dean has pointed out, to Bonhoeffer's "religionless-worldly understanding of the Christian faith."[31] Through it, we are drawn more and more deeply into our humanity and the life of the world. This movement, it should be noted, does not come at the expense of obedience to God but rather happens in concert with it. In his letter from May 20, Bonhoeffer writes, "God, the Eternal, wants to be loved with our whole heart . . . as a sort of *cantus firmus* to which the other voices of life resound in counterpoint."[32] Dean explains, "The type of polyphonic composition which Bonhoeffer had in mind involved adopting an existing plainsong or secular tune as the *cantus firmus* (lit. 'fixed melody') and adding over it other contrapuntal (from the Latin *contrapunctum*, 'against note') voices. The addition of these musical lines adds depth and texture to the composition and for Bonhoeffer points towards the multi-dimensionality of truly human life in Christ."[33] Given the single-mindedness he perceived in those around him at Tegel prison, Bonhoeffer's embrace of the polyphony of human life and the worldliness that comes with it becomes, perhaps somewhat paradoxically, an avenue for witness. Bonhoeffer writes, "I've almost made it a rule here for myself, when people here are trembling during an air raid, always just to talk about how much

---

[30]Bonhoeffer, "Letter to Eberhard Bethge, May 29, 1944," in *Dietrich Bonhoeffer Works, Volume 8*, 405.

[31]Robert J. Dean, *For the Life of the World: Jesus Christ and the Church in the Theologies of Dietrich Bonhoeffer and Stanley Hauerwas* (Eugene, OR: Pickwick, 2016), 176.

[32]"Letter to Eberhard Bethge, May 20, 1944," in *Dietrich Bonhoeffer Works, Volume 8*, 394.

[33]Dean, *For the Life of the World*, 177.

worse such an attack would be for smaller towns. One has to dislodge people from their one-track thinking—as it were, in 'preparation for' or 'enabling' faith."[34] A rhetoric of Christian witness shaped by Pentecost invites others to listen for the many counterpoints of human experience in the hopes that they might learn to recognize and follow the *cantus firmus* that anchors them all.

In addition to these insights of Lewis, Tutu, and Bonhoeffer, a Pentecost-informed witness also recognizes this vital truth: all of our attempts at Christian witness come to nothing apart from the power of the Spirit. It is only by the Spirit's power that the church's "many voices" and rhetorics, including those described throughout this book, can bring about the faith of their hearers. Both Dorothy L. Sayers and Marilynne Robinson shed light on this power.

As we explored in chapter two, in her book *The Mind of the Maker,* Sayers likens human creativity to the Trinity: a writer's Idea, Energy, and Power is analogous to Father, Son, and Spirit. Chapter two focused on Energy and the incarnation of the second person of the Godhead, but Sayers also has much to say about Power and the Spirit. In her "Pentecost" chapter of *The Mind of the Maker,* she describes how Power relates to the other two elements of the creative process, suggesting that Power is the impact or action that an Idea, once incarnated, has on a writer's audiences. She writes, "Before the Energy was revealed or incarnate it was, as we have seen, already present in Power within the creator's mind, but now that Power is released for communication to other men, and returns from their minds to his with a new response. It dwells in them and works upon them with creative energy, producing in them fresh manifestations of Power."[35] Sayers implies in this passage that she believes that the Holy Spirit's activity

---

[34]Bonhoeffer, "Letter to Eberhard Bethge, May 29, 1944," in *Dietrich Bonhoeffer Works, Volume 8,* 405.

[35]Dorothy Sayers, *The Mind of the Maker* (San Francisco: HarperCollins, 1987), 111.

involves the response brought about by the Word's call. It gives life to faith in the hearer. Significantly, however, the response is not only _created_ but also _creative_. Sayer's understanding of Pentecost's witness could even be described as _procreative_, insofar as it yields "fresh manifestations of Power." What Sayers is saying about Pentecost here suggests, for the purposes of my own project, that the rhetoric of Christian witness ought to invite and create possibilities for rhetorical activity and innovation among its audiences. Witness must bring forth witness.

Sayers's subsequent remarks encourage us to take our responsibility to witness in this manner seriously. She describes Power as "dangerous" and then writes: "Every word—even every idle word—will be accounted for at the day of judgment, because the word itself has power to bring judgment."[36] The witness of Pentecost is dangerous in part because we will be asked to account for it, but it is also dangerous because of its transformative potential. Using language that resonates with our exploration of _ēthos_ in chapter five, Sayers writes that Power "dwells in" our audience members and "works upon them."

On the topic of the transformation, Marilynne Robinson takes up the baton. Late in her book _Gilead_, we learn from Ames that Lila's initial visit to his church—the first moment the two saw each other, right in the middle of Ames's sermon—happened on a "blessed, rainy Pentecost."[37] Thinking about that astonishing moment of his life, Ames recalls a dream he once had.[38] In the dream, he and Boughton were searching for tadpoles in the river when Ames's grandfather approached, filled his hat with river water, drenched the boys, and departed, leaving the two "standing there in that glistening river, amazed at ourselves and shining like the apostles." Ames's dream

---

[36]Sayers, _Mind of the Maker_, 111.
[37]Marilynne Robinson, _Gilead: A Novel_ (New York: Farrar, Straus, and Giroux, 2004), 203
[38]Robinson, _Gilead_, 202-3.

reveals a truth about reality that helps him understand his first encounter with Lila: that "transformations just that abrupt do occur in this life, and they occur unsought and un-awaited, and they beggar your hopes and your deserving." In one moment Ames is fishing for tadpoles, and in the next he has received a kind of baptism. He is a persuasive pastor in one instant and then, seeing Lila, bewildered ever after. Interestingly, Ames's *reflections* about seeing Lila for the first time are not that different from the *content* of the sermon that he was giving as she walked through the door: "It has seemed to me sometimes as though the Lord breathes on this poor gray ember of Creation and it turns to radiance—for a moment or a year or the span of a life. And then it sinks back into itself again, and to look at it no one would know it had anything to do with fire, or light. That is what I said in the Pentecost sermon."[39]

The transformative power of Pentecost, Ames's sermon and his experience both suggest, comes at God's appointed time and not ours. For those interested in the rhetoric of Christian witness, this is a valuable insight worth keeping in mind. That said, by the end of the book, Ames has refined his views about his Pentecost message. He notes, "I have reflected on that sermon, and there is some truth in it. But the Lord is more constant and far more extravagant than it seems to imply. Wherever you turn your eyes the world can shine like transfiguration. You don't have to bring a thing to it except a little willingness to see."[40] Ames (and Robinson) seem to conclude that the Spirit's power is constantly flowing and ever transforming us and the world. As Christians, we just need eyes ready to perceive and, I might add, tongues prepared to speak.

All that said, while each of the figures in this book has something unique and important to teach us about the witness of Pentecost, it is

---

[39]Robinson, *Gilead*, 245.
[40]Robinson, *Gilead*, 245.

their collective witness—their many diverse voices, gathered together across the pages of this project—that speaks most forcefully to the essence of the season's witness. *Christian witness involves, and indeed requires, "speaking in tongues" together.* In making this claim, it is not my intention to enter into the longstanding interdenominational debate about the charism of glossolalia. Rather, I simply want to affirm the notion that, if the gospel of Jesus Christ is truly to reach the whole world, the church's witness must go forth in multiple languages, through a variety of mediums, by way of different genres and voices, using a host of rhetorics. It must, in other words, understand the reality of Pentecost not simply in terms of the specific practice of glossolalia but as a rhetorical paradigm for the collective *ēthos* of the whole body of Christ. It is true, of course, that the church has long recognized the importance of its polyvocality with respect to the world's languages (as our zeal for Bible translation efforts demonstrate); however, Christians have generally devoted less attention to cultivating and celebrating diverse rhetorics of witness. I have attempted to respond to this need by highlighting a few of the remarkable ways that our liturgical-rhetorical traditions have been put into practice over the last century. But there is still much more to do. The great diversity within the body of Christ has brought forth innumerable rhetorical resources, and I believe that we ought to continue to study these riches as we seek to witness faithfully to the good news.

Witnessing Worship

Dietrich Bonhoeffer begins his Pentecost 1943 letter to his parents by revealing his deep desire to celebrate the feast day by worshiping in church. Later in the letter, while still reflecting on Pentecost, Bonhoeffer makes a somewhat startling claim about *where* the "Babylonian confusion of languages" will be "overcome by the language God." *It is in the church.* He then adds that "all these are indeed very deep and important thoughts." The Spirit's power at Pentecost, Bonhoeffer's comments appear to imply, is less about the Word going out than it is about the Word drawing people in and reconciling them to one another. Based on Bonhoeffer's remarks here, it would seem that the witness of Pentecost happens *within and through* the worshiping body of Christ.[41]

Though Bonhoeffer's point may strike some readers as obvious, pastors and theologians sometimes discuss worship and witness as if the two actions are separate from each other. To give just one example, in his piece "The Church as Worshiping Community," theologian John Webster writes, "We may conveniently distinguish [the church's] activities into acts of the *church in gathering* and acts of the *church in dispersal,* that is, the acts of the church in its internal and its external orientations."[42] At times it is indeed worthwhile to make such a distinction. Differentiating acts of the church in gathering (worship) from acts of the church in dispersal (witness) may serve to guard against the hypocrisy Jesus warns us about in Matthew 6:1: "Beware of practicing your righteousness before other

---

[41]The letter discussed in this paragraph is found in Bonhoeffer, "Letter to Karl and Paula Bonhoeffer, Pentecost 1943, June 14," in *Dietrich Bonhoeffer Works, Volume 8,* 104-5.

[42]Webster continues, "The acts of the church in gathering are those acts by which the church is drawn towards the source of its life, and reinvested in the truth and goodness of the gospel. The acts of the church in dispersal are those acts in which the church follows the external impulse of its source of life, and is pushed beyond itself in testimony and service" ("The Church as Witnessing Community," *Scottish Bulletin of Evangelical Theology* 21, no. 1 [2003]: 29). John Stott describes the church's actions in a similar way, although—as he notes—he has a reason for doing so. Stott writes, "I sometimes wonder (although I exaggerate in order to make my point) if it would not be very healthy for church members to meet only on Sundays (for worship, fellowship and teaching) and not at all midweek. Then we would gather on Sundays and scatter for the rest of the week. We would come to Christ for worship and go for Christ in mission. And in that rhythm of Sunday-weekday, gathering-scattering, coming-going and worship-mission the church would express its holy worldliness, and its structure would conform to its double identity" (*The Living Church: Convictions of a Lifelong Pastor* [Downers Grove, IL: InterVarsity Press, 2007], 57). Importantly, Stott *does* complicate this distinction later by inviting us to consider whether or not aspects of our life together—including church decor, liturgies, programming, etc.—are "mobilized for mission" (59-62). I have found that collapsing distinctions between worship and witness in such ways often leads to fruitful conversations about both among Christians.

people in order to be seen by them, for then you will have no reward from your Father who is in heaven." Nevertheless, while Webster's distinction may be helpful on such occasions, accepting this convenience does risk obscuring the fact that all of the church's acts—whether in gathering or in dispersal—always involve both internal and external orientations.[43] As we go outward to witness, our witness orients us inward; as we come inward to worship, our worship orients us outward.[44]

The claim that worship and witness are not distinct from each other also finds traction in the work of theologian Stanley Hauerwas. As I already touched on in the previous chapter, Hauerwas has emphasized the importance of the gospel's embodiment *in* the church. The church must be a community in which people can see themselves living.[45] In discussing elsewhere what defines such a community,

---

[43]To be fair, Webster himself seems to acknowledge this point implicitly, in a passage that is characteristically forceful: "If the church is what it is because of the gospel, it will be most basically characterized by astonishment at the good news of Jesus. What will lie at the heart of all its undertakings will be the primitive response to Jesus' presence and proclamation: 'they were all amazed' (Mark 1:27). What is this amazement? It is being held by a reality—the reality of Jesus—which presents itself as pure gift, without desert or expectation; it is letting ourselves be taken up by that reality and its inherent authority, worth, and persuasiveness; it is having settled ideas and routines ruptured and transcended; it is being disconcerted by what is at once a matter of bewilderment and delight. *The life and proclamation of the church are 'evangelical' in so far as they are captivated in these ways by the good news*" ("Church as Witnessing Community," 29, emphasis added). Here, to be a witness involves an orientation that, in light of Webster's emphasis on astonishment and amazement, seems very worshipful indeed: we proclaim the good news of Jesus Christ insofar as we ourselves are "captivated . . . by the good news." Webster also seems to complicate his distinction between internal and external orientations when he writes, "Human society and culture are *enclosed* by the reality of the gospel" (23, emphasis added).

[44]In the second book of his Cultural Liturgies series, James K. A. Smith makes the second of these points particularly forcefully: "It's not a matter of choosing between worship *or* mission; nor are we faced with the false dichotomy of church *or* world, cathedral *or* city. To the contrary, we worship *for* mission; we gather *for* sending; we center ourselves in the practices of the body of Christ *for the sake of* the world; we are reformed in the cathedral to undertake our image-bearing commission to reform the city. So it is precisely an expansive sense of mission that requires formation. It is the missional *telos* of Christian *action* that requires us to be intentional about the formative power of Christian practices" (*Imagining the Kingdom* [Grand Rapids: Baker Academic, 2013], 154). See part two, chapter four of *Imagining the Kingdom* for a more in-depth discussion of the relationship between liturgy, Christian formation, and mission.

[45]Stanley Hauerwas, *With the Grain of the Universe: The Church's Witness and Natural Theology* (Grand Rapids: Brazos, 2013), 214.

Hauerwas emphasizes the importance of Christian character and other "'marks' through which we know that the church is church."[46] Two of the primary marks of the church that Hauerwas focuses on are the administration of the sacraments and the proclamation of the Word—both of which are, of course, tied to Christian worship practices.[47] But for Hauerwas, the line between worship and witness is blurred, for even as the sacramental and sermonic marks of the church transform the character of the community, they also distinguish Christians from the world and, in so doing, reveal Christ to it. In other words, the church's character is rhetorical. The Christian social ethic, writes Hauerwas, "shines as a beacon to others illuminating how life should be lived well."[48] To return to the rhetorical language I introduced in chapter five, we might say that worship creates the dwelling place (*ēthos*) where effective witness happens.[49] Such a view of Christian witness puts at least as much emphasis on the world's place in the church as it does on the church's place in the world.[50]

---

[46]Stanley Hauerwas, *A Community of Character* (Notre Dame: University of Notre Dame Press, 1981); *The Peaceable Kingdom* (Notre Dame: University of Notre Dame Press, 1983), 99.

[47]Hauerwas, *Peaceable Kingdom*, 107.

[48]Hauerwas, *Peaceable Kingdom*, 33-34.

[49]Drawing on Hauerwas, theologian Simon Chan also collapses the distinction between the church's worship practices and its missional activity: "Lives are transformed [through preaching and, by extension, the church's other liturgical practices] so that they become, in Stanley Hauerwas's term, 'a community of character.' This does not just mean being 'nice' people. What marks Christians as God's people is that they have become a community that worships God in spirit and in truth. This is what the church must aim at in mission. Mission does not seek to turn sinners into saved individuals; it seeks, rather, to turn disparate individuals into a worshiping community" (*Liturgical Theology: The Church as Worshiping Community* [Downers Grove, IL: InterVarsity Press, 2006], 45). Likewise, Michael G. Cartwright builds on Hauerwas's work to make the related point that worship practices and practices associated with the Christian year are features of the "*ethos* of Christian witness" ("Being Sent: Witness," in *The Blackwell Companion to Christian Ethics,* ed. Stanley Hauerwas and Samuel Wells [Malden, MA: Blackwell, 2004], 483, 484-85, 486). My book has tried to explain how this is so in more detail.

[50]Kevin Vanhoozer gets at this dynamic when he describes the church "as the 'theater of the gospel,' the place where the reconciliation achieved by the cross is to be played out in scenes large and small" (*The Drama of Doctrine: A Canonical Linguistic Approach to Christian Theology* [Louisville: Westminster John Knox, 2005], 32). Vanhoozer continues, "The church is the company of players gathered together to stage scenes of the kingdom of God for the sake of the

As we have seen throughout this book, worship and witness are connected in another significant way as well: our liturgical practices have something to teach us about what our witnessing ought to look like. As we have explored the rhetorical mastery of five heroes of Christian witness together, we have journeyed through the seasons of the Christian year from Advent to Pentecost and, simultaneously, observed liturgical practices such as the collect/call to worship, the recitation of the creed, the sermon, the confession of sin, and the Eucharist. We have, in other words, engaged in the practice of "keeping time," in terms of both the movement of the Christian year and the pacing of the weekly worship service.[51] In light of this journey, it is appropriate to bring this book to a conclusion with a brief benediction, which I have adapted from a blessing for the Day of Pentecost from the *Book of Occasional Services*.[52] Please receive these words as my prayer for you:

May God, who by the Holy Spirit caused those of many tongues to proclaim Jesus as Lord, strengthen your faith and equip you to bear witness to him in word and deed. Amen.

---

watching world. The direction of doctrine thus enables us, as individuals and as a church, to render the gospel public by leading lives in creative imitation of Christ" (32). In Vanhoozer's metaphor of the theater, the church can be understood as playing host to the world.

[51]Cartwright, "Being Sent," 484.

[52]Quoted in Philip Pfatteicher, *Journey into the Heart of God: Living the Liturgical Year* (Oxford: Oxford University Press, 2013), 268.

BIBLIOGRAPHY

Allen, John. *Rabble-rouser for Peace: The Authorized Biography of Desmond Tutu.* New York: Free Press, 2006.

Amorose, Thomas. "Resistance to Rhetoric in Christian Tradition." In *Renovating Rhetoric in Christian Tradition.* Edited by Elizabeth Vander Lei et al., 135-49. Pittsburgh: University of Pittsburgh Press, 2014.

Anderson, Greg M. "A Most Potent Rhetoric: C. S. Lewis, 'Congenital Rhetorician.'" In *C. S. Lewis: Life, Works, and Legacy.* Vol. 4, *Scholar, Teacher, and Public Intellectual.* Edited by Bruce L. Edwards, 195-228. Westport: Praeger, 2007.

Aristotle. *On Rhetoric: A Theory of Civic Discourse.* Translated by George Alexander Kennedy. New York: Oxford University Press, 1991.

Arnett, Ronald. *Dialogic Confession: Bonhoeffer's Rhetoric of Responsibility.* Carbondale: Southern Illinois University Press, 2005.

St. Augustine. *On Christian Teaching.* Oxford: Oxford University Press, 1997.

———. *The Confessions.* Translated by Maria Boulding, O.S.B. New York: Vintage, 1998.

Bakhtin, M. M. "Discourse in the Novel." In *The Dialogic Imagination: Four Essays.* Edited by Michael Holquist. Translated by Caryl Emerson and Michael Holquist, 259-422. Austin: University of Texas Press, 1981.

Battle, Michael. *Reconciliation: The Ubuntu Theology of Desmond Tutu.* Cleveland, OH: Pilgrim, 1997.

———. "Ubuntu: Learning from the African Worldview." *Sewanee Theological Review* 53, no. 4 (2010): 404-16.

Beitler, James. "Making More of the Middle Ground: Desmond Tutu and the *Ethos* of the South African Truth and Reconciliation Commission." *Relevant Rhetoric: A New Journal of Rhetorical Studies* 3, no. 1 (Spring 2012): http://relevantrhetoric.com/Making%20More%20of%20the%20Middle%20Ground.pdf.

———. _Remaking Transitional Justice in the United States: The Rhetorical Authorization of the Greensboro Truth and Reconciliation Commission._ New York: Springer, 2013.

———. "Response to 'George MacDonald in the Age of the Incarnation.'" In _George MacDonald in the Age of Miracles: Incarnation, Doubt, and Reenchantment,_ by Timothy Larsen, 37-47. Downers Grove, IL: InterVarsity Press, 2018.

———. Review of _Managing Vulnerability: South Africa's Struggle for a Democratic Rhetoric,_ by Richard C. Marback. _Rhetoric Review_ 32, no. 4 (2013): 490-93.

———. _Rhetorics of Interdependence: Composing the Ethos of the Greensboro Truth and Reconciliation Commission._ PhD diss., University of Michigan, 2009.

Bieber Lake, Christina. _Prophets of the Posthuman: American Fiction, Biotechnology, and the Ethics of Personhood._ Notre Dame: University of Notre Dame Press, 2013.

Boedy, Matthew. "Bonhoeffer's Performative Sensibilities in His Earliest Work." _The Heythrop Journal_ 53 (2012): 983-92.

———. "From Deliberation to Responsibility: Ethics, Invention, and Bonhoeffer in Technical Communication." _Technical Communication Quarterly_ 26, no. 2 (2017): 116-26.

Bonhoeffer, Dietrich. "After Ten Years." In _Dietrich Bonhoeffer Works, Volume 8: Letters and Papers from Prison._ Edited by John W. de Gruchy. Translated by Barbara and Martin Rumscheidt, 37-52. Minneapolis: Fortress, 2009.

———. "Ambassadors for Christ." In _Collected Sermons._ Edited by Isabel Best. Translated by Douglas W. Scott et al., 87-94. Minneapolis: Fortress, 2012.

———. _Christ the Center._ New York: Harper & Row, 1978.

———. "The Church and the Jewish Question." In _Dietrich Bonhoeffer: Witness to Jesus Christ._ Edited by John de Gruchy, 124-30. Minneapolis: Fortress, 1991.

———. "The Church and the Jewish Question." _Dietrich Bonhoeffer Works, Volume 12: Berlin: 1932-1933._ Edited by Larry L. Rasmussen. Translated by Isabel Best and David Higgins, 361-70. Minneapolis: Fortress, 2009.

———. "_Daily Text_ Meditation for Pentecost 1944." In _Dietrich Bonhoeffer Works, Volume 16: Conspiracy and Imprisonment: 1940-1945._ Edited by Mark S. Brocher. Translated by Lisa E. Dahill, 626-29. Minneapolis: Fortress, 2009.

———. "_Epiphany:_ A Theological Reflection." _Dietrich Bonhoeffer Works, Volume 15: Theological Education Underground: 1937-1940._ Edited by Victoria J. Barnett. Translated by Victoria J. Barnett et al., 534-37. Minneapolis: Fortress, 2012.

———. "Lectures on Christology (Student Notes)." _Dietrich Bonhoeffer Works, Volume 12: Berlin: 1932-1933._ Edited by Larry L. Rasmussen. Translated by Isabel Best and David Higgins, 299-360. Minneapolis: Fortress, 2009.

———. "Letter to Eberhard Bethge, May 20, 1944." In _Dietrich Bonhoeffer Works, Volume 8: Letters and Papers from Prison._ Edited by John W. de Gruchy. Translated by Barbara and Martin Rumscheidt, 393-94. Minneapolis: Fortress, 2009.

———. "Letter to Eberhard Bethge, May 29, 1944." In _Dietrich Bonhoeffer Works, Volume 8: Letters and Papers from Prison._ Edited by John W. de Gruchy. Translated by Barbara and Martin Rumscheidt, 404-7. Minneapolis: Fortress, 2009.

———. "Letter to Karl and Paula Bonhoeffer, Pentecost 1943, June 14." In _Dietrich Bonhoeffer Works, Volume 8: Letters and Papers from Prison._ Edited by John W. de Gruchy. Translated by Barbara and Martin Rumscheidt, 104-7. Minneapolis: Fortress, 2009.

———. "Letter to Renate and Eberhard Bethge, May 24, 1944." _Dietrich Bonhoeffer Works, Volume 8: Letters and Papers from Prison._ Edited by John W. de Gruchy. Translated by Barbara and Martin Rumscheidt, 400-401. Minneapolis: Fortress, 2009.

———. _Life Together._ Translated by John W. Doberstein. New York: HarperCollins, 1954.

———. "Practical Exercises in Homiletics" and "Lectures on Homiletics." _Dietrich Bonhoeffer Works, Volume 14: Theological Education at Finkenwalde: 1935-1937._ Edited by H. Gaylon Barker and Mark S. Brocker. Translated by Douglas W. Stott, 341-76, 487-535. Minneapolis: Fortress, 2013.

Bonhoeffer, Dietrich, and Clyde E. Fant. _Worldly Preaching: Lectures on Homiletics._ Rev. ed. New York: Crossroad, 1991.

Book of Common Prayer and Administration of the Sacraments and Other Rites and Ceremonies of the Church: Together with the Psalter or Psalms of David According to the Use of the Episcopal Church. New York: Seabury, 1979.

Brabazon, James. _Dorothy L. Sayers: A Biography._ New York: Charles Scribner's Sons, 1981.

Burke, Kenneth. _Language as Symbolic Action: Essays on Life, Literature, and Method._ Berkeley: University of California Press, 1966.

———. "The Rhetoric of Hitler's 'Battle.'" In _The Philosophy of Literary Form: Studies in Symbolic Action,_ 191-220. 3rd ed. Berkeley: University of California Press, 1973.

————. *A Rhetoric of Motives*. 2nd ed. Berkeley: University of California Press, 1969.

————. *A Rhetoric of Motives*. New York: Prentice Hall, 1950.

————. "Rhetoric—Old and New." *Journal of General Education* 5, no. 3 (1951): 202-9.

Carpenter, Humphrey. *The Inklings: C. S. Lewis, J. R. R. Tolkien, Charles Williams, and Their Friends*. Boston: Houghton Mifflin, 1979.

Cartwright, Michael G. "Being Sent: Witness." In *The Blackwell Companion to Christian Ethics*. Edited by Stanley Hauerwas and Samuel Wells, 481-94. Malden, MA: Blackwell, 2004.

Chan, Simon. *Liturgical Theology: The Church as Worshiping Community*. Downers Grove, IL: InterVarsity Press, 2006.

Charland, Maurice. "Constitutive Rhetoric: The Case of the Peuple Québécois." *Quarterly Journal of Speech* 73, no. 2 (1987): 133-50.

Charles, Ron. "Marilynne Robinson's 'Lila': An Exquisite Novel of Spiritual Redemption and Love." *The Washington Post*. September 30, 2014.

————. "Their Father's House." *The Washington Post*. September 7, 2008.

Chase, Kenneth R. "Christian Rhetorical Theory: A New (Re)Turn." *Journal of Communication and Religion* 36, no. 1 (2013): 25-49.

————. "Ethical Rhetoric and Divine Power: Reflections on Matthew 10:17-20 (and Parallels)." *Bulletin for Biblical Research* 22, no. 4 (2012): 199-218.

Cheney, George. *Rhetoric in an Organizational Society: Managing Multiple Identities*. Columbia: University of South Carolina Press, 1991.

Churchwell, Sarah. "Marilynne Robinson's *Lila*—A Great Achievement in US Fiction." *The Guardian*. November 7, 2014.

Cipriani, Nello. "Rhetoric." *Augustine Through the Ages: An Encyclopedia*. Edited by Allan D. Fitzgerald et al., 724-26. Grand Rapids: Eerdmans, 1999.

Clark, Gregory. *Rhetorical Landscapes in America: Variations on a Theme from Kenneth Burke*. Columbia: University of South Carolina Press, 2004.

Coetzee, Carli. "'They Never Wept, the Men of My Race': Antjie Krog's *Country of My Skull* and the White South African Signature." *Journal of Southern African Studies* 27, no. 4 (2001): 685-96.

Collins, David. *A Virtual Tour of the Parish Church of Fenchurch St. Paul: From The Nine Tailors by Dorothy Sayers*. West Sussex: The Dorothy L. Sayers Society, 2011.

Colón, Christine A. *Writing for the Masses: Dorothy L. Sayers and the Victorian Literary Tradition*. New York: Routledge, 2018.

Common Worship: Services and Prayers for the Church of England: Times and Seasons. London: Church House Publishing, 2006.

Como, James. *Branches to Heaven: The Geniuses of C. S. Lewis*. Dallas: Spence, 1998.

Corbett, Edward P. J. *Classical Rhetoric for the Modern Student*. Oxford: Oxford University Press, 1965.

Crouch, Andy. *Culture Making: Recovering Our Creative Calling*. Downers Grove, IL: InterVarsity Press, 2008.

Crowley, Sharon. *Toward a Civil Discourse: Rhetoric and Fundamentalism*. Pittsburgh: University of Pittsburgh Press, 2006.

Crowley, Sharon, and Debra Hawhee. *Ancient Rhetorics for Contemporary Students*. 5th ed. Boston: Pearson, 2012.

Cunningham, David. *Faithful Persuasion: In Aid of a Rhetoric of Christian Theology*. Notre Dame: University of Notre Dame Press, 1992.

Cunningham, Richard B. *C. S. Lewis: Defender of the Faith*. Philadelphia: Westminster, 1967.

Danker, Frederick William. *The Concise Greek-English Lexicon of the New Testament*. Chicago: University of Chicago Press, 2009.

Davis, Jeffry C., and Adam Q. Corbin. "Problematizing the Center: Affirming Christian Identities and the Complexity of Faith." *The Dangling Modifier* 21, no. 2 (2015): http://sites.psu.edu/thedanglingmodifier/?p=2284.

Dawn, Maggi. "Liturgy—It's *not* the Work of the People." *Maggidawn.net*, September 21, 2009.

Dean, Robert J. *For the Life of the World: Jesus Christ and the Church in the Theologies of Dietrich Bonhoeffer and Stanley Hauerwas*. Eugene, OR: Pickwick, 2016.

Deans, Thomas. "The Rhetoric of Jesus Writing in the Story of the Woman Accused of Adultery (John 7.53-8.11)." *College Composition and Communication* 65, no. 3 (2014): 406-29.

Derrida, Jacques. "Declarations of Independence." *New Political Science: A Journal of Politics and Culture* 15 (1986): 7-15.

"Dietrich Bonhoeffer-Prize for the South African Truth and Reconciliation Commission." *Evangelical Church in Germany*. Bulletin no. 2 (1999): https://archiv.ekd.de/english/1697-2699.html.

"Don v. Devil." *Time*. September 8, 1947, 65-66, 68-69, 72, 74.

Dorsett, Lyle W., ed. Introduction to *The Essential C. S. Lewis*, 1-17. New York: Collier/Macmillan, 1988.

Downing, Crystal. "The Orthodoxology of Dorothy L. Sayers." *VII* 22 (2005): 29-44.

———. *Writing Performances: The Stages of Dorothy L. Sayers.* New York: Palgrave Macmillan, 2004.

Doxtader, Erik. "The Faith and Struggle of Beginning (with) Words: On the Turn Between Reconciliation and Recognition." *Philosophy and Rhetoric* 40, no. 1 (2007): 119-46.

———. "Making Rhetorical History in a Time of Transition: The Occasion, Constitution, and Representation of South African Reconciliation." *Rhetoric & Public Affairs* 4, no. 2 (2001): 223-60.

———. "The Potential of Reconciliation's Beginning: A Reply." *Rhetoric & Public Affairs* 7, no. 3 (2004): 378-90.

———. "Reconciliation—a Rhetorical Concept/ion." *Quarterly Journal of Speech* 89, no. 4 (2003): 267-92.

———. *With Faith in the Works of Words: The Beginnings of Reconciliation in South Africa, 1985–1995.* East Lansing: Michigan State University Press, 2009.

Dreher, Rod. *The Benedict Option: A Strategy for Christians in a Post-Christian Nation.* New York: Penguin Random House, 2017.

Edwards, Bruce L. "A Thoroughly Converted Man: C. S. Lewis in the Public Square." In *The Pilgrim's Guide: C. S. Lewis and the Art of Witness.* Edited by David Mills, 27-40. Grand Rapids: Eerdmans, 1998.

Engebretson, Alex. "Marilynne Robinson's Singular Vision." *The Millions.* November 24, 2014.

———. *Understanding Marilynne Robinson.* Columbia: University of South Carolina Press, 2017.

Fahnestock, Jeanne, and Marie Secor. *A Rhetoric of Argument.* 3rd ed. New York: McGraw-Hill, 2004.

Fischer, Benjamin, and Philip C. Derbesy. "Literary Catholicity: An Alternative Reading of Influence in the Work of C. S. Lewis and G. K. Chesterton." *Religion and the Arts* 19, no. 4 (2015): 389-410.

Fleming, John V. "Literary Critic." In *The Cambridge Companion to C. S. Lewis.* Edited by Robert MacSwain and Michael Ward, 15-28. Cambridge: Cambridge University Press, 2010.

Fletcher, Christine M. "Vocation in Work: Dorothy L. Sayers and Economic Issues." *VII* 26 (2009): 53-80.

Ford, Andrew. *Homer: The Poetry of the Past.* Ithaca: Cornell University Press, 1992.

Fortenbaugh, William W. "Aristotle on Persuasion Through Character." *Rhetorica: A Journal of the History of Rhetoric* 10, no. 3 (1992): 207-44.

Gee, James Paul. *An Introduction to Discourse Analysis: Theory and Method.* 2nd ed. New York: Routledge, 2005.

Golden, James L., and Edward P. J. Corbett. *The Rhetoric of Blair, Campbell, and Whately.* Rev. ed. Carbondale: Southern Illinois University Press, 1990.

Greek New Testament. 4th rev. ed. Edited by Barbara Aland et al. Stuttgart: Deutsche Bibelgesellschaft, 1998.

Guinness, Os. *Fool's Talk: Recovering the Art of Christian Persuasion.* Downers Grove, IL: InterVarsity Press, 2015.

Hadden Hobbs, June. "Burial, Baptism, and Baseball: Typology and Memorialization in Marilynne Robinson's Gilead." *Christianity and Literature* 59, no. 2 (2010): 241-62.

Haddox, Thomas F. *Hard Sayings: The Rhetoric of Christian Orthodoxy in Late Modern Fiction.* Columbus: Ohio State University Press, 2013.

Halloran, S. Michael. "Aristotle's Concept of *Ethos,* or If Not His Somebody Else's." *Rhetoric Review* 1, no. 1 (1982): 58-63.

Harrison, William H. "Loving the Creation, Loving the Creator: Dorothy L. Sayers's Theology of Work." *Anglican Theological Review* 86, no. 2 (2004): 239-57.

Haswell, Janis, Richard Haswell, and Glenn Blalock. "Hospitality in College Composition Courses." *College Composition and Communication* 60, no. 4 (2009): 707-27.

Hatch, John B. *Race and Reconciliation: Redressing Wounds of Injustice.* Lanham, MD: Lexington, 2008.

Hauerwas, Stanley. *A Community of Character: Toward a Constructive Christian Social Ethic.* Notre Dame: University of Notre Dame Press, 1981.

——. *The Peaceable Kingdom: A Primer in Christian Ethics.* Notre Dame: University of Notre Dame Press, 1983.

——. *With the Grain of the Universe: The Church's Witness and Natural Theology.* Grand Rapids: Baker, 2013.

Haverkamp, Heidi. *Advent in Narnia: Reflections for the Season.* Louisville: Westminster John Knox, 2015.

Heck, Joel D. "*Praeparatio Evangelica.*" In *C. S. Lewis: Lightbearer in the Shadowlands: The Evangelistic Vision of C. S. Lewis.* Edited by Angus J. L. Menuge, 235-57. Wheaton: Crossway, 1997.

Holberg, Jennifer L. "'The Courage to See It': Toward an Understanding of Glory." *Christianity and Literature* 59, no. 2 (2010): 283-300.

Holiday, Judy. "In[ter]vention: Locating Rhetoric's *Ethos*." *Rhetoric Review* 28, no. 4 (2009): 388-405.

Hooper, Walter. Introduction to *C.S. Lewis, On Stories, and Other Essays on Literature*. Edited by Walter Hooper, ix-xxi. New York: Harcourt Brace, 1982.

———. Preface to C. S. Lewis, *God in the Dock: Essays on Theology and Ethics,* 7-17. Grand Rapids: Eerdmans, 1970.

Hungerford, Amy B. *Postmodern Belief: American Literature and Religion since 1960*. Princeton: Princeton University Press, 2010.

Hyatt, Douglas T. "Joy, the Call of God in Man: A Critical Appraisal of Lewis's Argument from Desire." In *C. S. Lewis: Lightbearer in the Shadowlands: The Evangelistic Vision of C. S. Lewis*. Edited by Angus J.L. Menuge, 305-28. Wheaton: Crossway, 1997.

Hyde, Michael J., ed. *The* Ethos *of Rhetoric*. Columbia: University of South Carolina Press, 2004.

Jacobs, Alan. *Looking Before and After: Testimony and the Christian Life*. Grand Rapids: Eerdmans, 2008.

———. *The Narnian: The Life and Imagination of C. S. Lewis*. San Francisco: HarperCollins, 2005.

Jamison, Leslie. "The Power of Grace." *The Atlantic,* October 2014.

Jasinski, James. "Heteroglossia." In *Sourcebook on Rhetoric: Key Concepts in Contemporary Rhetorical Studies*. Edited by James Jasinki, 295-99. Thousand Oaks, CA: Sage, 2002.

———. "Identification." In *Sourcebook on Rhetoric: Key Concepts in Contemporary Rhetorical Studies*. Edited by James Jasinki, 305-8. Thousand Oaks, CA: Sage, 2001.

———. *Sourcebook on Rhetoric: Key Concepts in Contemporary Rhetorical Studies*. Thousand Oaks, CA: Sage, 2001.

Johnson, Diana. "Moral of the Story." *The New York Times.* October 3, 2014.

Jost, Walter, and Wendy Olmsted, eds. *Rhetorical Invention and Religious Inquiry*. New Haven: Yale University Press, 2000.

Kalantzis, George. "A Witness to the Nations: Early Christianity and Narratives of Power." In *Christian Political Witness*. Edited by George Kalantzis and Gregory W. Lee, 90-111. Downers Grove, IL: InterVarsity Press, 2014.

Katula, Richard A. "Quintilian on the Art of Emotional Appeal. *Rhetoric Review* 22, no. 1 (2003): 5-15.

Kempis, Thomas à. *The Imitation of Christ*. New York: Random House, 1998.

Kennedy, George A. *Classical Rhetoric and Its Christian and Secular Tradition from Ancient to Modern Times.* Chapel Hill: University of North Carolina Press, 1980.

Kennerly, Michele. "Getting Carried Away: How Rhetorical Transport Gets Judgment Going." *Rhetoric Society Quarterly* 40, no. 3 (2010): 269-91.

Kidd, James. Review of *Lila* by Marilynne Robinson. *The Independent.* October 11, 2014.

Krog, Antjie. *Country of My Skull: Guilt, Sorrow, and the Limits of Forgiveness in the New South Africa.* New York: Three Rivers, 2000.

Larsen, Timothy. *George MacDonald in the Age of the Miracles: Incarnation, Doubt, and Reenchantment.* Downers Grove, IL: InterVarsity Press, 2018.

Leff, Michael C. "Hermeneutical Rhetoric." *Rethinking Rhetorical Theory, Criticism, and Pedagogy: The Living Art of Michael C. Leff.* Edited by Antonio de Velasco, John Angus Campbell, and David Henry. East Lansing: Michigan State University Press, 2016.

Lehmann, Paul L. "Faith and Worldliness in Bonhoeffer's Thought." In *Bonhoeffer in a World Come of Age*, edited by Peter Vorkink II, 25-45. Philadelphia: Fortress Press, 1968.

Lessl, Thomas. "The Legacy of C. S. Lewis and the Prospect of Religious Rhetoric." *Journal of Communication and Religion* 27, no. 1 (2004): 117-37.

Lewis, C. S. "Answers to Questions on Christianity." In *God in the Dock: Essays on Theology and Ethics.* Edited by Walter Hooper, 48-62. Grand Rapids: Eerdmans, 1970.

———. "Before We Can Communicate." In *God in the Dock: Essays on Theology and Ethics.* Edited by Walter Hooper, 254-57. Grand Rapids: Eerdmans, 1970.

———. "Christian Apologetics." In *God in the Dock: Essays on Theology and Ethics.* Edited by Walter Hooper, 89-103. Grand Rapids: Eerdmans, 1970.

———. "Christianity and Culture." In *Christian Reflections.* Edited by Walter Hooper, 12-36. Grand Rapids: Eerdmans, 1989.

———. "A Christmas Sermon for Pagans." *VII* 34 (2017): 47-50.

———. *The Collected Letters of C. S. Lewis.* Vol. 2. Edited by Walter Hooper. New York: HarperCollins, 2004.

———. *The Collected Letters of C. S. Lewis.* Vol. 3. Edited by Walter Hooper. New York: HarperCollins, 2007.

———. "Cross-Examination." In *God in the Dock: Essays on Theology and Ethics.* Edited by Walter Hooper, 258-67. Grand Rapids: Eerdmans, 1970.

———. "The Founding of the Oxford Socratic Club." In *God in the Dock: Essays on Theology and Ethics*. Edited by Walter Hooper, 126-28. Grand Rapids: Eerdmans, 1970.

———. *The Four Loves*. New York: Harcourt, 1988.

———. *God in the Dock: Essays on Theology and Ethics*. Edited by Walter Hooper. Grand Rapids: Eerdmans, 1970.

———. "God in the Dock." In *God in the Dock: Essays on Theology and Ethics*. Edited by Walter Hooper, 240-44. Grand Rapids: Eerdmans, 1970.

———. "The Grand Miracle." In *God in the Dock: Essays on Theology and Ethics*. Edited by Walter Hooper, 80-88. Grand Rapids: Eerdmans, 1970.

———. *The Great Divorce*. New York: Touchstone, 1996.

———. Introduction to George MacDonald, *Phantastes: A Faerie Romance*. Grand Rapids: Eerdmans, 2000.

———. *The Joyful Christian: 127 Readings*. New York: Touchstone, 1996.

———. "The Language of Religion." In *Christian Reflections*. Edited by Walter Hooper, 129-141. Grand Rapids: Eerdmans, 1967/1989.

———. *The Lion, the Witch and the Wardrobe*. New York: HarperCollins, 2001.

———. *Mere Christianity*. New York: Macmillan, 1977.

———. *Miracles: How God Intervenes in Nature and Human Affairs*. New York: Macmillan, 1978.

———. "Modern Translations of the Bible." In *God in the Dock: Essays on Theology and Ethics*. Edited by Walter Hooper, 229-33. Grand Rapids: Eerdmans, 1970.

———. "Must Our Image of God Go?" In *God in the Dock: Essays on Theology and Ethics*. Edited by Walter Hooper, 184-85. Grand Rapids: Eerdmans, 1970.

———. "On Stories." In *On Stories, and Other Essays on Literature*. Edited by Walter Hooper, 3-20. New York: Harcourt Brace Jovanovich, 1982.

———. "A Panegyric for Dorothy L. Sayers." In *On Stories, and Other Essays on Literature*. Edited by Walter Hooper, 91-95. New York: Harcourt Brace, 1982.

———. *A Preface to* Paradise Lost. New York: Oxford University Press, 1961.

———. "The Psalms." In *Christian Reflections*. Edited by Walter Hooper, 114-28. Grand Rapids: Eerdmans, 1989.

———. "Rejoinder to Dr Pittenger." In *God in the Dock: Essays on Theology and Ethics*. Edited by Walter Hooper, 177-83. Grand Rapids: Eerdmans, 1970.

———. "Religion without Dogma?" In *God in the Dock: Essays on Theology and Ethics*. Edited by Walter Hooper, 129-146. Grand Rapids: Eerdmans, 1970.

———. *Surprised by Joy: The Shape of My Early Life*. New York: Harcourt Brace & Company, 1955.

———. *The World's Last Night and Other Essays*. New York: Harcourt Brace Jovanovich, 1973.

Liutikas, Darius, and Alfonsas Motuzas. "The Pilgrimage to the Hill of Crosses: Devotional Practices and Identities." *Redefining Pilgrimage: New Perspectives on Historical and Contemporary Pilgrimages*. Edited by Antón M. Pazos, 103-26. Burlington: Ashgate, 2014.

Logan, Stephen. "Literary Theorist." In *The Cambridge Companion to C. S. Lewis*. Edited by Robert MacSwain and Michael Ward, 29-42. Cambridge: Cambridge University Press, 2010.

Marback, Richard C. *Managing Vulnerability: South Africa's Struggle for a Democratic Rhetoric*. Columbia: University of South Carolina Press, 2012.

Marsh, Charles. *Strange Glory: A Life of Dietrich Bonhoeffer*. New York: Alfred A. Knopf, 2014.

McBride, Jennifer M. *The Church for the World: A Theology of Public Witness*. Oxford: Oxford University Press, 2012.

———. *Radical Discipleship: A Liturgical Politics of the Gospel*. Minneapolis: Fortress, 2017.

Medhurst, Martin J. "Religious Belief and Scholarship: A Complex Relationship." *Journal of Communication & Religion* 27, no. 1 (2004): 40-47.

Menuge, Angus J. L., ed. *C. S. Lewis: Lightbearer in the Shadowlands: The Evangelistic Vision of C. S. Lewis*. Wheaton: Crossway, 1997.

———. "God's Chosen Instrument: The Temper of an Apostle." In *C. S. Lewis: Lightbearer in the Shadowlands: The Evangelistic Vision of C. S. Lewis*. Edited by Angus J.L. Menuge, 115-42. Wheaton: Crossway, 1997.

Metaxas, Eric. *Bonhoeffer: Pastor, Martyr, Prophet, Spy*. Nashville: Thomas Nelson, 2010.

Miller, Arthur B. "Aristotle on Habit (ἔθος) and Character (ἦθος): Implications for Rhetoric." *Speech Monographs* 41, no. 4 (1974): 309-16.

Mitchell, Christopher W. "Bearing the Weight of Glory." In *The Pilgrim's Guide: C. S. Lewis and the Art of Witness*. Edited by David Mills, 3-14. Grand Rapids: Eerdmans, 1998.

Morris, Colin. "Pilgrimage to Jerusalem in the Late Middle Ages." In *Pilgrimage: The English Experience from Becket to Bunyan*. Edited by Colin Morris and Peter Roberts, 141-63. New York: Cambridge University Press, 2002.

Moss, Laura. "'Nice Audible Crying': Editions, Testimonies, and *Country of My Skull*." *Research in African Literatures* 37, no. 4 (2006): 85-104.

Mouw, Richard J. *Uncommon Decency: Christian Civility in an Uncivil World.* 2nd ed. Downers Grove, IL: InterVarsity Press, 2010.

Muehlhoff, Tim, and Richard Langer. *Winsome Persuasion: Christian Influence in a Post-Christian World.* Downers Grove, IL: InterVarsity Press, 2017.

Newbigin, Lesslie. *The Gospel in a Pluralist Society.* Grand Rapids: Eerdmans, 1989.

Nienkamp, Jean, ed. Introduction to *Plato on Rhetoric and Language: Four Key Dialogues,* 1-19. Mahwah, NJ: Hermagoras, 1999.

Noble, Alan. *Disruptive Witness: Speaking Truth in a Distracted Age.* Downers Grove, IL: InterVarsity Press, 2018.

O'Connell, Mark. "The First Church of Marilynne Robinson." *The New Yorker.* May 30, 2012.

O'Donnell, Angela Alaimo. "This Blessed Place: The Faithful Fiction of Marilynne Robinson." *America Magazine.* April 27, 2015.

O'Gorman, Ned. "'Telling the Truth': Dietrich Bonhoeffer's Rhetorical Discourse Ethic." *The Journal of Communication and Religion* 28, no. 2 (2005): 224-48.

Oxford English Dictionary. S.v. "seasoned." Oxford: Oxford University Press, 2016.

————. S.v. "win." Oxford: Oxford University Press, 2016.

————. S.v. "winsome." Oxford: Oxford University Press, 2016.

Oswald, Alice. *Memorial: A Version of Homer's Iliad.* New York: W. W. Norton, 2011.

————. "The Unbearable Brightness of Speaking." *The New Statesman.* October 17, 2011.

Painter, Rebecca M. "Further Thoughts on a Prodigal Son Who Cannot Come Home, on Loneliness and Grace: An Interview with Marilynne Robinson." *Christianity and Literature* 58, no. 3 (2009): 484-92.

————. "Loyalty Meets Prodigality: The Reality of Grace in Marilynne Robinson's Fiction." *Christianity and Literature* 59, no. 2 (2010): 321-40.

Pauw, Amy Plantinga. *Church in Ordinary Time: A Wisdom Ecclesiology.* Grand Rapids: Eerdmans, 2017.

Pelikan, Jaroslav. *Divine Rhetoric: The Sermon on the Mount as Message and as Model in Augustine, Chrysostom and Luther.* Crestwood, NY: St. Vladimir's Seminary Press, 2000.

Perelman, Chaïm, and Lucie Olbrechts-Tyteca. *The New Rhetoric: A Treatise on Argumentation.* Notre Dame: University of Notre Dame Press, 1969.

Pfatteicher, Philip. *Journey into the Heart of God: Living the Liturgical Year.* Oxford: Oxford University Press, 2013.

Philpott, Daniel. "Beyond Politics as Usual: Is Reconciliation Compatible with Liberalism?" In *The Politics of Past Evil: Religion, Reconciliation, and the Dilemmas of Transitional Justice.* Edited by Daniel Philpott, 11-44. Notre Dame: University of Notre Dame Press, 2006.

Plato. *Gorgias.* In *Plato on Rhetoric and Language: Four Key Dialogues.* Edited by Jean Nienkamp. Translated by Donald J. Zeyl, 85-164. Mahwah, NJ: Lawrence Erlbaum, 1999.

Quintilian. *Quintilian's Institutes of Oratory.* Edited by Lee Honeycutt. Translated by John Selby Watson. http://rhetoric.byu.edu/Primary%20Texts/Quintilian.htm.

Rahim, Sameer. "Quiet Epiphanies." *The Telegraph.* July 29, 2015.

Ramus, Peter. *Peter Ramus's Attack on Cicero: Text and Translation of Ramus's Brutinae Quaestiones.* Edited by James J. Murphy. Translated by Carole Newlands. Davis, CA: Hermagoras, 1992.

Rasmussen, Larry. "The Ethics of Responsible Action." In *The Cambridge Companion to Dietrich Bonhoeffer,* 206-25. Cambridge: Cambridge University Press, 2006.

Rasmussen, Larry, and Renate Bethge. *Dietrich Bonhoeffer: His Significance for North Americans.* Minneapolis: Fortress, 1990.

Ratcliffe, Krista. *Rhetorical Listening: Identification, Gender, Whiteness.* Carbondale: Southern Illinois University Press, 2005.

Reid, Robert Stephen. "A Rhetoric of Contemporary Christian Discourse." In *Journal of Communication and Religion* 31, no. 2 (2008): 109-142.

Resner, André, Jr. *Preacher and Cross: Person and Message in Theology and Rhetoric.* Grand Rapids: Eerdmans, 1999.

Reynolds, Barbara. *Dorothy L. Sayers: Her Life and Soul.* New York: St. Martin's, 1993.

———. "Fifty Years On: Dorothy L. Sayers and Dante." *VII* 13 (1996): 3-6.

———. *The Passionate Intellect: Dorothy L. Sayers' Encounter with Dante.* Kent, OH: Kent State University Press, 1989.

Reynolds, Nedra. "*Ethos* as Location: New Sites for Understanding Discursive Authority." *Rhetoric Review* 11, no. 2 (1993): 325-38.

Riley, Catherine. "The Rhetorical Dimensions of Preaching: Preachers as Rhetors and Rhetoricians." Rhetoric Society of America Conference, Atlanta, May 2016.

Robinson, John A.T. *Honest to God.* Philadelphia: Westminster, 1963.

Robinson, Marilynne. "Bonhoeffer." In *The Death of Adam: Essays on Modern Thought,* 108-25. New York: Picador, 2005.

———. *Gilead: A Novel.* New York: Farrar, Straus, and Giroux, 2004.

———. *Home: A Novel.* New York: Farrar, Straus, and Giroux, 2008.

———. *Lila: A Novel.* New York: Farrar, Straus, and Giroux, 2014.

———. "Marguerite de Navarre." In *The Death of Adam: Essays on Modern Thought,* 174-206. New York: Picador, 2005.

Root, Jerry. *C. S. Lewis and a Problem of Evil: An Investigation of a Pervasive Theme.* Eugene, OR: Pickwick, 2009.

———. "Tools Inadequate and Incomplete: C. S. Lewis and the Great Religions." *The Pilgrim's Guide: C. S. Lewis and the Art of Witness.* Edited by David Mills, 221-35. Grand Rapids: Eerdmans, 1998.

Rossow, Francis C. "Old Wine in New Wineskins." In *C. S. Lewis: Lightbearer in the Shadowlands: The Evangelistic Vision of C. S. Lewis.* Edited by Angus J. L. Menuge, 259-78. Wheaton: Crossway, 1997.

Ryken, Philip G. "Winsome Evangelist: The Influence of C. S. Lewis." In *C. S. Lewis: Lightbearer in the Shadowlands: The Evangelistic Vision of C. S. Lewis.* Edited by Angus J.L. Menuge, 55-78. Wheaton: Crossway, 1997.

Salazar, Philippe-Joseph. *An African Athens: Rhetoric and the Shaping of Democracy in South Africa.* Mahwah, NJ: L. Erlbaum, 2002.

Sayers, Dorothy L. "Creed or Chaos?" In *Creed or Chaos? Why Christians Must Choose Either Dogma or Disaster (Or, Why It Really Does Matter What You Believe),* 37-73. Manchester, NH: Sophia Institute, 1999.

———. *He That Should Come: A Nativity Play in One Act.* Eugene, OR: Wipf & Stock, 2011.

———. Introduction to *The Man Born To Be King: A Play-Cycle on the Life of Our Lord and Saviour JESUS CHRIST,* 11-31. San Francisco: Ignatius, 1990.

———. *Introductory Papers on Dante.* Eugene, OR: Wipf & Stock, 1954.

———. Letter to E. Day. January 20, 1939. Correspondence and fan mail related to *He That Should Come.* Last names A-L. *He That Should Come* Archive, box 1, folder 4. The Marion E. Wade Center, Wheaton College, Wheaton, IL.

———. Letter to Mrs. F. Bayley. January 2, 1939. Correspondence and fan mail related to *He That Should Come.* Last names A-L. *He That Should Come* Archive, box 1, folder 4. The Marion E. Wade Center, Wheaton College, Wheaton, IL.

———. "Letter to James Welch, 11 February 1943." In *The Christ of the Creeds and Other Broadcast Messages to the British People during World War II,* 72-75. West Sussex: Dorothy L. Sayers Society, 2008.

———. Letter to Rev. T. A. Agins, O.S.B. January 19, 1939. Correspondence and fan mail related to *He That Should Come.* Last names A-L. *He That Should Come* Archive, box 1, folder 4. The Marion E. Wade Center, Wheaton College, Wheaton, IL.

———. "The Lost Tools of Learning." In *A Matter of Eternity: Selections from the Writings of Dorothy L. Sayers.* Grand Rapids: Eerdmans, 1973.

———. *The Man Born to Be King: A Play-Cycle on the Life of our Lord and Savior JESUS CHRIST.* Grand Rapids: Eerdmans, 1979.

———. *The Mind of the Maker.* San Francisco: HarperCollins, 1987.

———. *The Nine Tailors.* New York: Harcourt Brace, 1934.

———. "Playwrights Are Not Evangelists." *World Theatre* 5 (1955–1956): 61-66.

———. "The Religions Behind the Nations." In *The Christ of the Creeds and Other Broadcast Messages to the British People during World War II*, 43-48. West Sussex: Dorothy L. Sayers Society, 2008.

———. "Why Work?" *Letters to a Diminished Church: Passionate Arguments for the Relevance of Christianity.* Nashville: Thomas Nelson, 2004.

———. *The Zeal of Thy House.* Eugene, OR: Wipf & Stock, 2011.

Schaffer, Kay, and Sidonie Smith. "Human Rights, Storytelling, and the Position of the Beneficiary: Antjie Krog's *Country of My Skull.*" *PMLA* 121, no. 5 (2006): 1577-84.

Schine, Cathleen. "A Triumph of Love." *The New York Review of Books* 61, no. 16 (2014).

Schrag, Calvin O. Foreword to *The* Ethos *of Rhetoric.* Edited by Michael J. Hyde, vii-viii. Columbia: University of South Carolina Press, 2004.

Schultze, Quentin J. Foreword to *Winsome Persuasion: Christian Influence in a Post-Christian World,* by Tim Muehlhoff and Richard Langer, ix-xiii. Downers Grove, IL: InterVarsity Press, 2017.

Scott, A. O. "Return of the Prodigal Son." *The New York Times.* September 19, 2008.

Siefker Bailey, Lisa M. "Fraught with Fire: Race and Theology in Marilynne Robinson's *Gilead.*" *Christianity and Literature* 59, no. 2 (2010): 265-82.

Simmons, Laura K. *Creed Without Chaos: Exploring Theology in the Writings of Dorothy L. Sayers.* Grand Rapids: Baker, 2005.

Smith, Craig R. "*Ethos* Dwells Pervasively: A Hermeneutic Reading of Aristotle on Credibility." In *The* Ethos *of Rhetoric.* Edited by Michael J. Hyde, 1-19. Columbia: University of South Carolina Press, 2004.

Smith, James K. A. *Awaiting the Kingdom: Reforming Public Theology.* Grand Rapids: Baker Academic, 2017.

———. *Desiring the Kingdom: Worship, Worldview, and Cultural Formation.* Grand Rapids: Baker Academic, 2009.

———. *Imagining the Kingdom: How Worship Works.* Grand Rapids: Baker Academic, 2013.

———. "The Lost Art of Persuasion." *Comment Magazine,* Spring 2013, 2-3.

———. *You Are What You Love: The Spiritual Power of Habit.* Grand Rapids: Brazos Press, 2016.

Steiner, Mark Allan. "Reconceptualizing Christian Public Engagement: 'Faithful Witness' and the American Evangelical Tradition." *Journal of Communication and Religion* 32, no. 2 (2009): 289-318.

Stott, John. *The Living Church: Convictions of a Lifelong Pastor.* Downers Grove, IL: InterVarsity Press, 2007.

Stroud, Dean G., ed. *Preaching in Hitler's Shadow: Sermons of Resistance in the Third Reich.* Grand Rapids: William B. Eerdmans Publishing Company, 2013.

Tandy, Gary L. *The Rhetoric of Certitude: C. S. Lewis's Nonfiction Prose.* Kent, OH: Kent State University Press, 2009.

Tell, Dave. "Augustine and the 'Chair of Lies': Rhetoric in *The Confessions.*" *Rhetorica: A Journal of the History of Rhetoric* 38, no. 4 (2010): 384-407.

Thurmer, John. *Reluctant Evangelist: Papers on the Christian Thought of Dorothy L. Sayers.* West Sussex: Dorothy L. Sayers Society, 1996.

Tutu, Desmond. "Clarifying the Word: A Sermon by Desmond Tutu." In *Crucible of Fire: The Church Confronts Apartheid.* Edited by Jim Wallis and Joyce Hollyday, 32-39. Maryknoll, NY: Orbis, 1989.

———. "Deeper into God: Spirituality for the Struggle: An Interview with Desmond Tutu." In *Crucible of Fire: The Church Confronts Apartheid.* Edited by Jim Wallis and Joyce Hollyday, 62-69. Maryknoll, NY: Orbis, 1989.

———. Foreword by Chairperson. In *Truth and Reconciliation Commission of South Africa Report.* Vol. 1, 1-23. New York: Grove's Dictionaries, 1999.

———. *No Future Without Forgiveness.* New York: Doubleday, 1999.

———. *The Rainbow People of God: The Making of a Peaceful Revolution.* Edited by John Allen. New York: Doubleday, 1994.

———. "Reconciling Love: A Millennium Mandate." 2005–2006 Bryan Series Lectures on Spirit and Spirituality. Hege Library, Guilford College, Greensboro, NC. 2005.

Vander Lei, Elizabeth, Thomas Amorose, Beth Daniell, and Anne Ruggles Gere, eds. *Renovating Rhetoric in Christian Tradition.* Pittsburgh: University of Pittsburgh Press, 2014.

Vander Weele, Michael. "Marilynne Robinson's *Gilead* and the Difficult Gift of Human Exchange." *Christianity and Literature* 59, no. 2 (2010): 217-40.

Vanhoozer, Kevin J. *The Drama of Doctrine: A Canonical Linguistic Approach to Christian Theology*. Louisville: Westminster John Knox, 2005.

———. "Theology and the Condition of Postmodernity." In *The Cambridge Companion to Postmodern Theology*, 3-25. Cambridge: Cambridge University Press, 2003.

Wallis, Jim. *God's Politics: Why the Right Gets It Wrong and Left Doesn't Get It*. New York: HarperSanFrancisco, 2005.

———. "Into the Crucible of Fire: The Church Steps forward in South Africa." In *Crucible of Fire: The Church Confronts Apartheid*. Edited by Jim Wallis and Joyce Hollyday, 1-20. Maryknoll, NY: Orbis, 1989.

Wallis, Jim, and Joyce Hollyday, eds. *Crucible of Fire: The Church Confronts Apartheid*. Maryknoll, NY: Orbis, 1989.

Ward, Michael. "Escape to Wallaby Wood: Lewis's Depictions of Conversion." In *C. S. Lewis: Lightbearer in the Shadowlands: The Evangelistic Vision of C. S. Lewis*. Edited by Angus J. L. Menuge, 143-67. Wheaton: Crossway, 1997.

Weaver, Richard M. *The Ethics of Rhetoric*. Davis, CA: Hermagoras Press, 1985.

Webber, Robert E. *Ancient-Future Faith: Rethinking Evangelicalism for a Postmodern World*. Grand Rapids: Baker Academic, 1999.

———. *Ancient-Future Time: Forming Spirituality Through the Christian Year*. Grand Rapids: Baker Books, 2004.

———. *God Still Speaks: A Biblical View of Christian Communication*. Nashville: Thomas Nelson, 1980.

Webster, John. "The Church as Witnessing Community." *Scottish Bulletin of Evangelical Theology* 21, no. 1 (2003): 21-33.

White, James Boyd. *Justice as Translation: An Essay in Cultural and Legal Criticism*. Chicago: University of Chicago Press, 1990.

———. *Living Speech: Resisting the Empire of Force*. Princeton: Princeton University Press, 2006.

———. *When Words Lose Their Meaning: Constitutions and Reconstitutions of Language, Character, and Community*. Chicago: University of Chicago Press, 1984.

Whitlock, Gillian. "Consuming Passions: Reconciliation in Women's Intellectual Memoir." *Tulsa Studies in Women's Literature* 23, no. 1 (2004): 13-28.

Williams, Reggie L. "Dietrich Bonhoeffer, the Harlem Renaissance and the Black Christ." In *Bonhoeffer, Christ and Culture*. Edited by Keith L. Johnson and Timothy Larsen, 59-72. Downers Grove, IL: InterVarsity Press, 2013.

Williams, Rowan. "Native Speakers: Identity, Grace, and Homecoming." *Christianity and Literature* 61, no. 1 (2011): 7-18.

Wilson, John. Review of *Lila* by Marilynne Robinson. *The Chicago Tribune*. October 10, 2014.

Wolin, Ross. *The Rhetorical Imagination of Kenneth Burke*. Columbia: University of South Carolina Press, 2001.

Wolterstorff, Nicholas. "Christology, Christian Learning, and Christian Formation: Mark Noll's *Jesus Christ and the Life of the Mind*." *Books & Culture*. September–October 2012.

Wood, James. "The Homecoming." *The New Yorker*. September 8, 2008.

Wright, N. T. *Surprised by Hope: Rethinking Heaven, the Resurrection, and the Mission of the Church*. New York: HarperCollins, 2008.

Zodhiates, Spiros, ed. *The Complete Word Study Dictionary: New Testament*. Chattanooga, TN: AMG, 1992.

GENERAL INDEX

SCRIPTURE INDEX

Finding the Textbook You Need

The IVP Academic Textbook Selector
is an online tool for instantly finding the IVP books
suitable for over 250 courses across 24 disciplines.

ivpacademic.com